For God and His People

Ulrich Zwingli AND THE SWISS REFORMATION

Jean Henri Merle d'Aubigné

Translated by Henry White

Edited by Mark Sidwell, Ph.D.

BJU PRESS

Greenville, South Carolina

Library of Congress Cataloging-in-Publication Data

Merle d'Aubigné, J. H. (Jean Henri), 1794-1872
    [Histoire de la réformation du seizième siècle. English. Selections]
    For God and his people : Ulrich Zwingli and the Swiss Reformation / Jean Henri Merle
    d'Aubigné : translated by Henry White ; edited by Mark Sidwell.
        p. cm.
    Includes biographical references and index.
    ISBN 1-57924-399-1
    1. Zwingli, Ulrich, 1484-1531. 2. Reformation—Switzerland—Biography. 3.
    Switzerland—Church history—16th century. I. Sidwell, Mark, 1958- II. Title.

    BR345 .M4713 2000
    284.2'092—dc21
    [B]   00-040368

Photograph Credits
The following agencies and individuals have furnished materials to meet
the photographic needs of this textbook. We wish to express our gratitude to
them for their important contribution.

Digital Stock: cover photos
German Information Center: 150
Library of Congress: 266
courtesy of Mark Sidwell: 40
www. arttoday. com: 4, 144, 161, 247

NOTE:
The fact that materials produced by other publishers are referred to in this volume does
not constitute an endorsement by Bob Jones University Press of the content or theological position of materials produced by such publishers. The position of Bob Jones
University Press, and of the University itself, is well known. Any references and ancillary
materials are listed as an aid to the student or the teacher and in an attempt to maintain the
accepted academic standards of the publishing industry.

Cover designer: Duane A. Nichols
Maps by Jim Hargis
Project Editor: Debbie L. Parker

For God and His People: Ulrich Zwingli and the Swiss Reformation

15   14   13   12   11   10   9   8   7   6   5   4   3   2   1

Contents

"To know the limbs and leaps of history is hardly worth a cent. . . . The only thing which counts is that you become more certain of your God as you contemplate the past, and that you then show more courage in the face of present needs!"

—Ulrich Zwingli

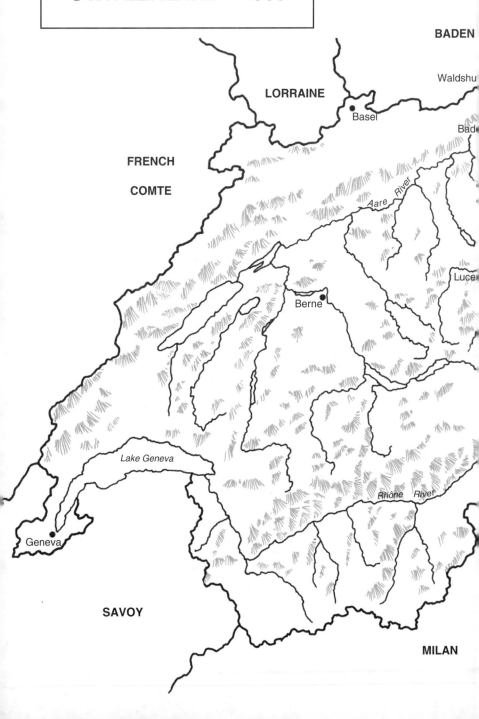

SWITZERLAND—1580

BADEN

Waldshu

LORRAINE

Basel

Bad

FRENCH

COMTE

Aare River

Luce

Berne

Lake Geneva

Rhône River

Geneva

SAVOY

MILAN

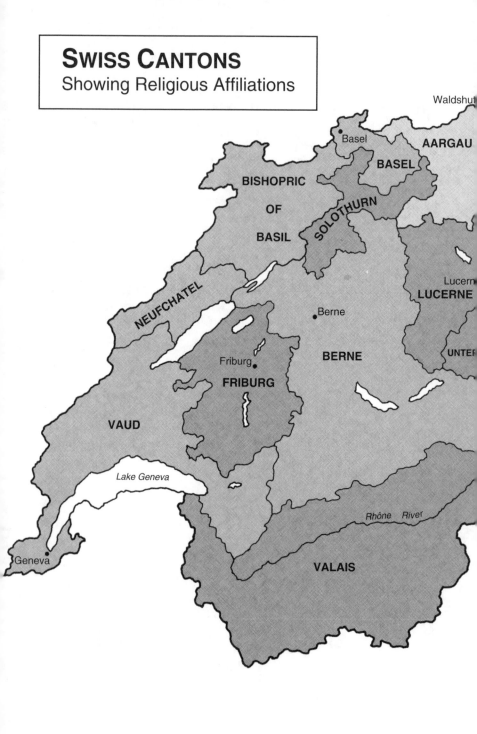

SWISS CANTONS
Showing Religious Affiliations

Waldshut

Basel

AARGAU

BASEL

BISHOPRIC

OF

BASIL

SOLOTHURN

NEUFCHATEL

Lucern
LUCERNE

Berne

UNTER

BERNE

Friburg

FRIBURG

VAUD

Lake Geneva

Rhône River

Geneva

VALAIS

Jean Henri Merle d'Aubigné (1794-1872)

Introduction
by Mark Sidwell

Jean Henri Merle d'Aubigné was born in 1794 in Geneva. His name represents the joining of two illustrious French families who had fled religious persecution in their native country. Probably the most famous of his ancestors was Theodore Agrippa d'Aubigné (1550-1630), French soldier, poet, and historian—a man "who fought with the pen and the sword" in the words of Jules Bonnet. D'Aubigné had formerly been a councilor to King Henry IV of France, the king who abandoned the Huguenot (French Protestant) faith to become a Catholic in order to take the French throne. In 1620, after the death of Henry IV, d'Aubigné left France for the haven of Geneva. Another ancestor of the historian, Jean-Louis Merle of Nîmes, fled France when King Louis XIV revoked the Edict of Nantes in 1685, thus taking away the Protestants' freedom of worship.

After these two families were finally joined in marriage, the historian's uncle and then his father joined the two names as well. He was born "Jean Henri Merle d'Aubigné," not simply "Jean Henri Merle." (This fact has often confused English readers, who sometimes refer to him simply as "d'Aubigné"; he is correctly referred to as "Merle d'Aubigné" or simply "Merle.") Thus, even the author's name represented a heritage of courageous faith against oppression.

Merle's family experienced tragedy when he was only five years old. He grew up during the era of the Napoleonic wars, and his home city of Geneva was soon annexed to Napoleon's French empire. Merle's father, Aimè-Robert Merle d'Aubigné, was a prosperous businessman who served the Napoleonic cause. In 1799 he disappeared while on a mission for Napoleon's government, probably the victim of enemy troops. Merle's mother was left to rear Jean Henri and his two brothers by herself.

Young Merle developed an interest in the ministry as a young man, although his family had originally planned for him to enter business, as his father had done. At the age of seventeen, Merle wrote in his journal, "If I enter commerce, I will be able to become rich and to give myself up to all pleasures; but perhaps I will abandon myself too much to the love of money, to evil pleasures, and then I will be lost for eternity. If on the other hand I embrace the holy ministry, I will be poor, and I will have a difficult life; but I will be obliged to seek God, to live in conformity to His will, and so my soul will be saved." Since study for the ministry exempted Merle from French military service, his mother supported his desire. Merle entered the Genevan Academy in 1813.

Geneva had been one of the great centers of the Reformation in the sixteenth century. It was the city of John Calvin, the giant of the Reformation second only to Martin Luther in importance. After living in Geneva for a time, Scottish reformer John Knox called the city under Calvin "the most perfect school of Christ that ever was in the earth since the days of the Apostles. In other places, I confess Christ to be truly preached; but manners and religion so sincerely reformed, I have not yet seen in any other place." From Geneva the recovered gospel of salvation through Christ alone spread across Europe.

By Merle's day, however, Geneva was no longer a center of Christian truth. Most of the ministers of the state church were Unitarians. They denied Christ's deity, the inspiration and authority of the Scriptures, and the natural sinfulness of man. Students for the ministry rarely studied Bible in the Genevan Academy. A classmate of Merle said, "During the four years I attended the theological teachers of Geneva, I did not, as part of my studies, read one single chapter of the Word of God, except a few Psalms and chapters, exclusively with a view to learning Hebrew, and . . . I did not receive one single lesson of exegesis of the Old and New Testaments."

Not all of the ministers in Geneva were liberal. Some, particularly in the rural areas outside the city limits, clung to the biblical faith of Calvin and the other reformers. Merle was much impressed with the testimony and preaching of orthodox Genevan minister J.S.I. Cellèrier, although Merle was not converted under his preaching. But just as God brought John Calvin from France to reform the city in the 1500s, so in the 1800s God brought to Geneva His instruments to carry revival to the city. And as Calvin's work in Geneva spread abroad, so the new revival eventually touched all of Europe.

The awakening in Geneva was actually one part—in many ways one of the earliest expressions—of a revival that touched Protestants in Switzerland, France, the Netherlands, and Germany. Known as the *réveil* (French for "awakening"), this revival saw the Holy Spirit draw earnest seekers after truth to Christ. Merle, however, was at first cold toward this movement.

When the revival broke out, one Genevan wrote a pamphlet that defended the deity of Christ and criticized the pastors of the state church of Geneva for their unbelief. Merle's fellow theological students chose him as their leader and spokesman to read publicly a letter protesting the pamphlet. Merle and all but two of his fellow students signed the protest.

But Merle's attitude changed under the ministry of a remarkable Scotsman named Robert Haldane (1764-1842). An independently wealthy businessman, Haldane devoted his time and money to furthering the cause of Christ wherever he found opportunity. On a visit to Geneva, Haldane was dismayed with how little even the theological students knew of the gospel. He decided to remedy that situation by renting rooms in Geneva and holding Bible studies with the students from the school of theology.

Some twenty or thirty students came to hear Haldane—over the objections of their Unitarian teachers. Although his French was not at all fluent, Haldane, with the help of the students who knew English, spoke on the Book of Romans. One of the attendees at these sessions said of Haldane, "He knew the Scriptures like a Christian who has had for his Teacher the same Holy Spirit by whom they were dictated." Another said, "He never wasted his time in arguing against our so-called reasonings, but at once pointed with his finger to the Bible, adding the simple words,

'Look here—how readest thou? There it stands written with the finger of God.'"

Merle d'Aubigné was among those students who listened with keen attention to the Scottish evangelist. Having been taught by his Unitarian teachers that man was naturally good, Merle had difficulty accepting the doctrine of the natural depravity of man's heart. After some study and discussion, Merle told Haldane, "Now I see that doctrine in the Bible."

"Yes," replied Haldane, "but do you see it in your heart?"

Merle said later, "That was but a simple question, but it came home to my conscience. It was the sword of the Spirit; and from that time I saw that my heart was corrupted, and knew from the Word of God that I can be saved by grace alone."

Merle was converted and noted later that "after having remained in the cheerless principles of Unitarianism until nearly the conclusion of my studies at the academy of Geneva, I had been seized by the Word of God." Years later, looking at the apartments where he and the others heard Haldane, Merle said, "There is the cradle of the Second Reformation of Geneva."

Merle finished his studies and was ordained in the state church in 1817. There was tension, however, between the leadership of the church and the supporters of the réveil. This unrest and the confusion it caused motivated Merle to go to Germany for further study.

The year 1817 was the three hundredth anniversary of the Reformation, three hundred years since Martin Luther had nailed his Ninety-five Theses to the door of the church of Wittenberg. The celebration fired the young Genevan's imagination. He stopped at Eisenach, the site of both Luther's birth and death. He visited Wartburg Castle on October 31, 1817, the actual anniversary of the nailing of the theses. There Merle viewed the castle where Luther had been kept a half-unwilling prisoner for his own protection. He saw the rooms in which Luther had done much of his translation work for the German Bible. His thoughts dwelt on the Reformation.

Later, on November 23, he wrote in his journal, "I want to compose a history of the Reformation. I want this history to be scholarly and to present facts not yet known; I want it to be profound and to unravel the causes and the effects of this great movement; I want it to be interesting and to make the authors of the transformation known by their letters, their writings, their words." Merle desired his history to be "truly Christian and suited to stimulate the religious spirit."

Merle went to the University of Berlin in 1817 to study. Among his teachers was August Neander, perhaps the leading church historian of the age. The young Genevan appreciated Neander's stress on the spiritual in history. Also Neander used biography to focus on outstanding individuals who represented the movements and forces that shaped the course of history. This emphasis appealed to Merle. He saw God's work in the individual as the basis of God's work in society, and Merle would later use Luther to typify the whole Reformation. Student and teacher enjoyed a certain theological sympathy, although Merle was more orthodox. "It was not possible to speak with Neander of inspiration, nor of irresistible grace, nor of eternal damnation," wrote Merle's daughter, "but one could agree wonderfully with him on church history."

After his study, Merle became pastor of a French-speaking church in Hamburg, Germany, in 1818. He won the hearts of his congregation with his evangelical, compassionate preaching. But he offended the leadership of the church, who preferred less "emotion" in their services. Merle then went to Brussels, today part of Belgium but at that time under Dutch control. From 1823 to 1831 he pastored a French-speaking church there. Merle preached with great eloquence and power, and the king and queen of the Netherlands were sometimes among his hearers. His work in Belgium ended, however, when the Belgians successfully revolted from Dutch control in 1830 and achieved their independence.

In 1831 Merle d'Aubigné returned to Geneva. There he joined the Société évangélique de Genève, originally a protest group standing for orthodoxy within Geneva's state church. The dominantly Unitarian leadership of the church opposed Merle and the other leaders of the Société and suspended them. Eventually, in 1849, the Société formed its own independent free church.

Perhaps the most important effort of the Société évangélique de Genève was to found a theological school to train men for the ministry—apart from the spiritually deadening atmosphere of the Genevan Academy. Thus, in 1831 Jean Henri Merle d'Aubigné became the new school's first president and its professor of church history. From then until his death in 1872, Merle taught—and touched—a stream of students who passed through his classroom. His commanding presence and stringent academic requirements led his students to nickname him "Jupiter," after the chief god of Roman mythology.

Merle taught, lectured, and traveled. He went all over Europe speaking at international conferences and promoting Christian causes. (When he visited London in 1862, Pastor C. H. Spurgeon of the Metropolitan Tabernacle shortened his sermon to allow Merle to briefly address the congregation.) During the bloody Austro-Italian War (1859), Merle called for Christians to minister to the wounded in time of war. "It is especially in times of war that Christians must show themselves children of peace," he wrote. The Société évangélique formed a committee to organize help for those suffering the ravages of war. Merle was a member of that committee, along with Jean Henri Dunant, who from this pioneer effort went on to become one of the founders of the International Red Cross.

But most of all, J. H. Merle d'Aubigné wrote.

Merle had published a few articles and sermons while he was a pastor, but with the new position in Geneva he launched into his dream of writing a history of the Reformation. He published the first volume in 1835. Sales in French were poor. Then the history was translated into English, and sales soared. (Merle said that the first three volumes sold only 4,000 copies in French but between 150,000 and 200,000 in English.) The enormous popularity of the English edition encouraged the historian to press forward with his project. In fact, as Merle continued to issue new volumes, he eventually published some volumes in English before issuing them in French.

Merle d'Aubigné wrote two sets: *The History of the Reformation in the Sixteenth Century* (5 volumes, 1835-53) and

The History of the Reformation in Europe in the Time of Calvin (8 volumes, 1863-78; the last three volumes edited and published by his son-in-law after Merle's death). The first set outsold the second by far, but both were surprisingly popular for a multivolume work of history. Merle also wrote a few other works, such as a defense of Oliver Cromwell, but it was his history of the Reformation that made him famous.

The appeal of Merle's work is the result of several factors. His style is flowing—and dramatic. This sense of drama is evident throughout and is heightened by the author's extensive use of original quotations from the persons he describes. Merle was not simply seeking dramatic effect in these quotations; he hoped to guarantee the greatest possible accuracy. He wrote, "The work of the historian is neither a work of the imagination like that of the poet, nor a mere conversation about times gone by, as some writers of our day appear to imagine. History is a faithful description of past events; and when the historian can relate them by making use of the language of those who took part in them, he is more certain of describing them just as they were."

Merle wrote during the growth of a movement in historical writing that sought to go back to the sources, to write "history as it really happened." Increasingly, European archives were opening and providing a wealth of materials for study, and Merle faithfully used those materials in his writing. Today we understand how difficult it is to achieve true objectivity in historical writing. The original sources an author quotes may themselves be in error, and a writer reveals his own views in the quotations he selects and how he arranges them. Nonetheless, Merle d'Aubigné relied much more heavily on the writings of the reformers and their opponents than he did on the contemporary writings of other historians. This quality gives his work a freshness and immediacy not always found in historical writing.

But for the Christian, Merle's appeal undoubtedly lies also in his personal faith and how that faith shaped his philosophy of history. He placed first and foremost God's providential control not only of the events of the Reformation but also of all history. In his preface to the first volume Merle wrote, "These volumes . . . lay down in the chief and foremost place this simple and pregnant principle: GOD IN HISTORY." He said later in that preface, "In history God should be acknowledged and proclaimed. The history of the world should be set forth as the annals of the government of the sovereign King."

In keeping with his stress on faith, Merle always wanted to include the "inner" aspect of history, not just trace the outward actions of his subjects. What the reformers *did* was important, but to the Genevan historian, what the reformers *thought* was also important—probably more so. "In my opinion," Merle wrote, "the very essence of the Reformation is its doctrines and its inward life." Merle believed that one cannot really understand the Reformation apart from faith and Scripture.

More than that, Merle believed that God accomplished the Reformation through Scripture. Merle wrote, "The only true reformation is that which emanates from the Word of God. The Holy Scriptures, by bearing witness to the incarnation, death, and resurrection of the Son of God, create in man by the Holy Ghost a faith which justifies him. That faith which produces in him a new life, unites him to Christ. . . . From the regeneration of individuals naturally results the regeneration of the church."

Readers of Merle's work should keep in mind his emphasis on the Reformation as a positive expression of God's will and Word. Critics often accuse him of being anti-Catholic. There is no question that he soundly criticizes much within Roman Catholicism, but he does so because he finds that system at odds with Scripture. Merle's goal was not primarily to attack the pope or the Roman Catholic church but to record what he saw as the triumph of God's truth in the Reformation. When the pope and church opposed that truth, Merle did not spare them. Merle must have heartily agreed with Luther when he quoted the reformer's words to Cardinal Cajetan: "My greatest joy will be to witness the triumph of what is according to God's Word."

Why does Merle's work still endure? The liveliness of his style, his extensive and remarkable use of original quotations, and the rich biographical color of his work make it enjoyable to read. More than that, Merle's evangelical fervor, his commitment to biblical truth, and his fundamental sympathy with the spirit of the

Reformation strike a responsive chord in the heart of the Christian.

Merle found common cause between himself and the Protestant Reformation. It is not surprising that he called the réveil the "Second Reformation of Geneva." The Reformation— whatever its profound social, political, and economic effects— was fundamentally a spiritual awakening, a revival of religion. Merle wrote about a phenomenon he had personally experienced. Without pressing the point too far, Jean Henri Merle d'Aubigné may have been writing not only history but also something of his autobiography when he traced the history of the Reformation.

Sources

Biéler, Blanche. *Un Fils du Refuge: Jean-Henri Merle d'Aubigné.* Geneva: Editions Labor, 1934.

Bonnet, Jules. *Notice sur la vie et les écrits de M. Merle d'Aubigné.* Paris: Grassart, 1874.

de Goltz, H. *Genève religieuse au dix-neuvième siècle.* Translated from the German by C. Malan-Sillem. Geneva: Henri Georg, 1862.

Good, James I. *History of the Swiss Reformed Church Since the Reformation.* Philadelphia: Publication and Sunday School Board of the Reformed Church in the United States, 1913.

Haldane, Alexander. *The Lives of Robert and James Haldane.* 1852. Reprint, Edinburgh: Banner of Truth Trust, 1990. See pp. 413-62.

Houghton, S. M. Introduction to *The Reformation in England,* by J. H. Merle d'Aubigné. Edinburgh: Banner of Truth Trust, 1962.

Merle d'Aubigné, J. H. *D'Aubigné and His Writings.* Edited by Robert Baird. New York: Baker and Scribner, 1846.

Roney, John. *The Inside of History: Jean Henri Merle d'Aubigné and Romantic Historiography.* Westport, Conn.: Greenwood Press, 1996.

———. "Jean Henri Merle d'Aubigné" In *Historians of the Christian Tradition,* edited by Michael Banman and Martin I. Klauber. Nashville: Broadman and Holman, 1995, pp. 167-89.

The Life of Ulrich Zwingli

1484, January 1—Ulrich Zwingli is born at Wildhaus
in the Tockenburg valley.

1498—Zwingli attends university at Vienna.

1502—Zwingli returns to Basel to teach and continue
his studies.

—Zwingli receives a Master of Arts degree.

1505—Thomas Wittembach comes to Basel and
influences Zwingli.

—Zwingli meets Leo Juda.

1506—Zwingli is ordained and becomes pastor at Glaris.

1513—Zwingli begins to study Greek in order to better
understand the Scriptures.

1514—Erasmus comes to Basel where Zwingli meets him,
Oswald Myconius, and John Oecolampadius.

1516—Zwingli is invited to Einsidlen as priest where he
begins to preach the gospel.

1517—Zwingli learns the epistles of Paul by heart.

1518—Zwingli comes to Zurich as people's priest
at the cathedral of Zurich.

1519, August–November—Zwingli nearly dies of the plague.

1520—The Great Council decrees that only the Word of God
should be preached.

1521—Zwingli meets Henry Bullinger and Gerold Meyer von
Knonau and his mother, Anna Reinhardt.

1522, April—Zwingli preaches against forced abstinence from
meat and publishes a treatise, *On Meats.*

July—Ministers at the meeting at Einsidlen
circulate in Lucerne two petitions against imposed celibacy of
priests.

1523, January 26—Cantons other than Zurich approve nineteen articles forbidding preaching of new or Lutheran doctrines.

January 29—Zwingli appears before the Great Council of Zurich to present his sixty-seven theses contending that salvation is found in Christ alone.

October 26—Zwingli argues before the Great Council for the removal of images.

1524, April 2—Zwingli marries Anna Reinhardt.

1525, April 11—Zwingli appears before the Great Council to demand the abolishment of the Mass and the reestablishment of the Lord's supper.

1526, May 21–April 8, 1527—The conference at Baden to dispute the doctrine of Zwingli draws the cantons of Berne and Basel to join the Reformation.

October—At the Colloquy of Marburg, Zwingli meets and disputes with Luther the extent of the Lord's Supper.

1528, January—The Council of Berne introduces the Reformation to Berne.

1529, April—The Five Cantons ally themselves with Austria.

June—In the First War of Kappel, Zurich arms itself against the Five Cantons.

June 26—A treaty of peace is obtained.

1531, January 8 and April 10—Two diets at Baden discuss the grievances of the Five Cantons and the evangelical cantons.

May 12—The diet at Arau decides to refuse to sell to the Five Cantons.

October—The Five Cantons march on Zurich.

October 11—Zwingli is killed in the Second War of Kappel.

Prologue

Switzerland at the Dawn
of the Reformation

Thirteen small republics, placed with their allies in the center of Europe, among mountains which seemed to form its citadel, composed a simple and brave nation. Who would have looked in those sequestered valleys for the men whom God would choose to be the liberators of the church conjointly with the children of the Germans? Who would have thought that small unknown cities—scarcely raised above barbarism, hidden behind inaccessible mountains, on the shores of lakes that had found no name in history—would surpass, as regards Christianity, even Jerusalem, Antioch, Ephesus, Corinth, and Rome? Nevertheless, such was the will of Him who "causeth it to rain upon one piece of land, and the piece of land whereupon it raineth not, withereth" (Amos 4:7).

Other circumstances besides seemed destined to oppose numerous obstacles to the progress of the Reformation in the bosom of the Swiss population. If the obstructions of power were to be dreaded in a monarchy, the precipitancy of the people was to be feared in a democracy.

But in Switzerland, also, the way had been prepared for the truth. It was a wild but generous stock, that had been sheltered in her deep valleys, to be grafted one day with a fruit of great value. Providence had scattered among these new people principles of courage, independence, and liberty, that were to be developed in all their majesty, so soon as the day of battle against Rome should arrive. The pope had conferred upon the Swiss the title "Protectors of the Liberty of the Church." But they seem to have understood this honorable appellation in a sense somewhat different from the pontiff. If their soldiers guarded the pope beneath the shadow of the ancient Capitol, their citizens carefully protected in the bosom of the Alps their own religious liberties against the assaults of the pope and of the clergy. Zurich was distinguished among all the states by its courageous resistance to the claims of Rome. Geneva, at the other extremity of Switzerland, was contending with its bishop. These two cities distinguished themselves above all the others in the great struggle that we have undertaken to describe.

But if the Helvetian towns were to be drawn into the reform movement, it was not to be the case with the inhabitants of the mountains. Knowledge had not yet reached them. These cantons, the founders of Swiss liberty, proud of the part they had taken in the great struggle for independence, were not easily disposed to imitate their younger brothers of the plain. Why should they change that faith under which they had expelled the Austrian and had consecrated by altars all the scenes of their triumphs? Their priests were the only enlightened guides to whom they could have recourse: their worship and their festivals relieved the monotony of their tranquil hours and agreeably disturbed the silence of their peaceful homes. They remained steadfast against all religious innovations.

At the moment when the decree of the Diet of Worms appeared, a continually increasing movement began to disturb the quiet valleys of Switzerland. The voices that resounded over the plains of Upper and Lower Saxony were re-echoed from the bosom of the Swiss mountains by the energetic voices of its priests, of its shepherds, and of the inhabitants of its warlike cities. The partisans of Rome were filled with apprehension, and exclaimed that a wide and terrible conspiracy was forming everywhere in the church against the church. The exulting friends of the gospel said that, as in spring the breath of life is felt from the shores of the sea to the mountaintop, so the Spirit of God was now melting throughout Christendom the ices of a lengthened winter and covering it with fresh flowers and verdure, from its lowest plains to its steepest and most barren rocks.

It was not Germany that communicated the light of truth to Switzerland, Switzerland to France, and France to England; all these countries received it from God, just as one part of the world does not communicate the light of day to the other, but the same brilliant orb imparts it direct to all the earth. Infinitely exalted above men, Christ, the Day-spring from on high, was at the epoch of the Reformation, as He had been at the establishment of Christianity, the divine fire whence emanated the life of the world. One sole and same doctrine was suddenly established in the sixteenth century at the hearths and altars of the most distant and dissimilar nations. It was everywhere the same spirit, everywhere producing the same faith.

The Reformations of Germany and of Switzerland both demonstrate this truth. Ulrich Zwingli had no communication with Martin Luther. There was no doubt a connecting link between these two men, but we must not look for it upon earth; it was from above. He who from heaven gave the truth to Luther, gave it to Zwingli also. Their bond of union was God. "I began to preach the gospel," says Zwingli, "in the year of grace 1516, that is to say, at a time when Luther's name had never been heard in this country. It is not from Luther that I learnt the doctrine of Christ, but from the Word of God. If Luther preaches Christ, he does what I am doing, and that is all."

But if the different reformations derived a striking unity from the same Spirit whence they all proceeded, they also received certain particular marks from the different nations that were affected. In Germany, the Reformation had to struggle with the will of princes; in Switzerland, against the wishes of the people. An assembly of men, more easily carried away than a single individual, is also more rapid in its decisions. The victory over the papacy, which cost years of struggle beyond the Rhine, required on this side but a few months and sometimes only a few days.

In Germany, the person of Luther towers imposingly above the Saxon people. He seems to be alone in his attacks upon the Roman colossus, and wherever the conflict is raging, we discern from afar his lofty stature rising high above the battle. Luther is the monarch, so to speak, of the revolution. In Switzerland, the struggle begins in different cantons at the same time. There is a confederation of reformers; their number surprises us. Doubtless one head overtops the others, but no one commands. It is a republican senate, in which all appear with their original features and distinct influences. They were a host: Zwingli, Capito, Haller, Oecolampadius, Myconius, Leo Juda, Farel, Calvin; their stage was Glaris, Basel, Zurich, Berne, Neuchâtel, Geneva, Lucerne, Schaffhausen, Appenzell, St. Gall, and the Grisons.

In the German Reformation there is but one stage, flat and uniform as the country itself. In Switzerland, the Reformation is divided, like the region itself, by its thousand mountains. Each valley, so to speak, has its own awakening, and each peak of the Alps its own light from heaven.

A lamentable epoch for the Swiss had begun after their exploits against the dukes of Burgundy. Europe, which had discovered the strength of their arms, had enticed them from their mountains and had robbed them of their independence by rendering them the arbitrators of the fate of nations on the battlefield. The hand of a Swiss pointed the sword at the breast of his fellow countryman on the plains of Italy and of France, and the intrigues of foreigners had filled with jealousy and dissension those lofty valleys of the Alps so long the abode of simplicity and peace. Attracted by the charms of gold, sons, laborers, and serving men stealthily quitted their Alpine pastures for the banks of the Rhône or the Po. Helvetian unity was broken under the slow steps of mules laden with gold.

The Reformation, for in Switzerland also it had its political bearings, proposed to restore the unity and the ancient virtues of the cantons. Its first cry was for the Swiss to rend the perfidious toils of the stranger and to embrace one another in close union at the foot of the cross. But its generous accents were unheeded. Rome, accustomed to purchase in these valleys the blood she shed to increase her power, rose in anger and excited Swiss against Swiss, and new passions arose to tear the body of the nation.

Switzerland needed a reform. It is now time to investigate the dawning of the new day in these valleys of the Alps.

Chapter 1
Birth of a Reformer

About the middle of the eleventh century, two hermits made their way from St. Gall toward the mountains that lie to the south of this ancient monastery, and they arrived at a desert valley, the Tockenburg, which is about ten leagues long. On the north, the lofty mountains of the Sentis, Sommerigkopf, and the Old Man separate this valley from the canton of Appenzell. On the south, the Kuhfirsten with its seven peaks rises between it and the Wallensee, Sargans, and the Grisons. On the east, the valley slopes away to the rays of the rising sun and displays the magnificent prospect of the Tyrolese Alps.

These two hermits, having reached the springs of the little river Thur, erected there two cells. By degrees the valley was peopled. On its most elevated portion (2,010 feet above the level of Lake Zurich), there arose around a church a village named Wildhaus, or the Wild-house. The fruits of the earth grow not upon these heights. A green turf of alpine freshness covers the whole valley, ascending the sides of the mountains, above which enormous masses of rock rise in savage grandeur to the skies.

About a quarter of a league from the church, by the side of a path that leads to the pasture grounds beyond the river, may still be seen a peasant's cottage. Tradition narrates that the wood necessary for its construction was felled on the very spot. Everything seems to indicate that it was built in the most remote times. The walls are thin. The windows are composed of small round panes of glass. The roof is formed of shingles, loaded with stones to prevent their being carried away by the wind. Before the house bubbles forth a limpid stream.

About the end of the fifteenth century, this house was inhabited by a man named Zwingli, the amman or bailiff of the parish. The family of the Zwinglis was ancient and in great esteem among the inhabitants of these mountains. Bartholomew, the bailiff's brother, the dean of Wesen, enjoyed a certain celebrity in the country. The wife of the amman of Wildhaus, Margaret Meili (whose brother John was somewhat later abbot of the convent of Fischingen in Thurgovia), had already borne him two sons, Henry and Klaus, when on New Year's Day, 1484 (seven weeks after the birth of Martin Luther), a third son, who was christened Ulrich, was born in this lonely chalet. Five other sons, John, Wolfgang, Bartholomew, James, and Andrew, and an only daughter, Anna, increased the number of this Alpine family.

No one in the whole district was more respected than the amman Zwingli. His character, his office, and his numerous children made him the patriarch of the mountains. He was a shepherd, as were his sons. No sooner had the first days of May clothed the mountains with verdure than the father and his children would set off for the pasture grounds with their flocks, rising gradually from station to station, and reaching in this way, by the end of July, the highest summits of the Alps. They then began to return gradually toward the valleys, and in autumn the whole population of the Wildhaus reentered their humble cottages.

Sometimes, during the summer, the young people who should have stayed at home, longing to enjoy the fresh breezes of the mountains, set out in companies for the chalets, accompanying their voices with the melodious notes of their rustic instruments, for all were musicians. When they reached the Alps, the shepherds welcomed them from afar with their horns and songs, and spread before them a repast of milk; and then the joyous troop, after many devious windings, returned to their valleys to the sound of the bagpipe. In his early youth, Ulrich doubtless sometimes shared in these amusements. He grew up at the foot of these rocks that seemed everlasting and whose summits pointed to the skies. "I have often thought," said one of his friends, "that being brought near to heaven on these sublime heights, he there contracted something very heavenly and divine."

Long were the winter evenings in the cottages of the Wildhaus. At such a season, the youthful Ulrich listened at the paternal hearth to the conversations between the bailiff and the elders of the parish. He heard them relate how the inhabitants of the valley had in former times groaned beneath a heavy yoke. He thrilled with joy at the thought of the independence the Tockenburg had won for itself and which its alliance with the Swiss had secured. The love of country kindled in his heart. Switzerland became dear to him, and if any one chanced to drop a word unfavorable to the confederates, the child would immediately rise up and warmly defend their cause. Often, too, might he be seen, during these long evenings, quietly seated at the feet of his pious grandmother, listening, with his eyes fixed on her, to her Scripture stories and her pious legends, and eagerly receiving them into his heart.

The good amman was charmed at the promising disposition of his son. He perceived that Ulrich might one day do something better than tend herds on Mount Sentis. One day he took him by the hand and led him to Wesen. He crossed the grassy flanks of the Ammon and descended the bold and savage rocks that border the Lake of Wallenstadt. On reaching the town, he entered the house of his brother, the dean, and entrusted the young mountaineer to his care, that he might examine his capacity. The dean soon loved his nephew like a son; and, charmed with his vivacity, he entrusted his education to a schoolmaster, who in a short time taught him all he knew himself. At ten years of age, the marks of a superior mind were already noticed in the young Ulrich. His father and his uncle resolved to send him to Basel.

When the child of the Tockenburg arrived in this celebrated city, a new world opened before him. The celebrity of the famous Council of Basel; the university which Pius II had founded in this city in 1460; the printing presses which then resuscitated the masterpieces of antiquity and circulated through the world the first fruits of the revival of letters; the residence of distinguished men, Wessel, Wittembach, and especially of that prince of scholars, that sun of the schools, Erasmus—all these men rendered Basel, at the epoch of the Reformation, one of the great centers of light in the West.

The city of Basel around the time of Zwingli

Ulrich was placed at St. Theodore's school. Gregory Bunzli, a man of feeling heart and gentleness rarely found at that period among teachers, was then at its head. Young Zwingli made rapid progress. The learned disputations, then in fashion among the doctors, had descended even to the children in the schools. Ulrich took part in them. He disciplined his growing powers against the pupils of other establishments, and he was always conqueror in these struggles, which were a prelude to those by which he was to overthrow the papacy in Switzerland. This success filled his elder rivals with jealousy. He soon outgrew the school of Basel, as he had that of Wesen.

Lupulus, a distinguished scholar, had just opened at Berne the first learned institution in Switzerland. The bailiff of Wildhaus and the priest of Wesen resolved to send the boy to it. Zwingli, in 1497, left the smiling plains of Basel and again approached those Upper Alps where his infancy had been spent and whose snowy tops, gilded by the sun, might be seen from Berne. Lupulus, himself a distinguished poet, introduced his pupil into the sanctuary of classic learning, a treasure then unknown, and whose threshold had been passed by only a few. The young neophyte ardently inhaled these perfumes of antiquity. His mind expanded; his style was formed. He became a poet.

He had studied polite letters at Berne. He had now to study philosophy, and for this purpose went to Vienna in Austria. The companions of Ulrich's studies and amusements in the capital of Austria were a young man of St. Gall, Joachim Vadian, whose genius promised to adorn Switzerland with a learned scholar and a distinguished statesman; Henry Loreti, of the canton of Glaris, better known as Glarean, who appeared destined to shine as a poet; and a young Swabian, John Heigerlin, the son of a blacksmith, and hence called Faber, a man of pliant character, proud of honors and renown, and who gave promise of all the qualities requisite to form a courtier.

Zwingli returned to Wildhaus in 1502. But on revisiting his native mountains, he felt that he had tasted of the cup of learning and that he could not live amidst the songs of his brothers and the lowing of their herds. Being now eighteen years of age, he again repaired to Basel to continue his literary pursuits. There, at once master and scholar, he taught in Saint Martin's school and studied at the university. From that time he was able to do without the assistance of his parents. Not long after, he took the degree of Master of Arts. An Alsatian, Wolfgang Capito by name, who was his elder by nine years, became one of his greatest friends.

Zwingli now applied to the study of scholastic divinity, for as he would one day be called to expose its sophistry, it was necessary that he should first explore its gloomy labyrinths. But the joyous student of the Sentis Mountains might be seen suddenly shaking off the dust of the schools and changing his philosophic toils for innocent amusements. He would take up one of his numerous musical instruments (the lute, harp, violin, flute, dulcimer, or hunting horn), draw from them some cheerful air, as in the pasture grounds of Lisighaus, and make his own chamber or that of his friends re-echo with the tunes of his native place or accompany them with his songs.

In his love for music he was a real child of the Tockenburg, a master among many. He played on other instruments besides those we have already named. Enthusiastic in the art of music, he spread a taste for it through the university. He liked by this means to relax his mind, fatigued by serious study, and to put himself in a condition to return with greater zeal to such arduous pursuits.

None possessed a livelier disposition, more amiable character, or more attractive conversational powers. He was like a vigorous Alpine tree, expanding in all its strength and beauty, and which, as yet unpruned, throws out its healthy branches in every direction. The time would come for these branches to shoot with fresh vigor toward heaven.

After having plunged into the scholastic divinity, he quitted its barren wastes with weariness and disgust, having only found therein a medley of confused ideas, empty babbling, vainglory, and barbarism, but not one atom of sound doctrine. "It is a mere loss of time," said he, and he waited his hour.

In November 1505, Thomas Wittembach, son of a burgomaster of Bienne, arrived at Basel. Hitherto Wittembach had been teaching at Tübingen. He was in the flower of life, sincere, pious, skilled in the liberal arts, the mathematics, and the knowledge of Scripture. Zwingli and all the youths of the academy immediately flocked around him. A life till then unknown animated his lectures, and prophetic words fell from his lips. "The hour is not far distant," said he, "in which the scholastic theology will be set aside, and the old doctrines of the church revived." "Christ's death," added he, "is the only ransom for our souls." Zwingli's heart eagerly received these seeds of life. This was at the period when classical studies were beginning everywhere to replace the Scholasticism of the Middle Ages. Zwingli, like his master and his friends, rushed into this new path.

Among the students who were most attentive to the lessons of the new doctor was a young man twenty-three years old, of small stature, of weak and sickly frame, but whose looks announced both gentleness and intrepidity. This was Leo Juda, the son of an Alsatian parish priest whose uncle had died at Rhodes fighting under the banners of the Teutonic knights in the defense of Christendom. Leo and Ulrich became intimate friends. Leo played on the dulcimer and had a very fine voice. Often did his chamber re-echo with the cheerful songs of these young friends of the arts. Leo Juda afterwards became Zwingli's colleague, and even death could not destroy so holy a friendship.

The office of pastor of Glaris became vacant at this time. One of the pope's youthful courtiers, Henri Goldli, who was already the possessor of several benefices, hastened to Glaris with the pontiff's letter of nomination. But the shepherds of Glaris, proud of the antiquity of their race and of their struggles in the cause of liberty, did not feel inclined to bend their heads before a slip of parchment from Rome. Wildhaus was not far from Glaris, and Wesen, of which Zwingli's uncle was the incumbent, was the place where these people held their markets. The reputation of the young master of arts of Basel had extended even to these mountains, and him the people of Glaris desired to have for their priest. They invited him in 1506. Zwingli was ordained at Constance by the bishop, preached his first sermon at Rapperswyl, read his first mass at Wildhaus on St. Michael's Day [late September] in the presence of all his relations and the friends of his family, and about the end of the year arrived at Glaris.

Chapter 2
Zwingli in Glaris

Zwingli immediately applied himself with zeal to the duties of his large parish. Yet he was but twenty-two years old, and often permitted himself to be led away by dissipation and by the relaxed ideas of the age. As a Catholic priest, he did not differ from all the surrounding clergy. But even at this time, when the evangelical doctrine had not changed his heart, he never gave rise to those scandals which often afflicted the church and always subjected his passions to the holy standard of the gospel.

A fondness for war at that time inflamed the tranquil valleys of Glaris. There dwelt the families of heroes whose blood had flowed on the field of battle. The aged warriors would relate to the youths, delighted at these recitals, their exploits in the wars of Burgundy and Swabia, and the combats of St. Jacques and of Ragaz. But it was no longer against the enemies of their independence that these warlike shepherds took up arms. They might be seen, at the voice of the king of France, of the emperor, of the duke of Milan, or even of the holy father himself, descending like an avalanche from the Alps and dashing with a noise of thunder against the troops drawn up in the plains.

One day as a poor boy named Matthew Schinner, who attended the school of Sion, in the Valais (in approximately the middle of the second half of the fifteenth century), was singing in the streets, he heard his name called by an old man. The latter, struck by the freedom with which the child answered his questions, said to him with that prophetic tone which a man is thought sometimes to possess on the brink of the grave: "Thou shalt be a bishop and a prince." These words struck the youthful mendicant, and from that moment a boundless ambition entered his soul. At Zurich and at Como, Schinner made such progress as to surprise his masters. He became a priest of a small parish in the Valais, rose rapidly, and later at Rome secured the bishopric of Sion for himself. This ambitious and crafty though often noble-minded and generous man never considered any dignity but as a step to mount still higher. He offered his services to Louis XII, at the same time naming his price. "It is too much for one man," said the king.

"I will show him," replied the exasperated bishop of Sion, "that I, alone, am worth many men." In effect, he turned toward Pope Julius II, who gladly welcomed him, and in 1510 Schinner succeeded in attaching the whole Swiss Confederation to the policy of this warlike pontiff. The bishop was rewarded by a cardinal's hat, and he smiled; he now saw but one step between him and the papal throne.

Schinner's eyes wandered continually over the cantons of Switzerland, and as soon as he discovered an influential man in any place, he hastened to attach him to himself. The pastor of Glaris attracted his attention, and Zwingli learnt erelong that the pope had granted him a yearly pension of fifty florins, to encourage him in his literary pursuits. His poverty did not permit him to buy books; this money, during the short time Ulrich received it, was entirely devoted to the purchase of classical or theological works, which he procured from Basel. Zwingli from that time attached himself to the cardinal, and thus entered the Roman party. Schinner and Julius II at last betrayed the object of their intrigues. Eight thousand Swiss, whom the eloquence of the cardinal-bishop had enlisted, crossed the Alps. But want of provisions made them return ingloriously to their mountains. They carried back with them the usual concomitants of these foreign wars—distrust, licentiousness, party spirit, violence, and disorders of every kind. Citizens refused to obey their magistrates; children their parents; agriculture and the cares of their flocks and herds were neglected; luxury and beggary increased side by side. The Confederation seemed on the brink of dissolution.

Then were the eyes of the young priest of Glaris opened, and his indignation burst forth. His powerful voice was raised to warn the people of the gulf into which they were about to fall. It was in the year 1510 that he published his poem entitled "The Labyrinth." It tells how, within the mazes of a mysterious garden, Minos has concealed the Minotaur, that monster, half-man, half-bull, whom he feeds with the bodies of the young Athenians. "This Minotaur," says Zwingli, "represents the sins, the vices, the irreligion, the foreign service of the Swiss, which devour the sons of the nation."

A bold man, Theseus, determines to rescue his country; but numerous obstacles arrest him: first, a one-eyed lion (this is Spain and Aragon); then a crowned eagle, whose beak opens to swallow him up (this is the Empire); then a cock, raising its crest, and seeming to challenge to the fight (this is France). The hero surmounts all these obstacles, reaches the monster, slays him, and saves his country.

"In like manner," exclaims the poet, "are men now wandering in a labyrinth, but, as they have no clue, they cannot regain the light. Nowhere do we find an imitation of Jesus Christ. A little glory leads us to risk our lives, torment our neighbor, and rush into disputes, war, and battle. . . . One might imagine that the furies had broken loose from the abyss of hell."

A Theseus, a reformer was needed. This Zwingli perceived clearly, and henceforth he felt a presentiment of his mission.

In April 1512, the confederates again arose at the voice of the cardinal for the defense of the church. Glaris was in the foremost rank. The whole parish took the field under their banner, with the landamman and their pastor. Zwingli was compelled to march with them. The army passed the Alps, and the cardinal appeared in the midst of the confederates decorated with the pontiff's present—a ducal cap ornamented with pearls and gold and surmounted by the Holy Ghost represented under the form of a dove. The Swiss scaled the ramparts of fortresses and the walls of cities, and in the presence of their enemies swam naked across rivers, halberds in hand.

The French were defeated at every point. Bells and trumpets pealed their notes of triumph. The people crowded around them from all quarters; the nobles furnished the army with wine and fruits in abundance. Monks and priests mounted the pulpits and proclaimed that the confederates were the people of God, who avenged the Bride of the Lord on her enemies. The pope, a prophet like Caiaphas of old, conferred on them the title of "Defenders of the Liberty of the Church."

This sojourn in Italy was not without its influence on Zwingli as regards his call to the Reformation. On his return from this campaign, he began to study Greek "in order to be able to draw from the fountainhead of truth the doctrines of Jesus Christ. I am determined to apply myself to Greek," wrote he to Vadian on February 23, 1513, "that no one shall be able to turn me aside from it, except God: I do it, not for glory, but for the love of sacred learning." Somewhat later, a worthy priest, who had been his schoolfellow, coming to see him said: "Master Ulrich, I am informed that you are falling into this new error; that you are a Lutheran."

"I am not a Lutheran," said Zwingli, "for I learned Greek before I had ever heard the name of Luther." To know Greek, to study the gospel in the original language, was, in Zwingli's opinion, the basis of the Reformation.

Zwingli went further than merely acknowledging at this early period the grand principle of evangelical Christianity, the infallible authority of Holy Scripture. He perceived, moreover, how we should determine the sense of the Divine Word: "They have a very mean idea of the gospel," said he, "who consider as frivolous, vain, and unjust, all that they imagine does not accord with their own reason. Men are not permitted to wrest the gospel at pleasure that it may square with their own sentiments and interpretation."

"Zwingli turned his eyes to heaven," says his best friend, Oswald Myconius, "for he would have no other interpreter than the Holy Ghost himself."

Such, at the commencement of his career, was the man whom certain persons have not hesitated to represent as having desired to subject the Bible to human reason. "Philosophy and divinity," said he, "were always raising objections. At last I said to myself: I must neglect all these matters, and look for God's will in his Word alone. I began earnestly to entreat the Lord to grant me his light, and although I read the Scriptures only, they became clearer to me than if I had read all the commentators."

He compared Scripture with itself, explaining obscure passages by those that are clear. He soon knew the Bible thoroughly, and particularly the New Testament. When Zwingli thus turned toward Holy Scripture, Switzerland took its first step toward the Reformation.

Zwingli did not, however, condemn the explanations of the most celebrated doctors. In afteryears he studied Origen, Ambrose, Jerome, Augustine, and Chrysostom, but not as authorities. "I study the doctors," said he, "with the same end as when we ask a friend: How do you understand this passage?" Holy Scripture, in his opinion, was the touchstone by which to test the holiest doctors themselves.

Zwingli's course was slow, but progressive. He did not arrive at the truth, like Martin Luther, by those storms which impel the soul to run hastily to its harbor of refuge. He reached it by the peaceful influence of Scripture, whose power expands gradually in the heart. Luther attained the wished-for shore through the storms of the wide ocean; Zwingli, by gliding softly down the stream.

About this period, one of Erasmus's poems, in which Jesus Christ addresses mankind perishing through their own fault, made a deep impression on Zwingli. Alone in his closet, he repeated to himself that passage in which Jesus complains that men do not seek every grace from him, although He is the source of all that is good. "*All*," said he, "*all*." And this word was ever present to his mind. "Are there, then, any creatures, any saints, of whom we should beg assistance? No: Christ is our only treasure."

Zwingli did not restrict himself to the study of Christian letters. One of the characteristic features of the reformers of the sixteenth century is their profound study of the Greek and Roman writers. The poems of Hesiod, Homer, and Pindar possessed great charms for Zwingli, and he has left some writings about the two last poets. It seemed to him that Pindar spoke of the gods in so sublime a strain that he must have felt a presentiment of the true God. He studied Demosthenes and Cicero thoroughly, and in their writings learnt the art of oratory and the duties of a citizen. He called Seneca a holy man. The child of the Swiss mountains delighted also to investigate the mysteries of nature in the works of Pliny. Thucydides, Sallust, Livy, Caesar, Suetonius, Plutarch, and Tacitus taught him the knowledge of mankind.

He has been reproached with his enthusiasm for the great men of antiquity, and it is true that some of his expressions on this subject admit of no justification. But if he honored them so highly, it was because he fancied he discerned in them not mere human virtues but the influence of the Holy Ghost. In his opinion, God's influence, far from being limited in ancient times by the boundaries of Palestine, extended over the whole world. "Plato," said he, "has also drunk at this heavenly spring. And if the two Catos, Scipio, and Camillus had not been truly religious, could they have been so high-minded?"

Zwingli communicated a taste for letters to all around him. Many intelligent young men were educated at his school. "You have offered me not only books, but yourself also," wrote Valentine Tschudi, son of one of the heroes in the Burgundian wars. And this young man, who had already studied at Vienna and Basel under the most celebrated doctors, added, "I have found no one who could explain the classic authors with such acumen and profundity as yourself." Tschudi went to Paris, and thus was able to compare the spirit that prevailed in this university with that which he had found in a narrow valley of the Alps. "In what frivolities do they educate the French youth!" said he. "No poison can equal the sophistical art that they are taught. It dulls the senses, weakens the judgment, and brutalizes the man, who then becomes, as it were, a mere echo, an empty sound. Ten women could not make head against one of these rhetoricians. Even in their prayers, I am certain, they bring their sophisms before God, and by their syllogisms presume to constrain the Holy Spirit to answer them."

Such were at that time Paris, the intellectual metropolis of Christendom, and Glaris, a village of herdmen among the Alps. One ray of light from God's Word enlightens more than all the wisdom of man.

Chapter 3
Myconius and Oecolampadius

A great man of that age, Desiderius Erasmus, exercised much influence over Zwingli. No sooner did one of his writings appear than Zwingli hastened to purchase it. In 1514 Erasmus arrived in Basel, where the bishop received him with every mark of esteem. All the friends of learning immediately assembled around him. But the prince of the schools had easily discovered him who was to be the glory of Switzerland. "I congratulate the Helvetians," wrote he to Zwingli, "that you are laboring to polish and civilize them by your studies and your morals, which are alike of the highest order."

Zwingli earnestly longed to see Erasmus. "Spaniards and Gauls went to Rome to see Livy," said he, and set out. On arriving at Basel, he found there a man about forty years of age, of small stature, weak frame, and delicate appearance, but exceedingly amiable and polite. It was Erasmus. His agreeable manners soon banished Zwingli's timidity; the power of his genius subdued him. "Poor as Aeschines," said Zwingli, "when each of Socrates' disciples offered their master a present, I give you what Aeschines gave. . . . I give you myself!"

Among the men of learning who then formed the court of Erasmus, Zwingli noticed Oswald Geisshussler, a young man of Lucerne, twenty-seven years old. Erasmus hellenized his name and called him Myconius. Oswald, after studying at Rothwyl with a youth of his own age named Berthold Haller, and next at Berne and at Basel, had become rector of Saint Theodore's school, and afterwards of Saint Peter's in the latter city. The humble schoolmaster, though possessed of a scanty income, had married a young woman whose simplicity and purity of mind won all hearts.

We have already seen that this was a time of trouble in Switzerland, in which foreign wars gave rise to violent disorders, and the soldiers, returning to their country, brought back with them their campaigning habits of licentiousness and brutality. One dark and cloudy day in winter, some of these ruffians at-tacked Myconius's quiet dwelling in his absence. They knocked at the door, threw stones, and called for his modest wife in the most indecent language. At last they dashed in the windows, and entering the schoolroom, broke everything they could find, and then retired.

Oswald returned shortly after. His son, little Felix, ran to meet him with loud cries, and his wife, unable to speak, made frightened signs. He perceived what had happened. At the same moment, a noise was heard in the street. Unable to control his feelings, the schoolmaster seized a weapon and pursued the riot-ers to the cemetery. They took refuge within it, prepared to de-fend themselves. Three of their number fell upon Myconius and wounded him; and while his wound was being dressed, those wretches again broke into his house with furious cries. Such were the scenes that took place in the cities of Switzerland at the be-ginning of the sixteenth century, before the Reformation had soft-ened and disciplined manners.

The integrity of Oswald Myconius, his thirst for knowledge and virtue, brought him into contact with Zwingli. The rector of the school of Basel recognized the superiority of the priest of Glaris. In his humility he shrank from the praises lavished on him both by Zwingli and Erasmus. The latter would often say, "I look upon you schoolmasters as the peers of kings." But the modest Myconius was of a different opinion. "I do but crawl upon the earth. From my childhood, there has been something humble and mean about me."

A preacher who had arrived in Basel at nearly the same time as Zwingli was then attracting general attention. Of a mild and peaceful disposition, he loved a tranquil life. Slow and circum-spect in action, his chief delight was to labor in his study and to promote concord among all Christians. His name was John Hausschein, in Greek *Oecolampadius*, or "the light of the house." He was born in Franconia, of rich parents, a year before Zwingli.

His pious mother desired to consecrate to learning and to God the only child that Providence had left her. His father at first destined him to business and then to jurisprudence. But after Oecolampadius had returned to Bologna, where he had been studying the law, the Lord, who was pleased to make him a light in the church, called him to the study of theology. He was preaching in his native town when Wolfgang Capito, who had known him at Heidelberg, got him appointed preacher at Basel. He there proclaimed Christ with an eloquence which filled his hearers with admiration. Erasmus admitted him into his intimacy.

Oecolampadius was charmed with the hours he passed in the society of this great genius. "There is but one thing," said the monarch of learning to him, "that we should look for in Holy Scripture, and that is Jesus Christ." He gave the youthful preacher, as a memorial of his friendship, the commencement of the Gospel of St. John. Oecolampadius would often kiss this pledge of so valued an affection, and kept it suspended to his crucifix, "in order," said he, "that I may always remember Erasmus in my prayers."

Zwingli returned to his native mountains, his heart and mind full of all he had seen and heard at Basel. "I should be unable to sleep," wrote he to Erasmus shortly after his return, "if I had not held some conversation with you. There is nothing I am prouder of than of having seen Erasmus."

Zwingli had received a new impulse. Such journeys often exercise a great influence over the career of a Christian. Zwingli's pupils were delighted to see him increase in knowledge and in wisdom. The old respected him as a courageous patriot; the faithful pastors, as a zealous minister of the Lord. Nothing was done in the country without his being first consulted. All good people hoped that the ancient virtues of Switzerland would one day be revived by him.

Francis I, having ascended the throne, desired to avenge in Italy the honor of the French name. The pope, in consternation, endeavored to win over the cantons. Thus, in 1515, Ulrich again visited the plains of Italy in the midst of the phalanxes of his countrymen. But the dissensions that the intrigues of the French sowed in the confederate army wrung his heart. Often might he be seen in the midst of the camp haranguing with energy, and at the same time with great wisdom, an audience armed from head to foot, and ready to fight.

On September 8, five days before the battle of Marignan, he preached in the square of Monza, where the Swiss soldiers who had remained faithful to their colors were assembled. "If we had then, and even later, followed Zwingli's advice," said Werner Steiner of Zug, "what evils would our country have been spared!" But all ears were shut against the voice of concord, prudence, and submission. The impetuous eloquence of Cardinal Schinner electrified the confederates and impelled them to rush like a torrent to the fatal field of Marignan. The flower of the Helvetian youth perished there.

Zwingli, who had been unable to prevent such disasters, threw himself, in the cause of Rome, into the midst of danger. His hand wielded the sword. A melancholy error! A minister of Christ, he forgot more than once that he should fight only with the weapons of the Spirit, and he was destined to see fulfilled, in his own person, this prophecy of our Lord: They that take the sword, shall perish with the sword.

This second visit to Italy was not unprofitable to Zwingli. He remarked the difference between the Ambrosian ritual in use at Milan and that of Rome. He collected and compared with each other the most ancient canons of the Mass. Thus a spirit of inquiry was developed in him, even amid the tumult of camps. At the same time the sight of the children of his fatherland, led beyond the Alps and delivered up to slaughter like their herds, filled him with indignation. It was a common saying, that "the flesh of the confederates was cheaper than that of their kine." The faithlessness and ambition of the pope, the avarice and ignorance of the priests, the licentiousness and dissipation of the monks, the pride and luxury of the prelates, the corruption and venality that infected the Swiss on every side—all these evils forced themselves upon his attention, and made him feel more keenly than ever the necessity of a reform in the church.

From this time Zwingli preached the Word of God more clearly. He explained the portions of the Gospels and Epistles selected for the public services, always comparing scripture with scripture. He spoke with animation and with power, and he pursued with his hearers the same course that God had adopted with him. He did not, like Martin Luther, expose the sores of the church. But in proportion as the study of the Bible manifested to him any useful lesson, he communicated it to his flock. He endeavoured to instill the truth into their hearts, and then relied on it for the result that it was destined to produce. "If the people understand what is true," thought he, "they will soon discern what is false." This maxim is good for the commencement of a reformation, but there comes a time when error should be boldly pointed out. This Zwingli knew full well. "The spring is the season for sowing," said he, and it was then springtime with him.

Had Zwingli remained at Glaris, he might possibly have been a mere man of the age. Party intrigue, political prejudices, the empire, France, and the duke of Milan, might have almost absorbed his life. God never leaves in the midst of the tumult of the world those whom he is training for his people. He leads them aside. He places them in some retirement, where they find themselves face to face with God and themselves, and whence they derive inexhaustible instruction. The Son of God Himself, a type in this respect of the course He pursues with his servants, passed forty days in the wilderness.

It was now time to withdraw Zwingli from this political movement which, by constant repetition in his soul, would have quenched the Spirit of God. The hour had come to prepare him for another stage than that on which courtiers, cabinets, and factions contended, and where he would have uselessly wasted a strength worthy of a higher occupation. His fellow countrymen had need of something better. It was necessary that a new life should now descend from heaven, and that the instrument of its transmission should unlearn the things of earth, to learn those of heaven. God at this time removed him from among the factions of Glaris and conducted him to the solitude of a hermitage. He confined within the narrow walls of an abbey this generous seed of the Reformation, which, soon transplanted to a better soil, was to cover the mountains with its shadow.

Chapter 4
Zwingli at Einsidlen

About the middle of the ninth century, a German monk, Meinrad of Hohenzollern, had passed between the lakes of Zurich and Wallenstadt and halted on a little hill in front of an amphitheater of pines, where he built a cell. Ruffians imbrued their hands in the blood of the saint. The polluted cell long remained deserted. About the end of the tenth century, a convent and church in honor of the virgin were built on this sacred spot.

About midnight on the eve of the day of consecration, the bishop of Constance and his priests were at prayers in the church. A heavenly strain, proceeding from invisible beings, suddenly resounded through the chapel. They listened prostrate and with admiration. On the morrow, as the bishop was about to consecrate the building, a voice repeated thrice: "Stop! Stop! God Himself has consecrated it!" Christ in person (it was said) had blessed it during the night. The strains they had heard were those of angels, apostles, and saints, and the virgin standing above the altar shone with the brightness of lightning.

A bull of Leo VIII had forbidden the faithful to doubt the truth of this legend. From that time, an immense crowd of pilgrims had annually visited our Lady of the Hermits for the festival of "The Consecration of the Angels." Delphi and Ephesus in ancient times, and Loretto in more recent days, have alone equaled the renown of Einsidlen. It was in this extraordinary place that, in 1516, Ulrich Zwingli was invited to be priest and preacher.

Zwingli did not hesitate. "It is neither ambition nor covetousness," said he, "that takes me there, but the intrigues of the French." Reasons of a higher kind determined him. On the one hand, having more solitude, more tranquillity, and a less extensive parish, he would be able to devote more time to study and meditation; on the other, this resort of pilgrims offered him an easy means of spreading a knowledge of Jesus Christ into the most distant countries.

Conrad of Rechberg, a gentleman descended from an ancient family, serious, frank, intrepid, and sometimes perhaps a little rough, was one of the most celebrated huntsmen of the country to which Zwingli was going. In one of his farms (the Silthal), he raised a breed of horses that became famous in Italy. Such was the abbot of Our Lady of the Hermits.

Rechberg held in equal detestation the pretensions of Rome and theological discussions. One day when, during a visitation of the order, some observations were made to him: "I am master here, and not you," said he, somewhat rudely. "Go your ways." At another time, as Leo Juda was discussing some intricate question at table with the administrator of the convent, the hunting abbot exclaimed, "Leave off your disputes! I cry with David: Have mercy upon me, O God, according to thy lovingkindness, and enter not into judgment with thy servant. I desire to know nothing more."

The manager of the monastery was Baron Theobald of Geroldsek, a man of mild character, sincere piety, and great love for letters. His favorite plan was to assemble in his convent a body of learned men, and with this view he had invited Zwingli. Eager for instruction and reading, he begged his new friend to direct him. "Study the Holy Scriptures," replied Zwingli, "and that you may better understand them, read Saint Jerome. However, a time will come (and that soon, with God's help) when Christians will not set great store either by Saint Jerome or any other doctor, but solely by the Word of God." Geroldsek's conduct gave indication of his progress in faith. He permitted the nuns in a convent depending on Einsidlen to read the Bible in the common tongue, and some years later Geroldsek went and lived at Zurich beside Zwingli and died with him on the field of Kappel.

The same charm erelong tenderly attached to Zwingli, not only Geroldsek, but also Zink the chaplain, the worthy Oexlin, Lucas, and other inmates of the abbey. These studious men, far from the tumult of parties, used to unite in reading the Scriptures, the fathers of the church, the masterpieces of antiquity, and the writings of the restorers of learning.

This interesting circle was often increased by friends from distant parts. Among others, Capito one day arrived at Einsidlen. The two old friends of Basel walked over the convent together and strolled about its wild environs, absorbed in conversation, examining the Scriptures, and seeking to learn God's will. There was one point upon which they were agreed, and it was this: "The pope of Rome must fall!" Capito was at this time a bolder man than he was afterwards.

In this calm retreat Zwingli enjoyed rest, leisure, books, and friends, and grew in understanding and in faith. It was then (May 1517) that he commenced a work that proved very useful to him. As in ancient days the kings of Israel transcribed God's law with their own hands, so Zwingli with his copied out the Epistles of St. Paul. At that time there existed none but voluminous editions of the New Testament, and Zwingli wished to be able to carry it with him always. He learned these Epistles by heart, and somewhat later the other books of the New Testament and part of the Old. His soul thus grew daily more attached to the supreme authority of the Word of God. He was not content simply to acknowledge this authority. He resolved sincerely to subject his life to it. He entered gradually into a more Christian path.

The purpose for which he had been brought into this desert was being accomplished. Doubtless, it was not until his residence at Zurich that the power of a Christian life penetrated all his being, but already at Einsidlen he had made evident progress in sanctification. At Glaris, he had been seen to take part in worldly amusements. At Einsidlen, he sought more and more after a life pure from every stain and from all worldliness. He began to have a better understanding of the great spiritual interests of the people and learned by degrees what God designed to teach him.

Providence, in bringing him to Einsidlen, had also other aims. He was to have a nearer view of the superstitions and abuses which had invaded the church. The image of the virgin, carefully preserved in the monastery, had, it was said, the power of working miracles. Over the gate of the abbey might be read this presumptuous inscription: "Here a plenary remission of sins may be obtained." A crowd of pilgrims flocked to Einsidlen from every part of Christendom to merit this grace by their pilgrimage at the festival of the virgin. The church, the abbey, and all the valley were filled with her devout worshippers. But it was particularly at the great feast of "The Consecration of the Angels" that the crowd thronged the hermitage. Many thousand individuals of both sexes climbed in long files the slopes of the mountain leading to the oratory, singing hymns or counting their beads. These devout pilgrims crowded eagerly into the church, imagining themselves nearer to God there than elsewhere.

In this monastery Zwingli completed his education as a reformer. God alone is the source of salvation, and He is everywhere. This was what he learned at Einsidlen, and these two truths became the fundamental articles of Zwingli's theology. The seriousness he had acquired in his soul soon manifested itself in his actions. Struck by the knowledge of so many evils, he resolved to oppose them boldly. He did not hesitate between his conscience and his interests. He stood forth with courage, and his energetic eloquence uncompromisingly attacked the superstitions of the crowd that surrounded him. "Do not imagine," said he from the pulpit, "that God is in this temple more than in any other part of creation. Whatever be the country in which you dwell, God is around you, and hears you as well as at Our Lady's [sic] of Einsidlen. Can unprofitable works, long pilgrimages, offerings, images, the invocation of the virgin or of the saints, secure for you the grace of God? . . . What avails the multitude of words with which we embody our prayers? What efficacy has a glossy cowl, a smooth-shorn head, a long and flowing robe, or gold-embroidered slippers! . . . God looks at the heart, and our hearts are far from Him!"

But Zwingli desired to do more than merely inveigh against superstition. He wished to satisfy the ardent yearnings for reconciliation with God, experienced by many pilgrims who flocked to the chapel of Our Lady of Einsidlen. "Christ," exclaimed he, like John the Baptist in this new desert of the mountains of Judea, "who was once offered upon the cross, is the sacrifice and victim, that had made satisfaction for the sins of believers to all eternity."

Thus Zwingli advanced. On the day when such bold language was first heard in the most venerated sanctuary of Switzerland, the standard uplifted against Rome began to rise more distinctly above its mountains, and there was, so to speak, an earthquake of reformation that shook her very foundations.

In effect, universal astonishment filled the crowd as they listened to the words of the eloquent priest. Some withdrew in horror. Others hesitated between the faith of their sires and this doctrine which was to ensure peace. Many went to Jesus, who was preached to them as meek and gentle, and they carried back the tapers they had brought to present to the virgin. A crowd of pilgrims returned to their homes, everywhere announcing what they had heard at Einsidlen: "Christ *alone* saves, and He saves *everywhere.*" Often whole bands, amazed at these reports, turned back without completing their pilgrimage. Mary's worshipers diminished in number daily. It was their offerings that made up in great measure the stipends of Zwingli and Geroldsek. But this bold witness to the truth felt happy in impoverishing himself, if he could spiritually enrich souls.

Among Zwingli's numerous hearers at the feast of Whitsuntide in 1518 was Gaspard Hedio, doctor of divinity at Basel, a learned man, of mild character and active charity. Zwingli was preaching on the narrative of the paralytic (Luke 5), in which occurs this declaration of our Lord: "The Son of Man hath power upon earth to forgive sins"—words well adapted to strike the crowd assembled in the temple of the virgin. The preacher's sermon stirred, charmed, and inspired his congregation, and particularly the Basel doctor. For a long while after, Hedio was accustomed to speak of it with admiration. "How beautiful is this discourse," said he. "How profound, solemn, copious, penetrating, and evangelical! How it reminds us of the force of the ancient doctors!"

From this moment, Hedio admired and loved Zwingli. He would have liked to have spoken with him. He wandered around the abbey, yet dared not advance, being held back (he says) by superstitious timidity. He remounted his horse and retired slowly, often turning his head toward the walls that enclosed so great a treasure, and bearing away in his heart the keenest regret.

Thus preached Zwingli, certainly with less force, but with more moderation and not less success than Luther. He precipitated nothing. He shocked men's minds far less than the Saxon reformer. He expected everything from the power of truth. He behaved with the same discretion in his communication with the heads of the church. Far from showing himself immediately as their adversary like Luther, he long remained their friend. The latter humored him exceedingly, not only on account of his learning and talents, but especially because of his attachment to the political party of the pope and the influence such a man as Zwingli possessed in a republican state.

Several cantons, indeed, disgusted with the papal service, were on the point of breaking with it. But the legates flattered themselves in thinking they would retain many by gaining Zwingli, as they had already gained Erasmus, by pensions and honors. The legates Ennius and Pucci paid frequent visits to Einsidlen, whence, considering its vicinity to the democratic cantons, their negotiations with these states were easier. But Zwingli, far from sacrificing the truth to the demands and offers of Rome, let no opportunity escape of defending the gospel. The famous Schinner, whose diocese was then in a disturbed state, spent some time at Einsidlen. "The popedom," said Zwingli one day, "reposes on a bad foundation. Apply yourselves to the work. Reject all errors and abuses, or else you will see the whole edifice fall with a tremendous crash."

He spoke with the same freedom to Cardinal Pucci. Four times he returned to the charge. "With God's aid," said he, "I will continue to preach the gospel, and this preaching will make Rome totter." He then explained to the prelate what ought to be done in order to save the church. Pucci promised everything but did nothing. Zwingli declared that he would resign the pope's pension. The legate entreated him to keep it, and Zwingli, who had no intention at that time of setting himself in open hostility against the head of the church, consented to receive it for three years longer. "But do not imagine," added he, "that for love of money I retract a single syllable of the truth." Pucci, in alarm, procured for the reformer the nomination of acolyte to the pope. This was a step to further honors.

Rome aimed at frightening Luther by her judgments and gaining Zwingli by her favors. Against the one she hurled her excommunications; to the other she cast her gold and splendors. These were two different ways of attaining the same end, and of silencing the bold tongues that dared proclaim the Word of God in Germany and in Switzerland. The latter was the more skillful policy, but neither was successful. The emancipated souls of the preachers of the truth were equally beyond the reach of vengeance or of favor.

Another Swiss prelate, Hugo of Landenberg, bishop of Constance, about this time excited hopes in Zwingli's breast. He ordered a general visitation of the churches. But Landenberg, a man of no decision of character, permitted himself to be guided at one time by Faber, his vicar, and at another by a vicious woman whose influence he could not shake off. Sometimes he appeared to honor the gospel, and yet he looked upon any man as a disturber of the people who ventured to preach it boldly. He was one of those men, too common in the church, who, although they prefer truth to error, show more regard to error than to truth, and often end by turning against those by whose sides they should have fought. Zwingli applied to him, but in vain. He was destined to make the same experiment as Luther, and to acknowledge that it was useless to invoke the assistance of the heads of the church, and that the only way of reviving Christianity was to act as a faithful teacher of the Word of God. The opportunity soon came.

Along the heights of Saint Gothard, over those elevated roads that have been cut with incredible toil through the steep rocks that separate Switzerland from Italy, journeyed a Franciscan monk in the month of August 1518. Emerging from an Italian monastery, he was the bearer of the papal indulgences which he had been empowered to sell to the good Christians of the Helvetic Confederation.

The brilliant successes gained under the two preceding popes had conferred honor on this scandalous traffic. Accompanied by men appointed to puff up the wares he had for sale, he crossed these snows and icy glaciers as old as the world. This greedy train, whose appearance was wretched enough, not ill resembling a band of adventurers in search of plunder, advanced silently to the noise of the impetuous torrents that form the Rhine, the Rhône, the Ticino, and other rivers, meditating the spoliation of the simple inhabitants of Switzerland.

Samson, for such was the Franciscan's name, and his troop arrived first in Uri, and there opened their trade. They soon finished with these poor mountaineers, and then passed on to Schwytz. Zwingli resided in this canton—and here combat was to take place between the two servants of two very different masters. "I can pardon all sins," said the Italian monk, the Tetzel of Switzerland, addressing the inhabitants of the capital. "Heaven and hell are subject to my power, and I sell the merits of Christ to any who will purchase them by buying an indulgence for ready money."

Zwingli's zeal took fire as he heard of these discourses. He preached with energy, saying, "Jesus Christ, the Son of God, has said, 'Come *unto me* all ye that are weary and heaven laden, and I will give you rest.' Is it not, then, most presumptuous folly and senseless temerity to declare, on the contrary, 'Buy letters of indulgence! Hasten to Rome! Give to the monks! Sacrifice to the priests! And if thou doest these things, I absolve thee from thy sins?' Jesus Christ is the only oblation, the only sacrifice, the only way!"

Throughout Schwytz, Samson erelong was called a cheat and seducer. He took the road to Zug, and for a time the two champions did not meet.

Scarcely had Samson left Schwytz when Stapfer, a citizen of this canton, a man of distinguished character and afterwards secretary of state, was suddenly reduced with his family to great distress. "Alas!" said he, addressing Zwingli in his anguish, "I know not how to satisfy my hunger, and that of my poor children."

Zwingli every day carried Stapfer abundant supplies. "It is God," said he, desirous of taking no praise to himself, "who begets charity in the faithful, and gives at once the thought, the resolve, and the work itself. Whatever good work the just man doeth, it is God who doeth it by His own power." Stapfer remained attached to Zwingli all his life, and when four years later he had become secretary of state at Schwytz, and felt impelled by more elevated desires, he turned toward Zwingli, saying with nobleness and candor, "Since it was you who provided for my temporal wants, how much more may I now expect from you the food that shall satisfy my soul!"

Zwingli's friends increased in number. But the priest of Einsidlen had no friend more devoted than Oswald Myconius. Oswald had quitted Basel in 1516 to superintend the cathedral school at Zurich. At that time this city possessed neither learned men nor learned schools. Oswald labored, in conjunction with several other well-disposed men, among whom was Utinger, the pope's notary, to rescue the Zurich people from their ignorance, and to initiate them in the literature of the ancients. At the same time he upheld the immutable truth of the Holy Scriptures, and declared that if the pope and the emperor command anything in opposition to the gospel, man is bound to obey God alone, who is above the emperor and the pope.

Chapter 5
Zwingli Comes to Zurich

Seven centuries before, Charlemagne had attached a college of canons to the cathedral of Zurich, the school belonging to which was under the direction of Myconius. These canons having declined from their primitive institutions and desiring to enjoy their benefices in the sweets of an indolent life, used to elect a priest to whom they confided the preaching and the cure of souls. This post became vacant shortly after the arrival of Myconius, who immediately thought of his friend. Zwingli's exterior was in his favor. He was a handsome man, of graceful manners and pleasing conversation. He had already become celebrated for his eloquence and excelled throughout the Confederation by the splendor of his genius.

Myconius spoke of him to Felix Frey, the provost of the chapter, who was prepossessed by Zwingli's talents and appearance; to Utinger, an old man, highly respected; and to the canon Hoffmann, a person of upright and open character, who, from having long preached against the foreign service, was already well disposed in Ulrich's favor. Other Zurichers had, on different occasions, heard Zwingli at Einsidlen and had returned full of admiration.

The election of a preacher for the cathedral soon put everybody in Zurich in motion. The different parties began to bestir themselves. Many labored day and night to procure the election of the eloquent preacher of Our Lady of the Hermits. Myconius informed his friend of this. "Wednesday next, I shall go and dine at Zurich," replied Zwingli, "and then we will talk this matter over." He came accordingly.

While he was paying a visit to one of the canons, the latter said, "Can you not come and preach the Word of God among us?"

"I can," replied he, "but I will not come, unless I am called." He then returned to his abbey.

This visit spread alarm in the camp of his enemies. All agreed in extolling to the clouds the extent of his acquirements, but some said, "He is too fond of music!" Others, "He loves company and pleasure!" And others again, "He was once too intimate with persons of light conduct!" One man even accused him of seduction. Zwingli was not blameless, and although less erring than the ecclesiastics of his day, he had more than once, in the first years of his ministry, allowed himself to be led astray by the passions of youth. We cannot easily form an idea of the influence upon the soul of the corrupt atmosphere in which it lives. There existed in the papacy, and among the priests, disorders that were established, allowed, and authorized, as conformable to the laws of nature. Disorder had come to be the generally admitted order of things.

Myconius exerted an unwearying activity in his friend's behalf. He employed all his powers to justify him, and luckily succeeded. He visited the Burgomaster Roust, Hoffmann, Frey, and Utinger. He lauded the probity, decorum, and purity of Zwingli's conduct and confirmed the Zurichers in the favorable impression they entertained toward the priest of Einsidlen. Little credit was paid to the stories of his adversaries. The most influential men said that Zwingli would be preacher at Zurich. The canons said the same, but in an undertone.

"Hope on," wrote Myconius with a rising heart; "hope on, for I hope." He nevertheless informed him of the accusations of his enemies. Although Zwingli had not yet become altogether a new man, he was one of those whose conscience is awakened, who may fall into sin, but never without a struggle and without remorse. Often had he resolved to lead a holy life, alone among his kind, in the midst of the world. But when he found himself accused, he would not boast of being without sin. "Having no one to walk with me in the resolutions I had formed," wrote he to the canon Utinger, "many even of those about me being offended at them, alas! I fell, and like the dog of which St. Peter speaks (II Pet. 2:22), I turned again to my vomit. The Lord knows with what shame and anguish I have dragged these faults from the bottom of my heart, and laid them before that great Being to whom, however, I confess my wretchedness far more willingly than to man." But if Zwingli acknowledged himself a sinner, he vindicated himself from the odious accusations that had been made against him. He declared that he had always banished the thought of adultery or seducing the innocent—grievous excesses which were then too common. "I call to witness," says he, "all those with whom I have ever lived."

The election took place on December 11. Zwingli was appointed by a majority of seventeen votes out of twenty-four. It was time that the Reformation began in Switzerland. The chosen instrument that Providence had been preparing for three years in the hermitage of Einsidlen was ready. The hour was come for him to be stationed elsewhere. God selected in Helvetia the city of Zurich, regarded as the head of the Confederation, there to station Zwingli. In that place he would be in communication not only with one of the most intelligent and simple-hearted, the strongest and the most energetic people in Switzerland, but also still more with all the cantons that collected around this ancient and powerful state. The hand that had led a young herdsman from the Sentis to the school of Wesen was now setting him, mighty in word and in deed, in the face of all, that he might regenerate his nation. Zurich was about to become the center of light to the whole of Switzerland.

It was a day of mingled joy and sorrow at Einsidlen, when its inmates were informed of Zwingli's nomination. The society which had been formed there was about to be broken up by the removal of its most valuable member, and who could say that superstition might not again prevail in this ancient resort of pilgrims? The state council of Schwytz transmitted to Ulrich the expression of their sentiments, styling him, "reverend, most learned, very gracious lord and good friend."

"Give us at least a successor worthy of yourself," said the heartbroken Theobald of Geroldsek to Zwingli.

"I have a little lion for you," replied he, "one who is prudent and deep in the mysteries of Scripture." It was Leo Juda, that mild and intrepid man, with whom Zwingli had been so intimate at

Basel. Leo accepted this invitation which brought him nearer his dear Ulrich. The latter embraced his friends, quitted the solitude of Einsidlen, and arrived at that delightful spot where rises the cheerful and animated city of Zurich, with its amphitheater of hills, covered with vineyards, or adorned with pastures and orchards, and crowned with forests above which appear the highest summits of the Albis.

Zurich, the center of the political interests of Switzerland, and in which were often collected the most influential men in the nation, was the spot best adapted for acting upon Helvetia and scattering the seeds of truth through all the cantons. Accordingly, the friends of learning and of the Bible joyfully hailed Zwingli's nomination. At Paris, in particular, the Swiss students, who were very numerous, thrilled with joy at this intelligence. But if at Zurich a great victory lay before Zwingli, he had also to expect a hard struggle. Glarean wrote to him from Paris: "I foresee that your learning will excite great hatred; but be of good cheer, and like Hercules you will subdue the monsters."

On December 27, 1518, Zwingli arrived at Zurich and alighted at the hotel of Einsidlen. He received a hearty and an honorable welcome. The canons immediately assembled and invited him to take his place among them. Felix Frey presided. The canons, friends or enemies to Zwingli, sat indiscriminately around their provost. Unusual excitement prevailed in the assembly, for everyone felt, unconsciously perhaps, how serious was the beginning of this ministry. As they feared the innovating spirit of the young priest, it was agreed to explain to him the most important duties of his charge. "You will make every exertion," they said to him gravely, "to collect the revenues of the chapter, without overlooking the least. You will exhort the faithful, both from the pulpit and in the confessional, to pay all tithes and dues and to show by their offerings their affection to the church. You will be diligent in increasing the income arising from the sick, from masses, and in general from every ecclesiastical ordinance."

The chapter added, "As for the administration of the sacraments, the preaching and the care of the flock, these are also the duties of the chaplain. But for these you may employ a substitute, particularly in preaching. You should administer the sacraments to none but persons of note, and only when called upon. You are forbidden to do so without distinction of persons."

What a regulation for Zwingli! Money, money, nothing but money. Did Christ establish his ministry for this? Prudence, however, moderated his zeal. He knew that he could not at once deposit the seed in the earth, behold the tree grow up, and gather its fruits. Without any remark on the duties imposed upon him, Zwingli, after humbly expressing his gratitude for their flattering selection, announced what he intended doing. "The life of Christ," said he, "has been too long hidden from the people. I shall preach upon the whole of the Gospel of St. Matthew, chapter after chapter, according to the inspiration of the Holy Ghost, without human commentaries, drawing solely from the fountains of Scripture, sounding its depths, comparing one passage with another, and seeking for understanding by constant and earnest prayer. It is to God's glory, to the praise of his only Son, to the real salvation of souls, and to their edification in the true faith, that I shall consecrate my ministry."

Language so novel made a deep impression on the chapter. Some testified their joy, but the majority evinced sorrow. "This way of preaching is an innovation," exclaimed they. "One innovation will lead to another, and where shall we stop?" The canon Hoffmann, especially, thought it his duty to prevent the melancholy consequences of an election for which he himself had been so earnest. "This explanation of Scripture," said he, "will be more injurious than useful to the people."

"It is not a new manner," replied Zwingli; "it is the old custom. Call to mind the homilies of Chrysostom on St. Matthew and of Augustine on St. John. Besides, I will speak with moderation and give no persons just cause to complain of it."

Thus did Zwingli abandon the exclusive use of the fragments of the Gospels read since the time of Charlemagne. By restoring the Holy Scriptures to their ancient rights, he bound the Reformation from the very commencement of his ministry to the primitive times of Christianity and laid a foundation by which future ages might study the Word of God. But we may go further. The firm and independent position he took up as regards the

Gospel announced a new work. The figure of the reformer stood in bold outline before the eyes of his people, and the reform advanced.

On Saturday, the first day of the year 1519, and his thirty-fifth birthday, Zwingli went into the cathedral pulpit. A great crowd, eager to see this celebrated man and to hear this new gospel, which was a general topic of conversation, crowded the temple. "It is to Christ," said Zwingli, "that I desire to lead you; to Christ, the true source of salvation. His Divine Word is the only food that I wish to set before your hearts and souls." He then gave out that on the following day, the first Sunday in the year, he would begin to explain the Gospel according to St. Matthew.

The next morning, the preacher and a still more numerous congregation were at their posts. Zwingli opened the Gospel—so long a sealed book—and read the first page. Discoursing on the history of the patriarchs and prophets (the first chapter of St. Matthew), he explained it in such a manner that his wondering and enraptured hearers exclaimed, "We never heard the like of this before!"

He continued thus to explain St. Matthew according to the Greek text. He showed how all the Bible found at once its explanation and its application in the very nature of man. Setting forth the highest truths of the gospel in simple language, his preaching reached all classes, the wise and learned, as well as the ignorant and foolish. He extolled the infinite mercies of God the Father and exhorted all his hearers to place their sole trust in Jesus Christ as their only Savior.

At the same time, he called them most earnestly to repentance. He forcibly attacked the prevailing errors among his people and inveighed courageously against luxury, intemperance, costly garments, the oppression of the poor, idleness, foreign service, and pensions from the princes. "In the pulpit," said one of his contemporaries, "he spared no one, neither pope, emperor, kings, dukes, princes, lords, nor even the confederates themselves. All his strength and all the delight of his heart was in God, and accordingly he exhorted all the city of Zurich to trust solely in Him."

It was impossible that the gospel could be preached in Zurich to no purpose. An ever increasing multitude of all classes, and particularly of the lower orders, flocked to hear him. Many Zurichers had ceased to frequent the public worship. "I derive no instruction from the sermons of these priests," said Fusslin, the poet, historian, and councilor of state. "They do not preach the things belonging to salvation, because they understand them not. I can see in these men nothing but avarice and licentiousness." Henry Rauschlin, treasurer of state, a constant reader of Scripture, thought the same: "The priests met in thousands at the Council of Constance . . . to burn the best of them all." These distinguished men, attracted by curiosity, came to hear Zwingli's first sermon. On their features might be read the emotion with which they listened to the preacher. "Glory be to God!" said they, as they retired. "This man is a preacher of the truth. He will be our Moses to lead us forth from this Egyptian darkness."

From this moment they became the intimate friends of the reformer. "Ye mighty ones of the world," said Fusslin, "cease to proscribe the doctrine of Christ! When Christ, the Son of God, had been put to death, fishermen rose up to fill his place. And now, if you destroy the preachers of the truth, you will see glaziers, millers, potters, founders, shoemakers, and tailors teaching in their stead."

For a time there was but one cry of admiration in Zurich; but as soon as the first moments of enthusiasm were passed, the adversaries resumed their courage. Many well-meaning men, alarmed by the fear of a reformation, gradually became estranged from Zwingli. The violence of the monks, suppressed for a while, burst forth again, and the college of the canons resounded with complaints. Zwingli was immovable. His friends, as they contemplated his courage, imagined they saw a man of the apostolic age reappearing before them. Among his enemies, some laughed and joked, others gave utterance to violent threats, but he endured all with Christian patience. "If we desire to gain over the wicked to Jesus Christ," he was accustomed to say, "we must shut our eyes against many things."

His character and his deportment toward all men contributed, as much as his discourses, to win their hearts. He was at once a true Christian and a true republican. The equality of mankind was not with him a mere conventional term. It was written in his heart and shown by his life. He had neither that pharisaical pride nor that monastic coarseness which offend equally the simple and the wise of this world. They felt attracted toward him and were at ease in his society. Bold and energetic in the pulpit, he was affable to all whom he met in the streets or public places. He was often seen in the halls where the companies and trades used to meet, explaining to the citizens the chief features of the Christian doctrine or conversing familiarly with them.

He addressed peasants and patricians with the same cordiality. "He invited the country people to dine with him," said one of his most violent enemies, "walked with them, talked to them of God, put the Devil in their hearts and his books into their pockets. He succeeded so well that the notables of Zurich used to visit the peasants, drink with them, show them about the city, and pay them every mark of attention."

He continued to cultivate music "with moderation," says Bullinger. Nevertheless, the opponents of the gospel took advantage of this and called him "the evangelical lute player and fifer."

Faber having one day censured him for this taste, he replied with noble frankness: "My dear Faber, you do not know what music is. True, I have learnt to play on the lute, the violin, and other instruments, and they serve me to quiet little children. But you are too holy for music! . . . Do you not know that David was a skillful player on the harp, and how by this means he drove the evil spirit out of Saul? . . . Ah! if you did but know the sounds of the heavenly lyre, the wicked spirit of ambition and love of riches which possesses you would soon depart from you likewise."

Perhaps this may have been a weakness in Zwingli. Still it was with a spirit of cheerfulness and evangelical liberty that he cultivated this art, which religion has always associated with her sublimest devotion. He set to music some of his Christian poems and was not ashamed from time to time to amuse the little ones of his flock with his lute. He conducted himself in the same kindly manner toward the poor. "He would eat and drink with all who invited him," says one of his contemporaries. "He despised no one. He was compassionate to the poor, always steadfast and cheerful in good and evil fortune. No misfortune alarmed him. His conversation was at all times full of consolation, and his heart firm." Thus Zwingli's popularity was ever on the increase. Sitting by times at the tables of the poor and at the banquets of the rich, as his Master had done in former days, he everywhere did the work to which God had called him.

He was indefatigable in study. From daybreak until ten o'clock he used to read, write, and translate. At that time Hebrew was the special object of his studies. After dinner he listened to those who had any news to give him or who required his advice. He then would walk out with some of his friends and visit his flock. At two o'clock he resumed his studies. He took a short walk after supper, and then wrote his letters, which often occupied him till midnight. He always worked standing and never permitted himself to be disturbed except for some very important cause.

Portrait of Ulrich Zwingli, based on a woodcut that is the only known
representation of Zwingli done in his lifetime

Chapter 6
Samson and the Indulgence Traffic

An opportunity of displaying Zwingli's zeal in a new vocation presented itself. Samson, the famous indulgence merchant, was slowly approaching Zurich. This wretched trafficker had left Schwytz and arrived at Zug on September 20, 1518, and had remained there three days. An immense crowd had gathered around him. The poorest were the most eager and thus prevented the rich from getting near him. This did not suit the monk's views, and accordingly, one of his attendants began to cry out to the populace, "Good folks, do not crowd so much! Make way for those who have money! We will afterwards endeavour to satisfy those who have none."

From Zug, Samson and his band proceeded to Lucerne; from Lucerne to Unterwalden; and then, after crossing fertile mountains and rich valleys, skirting the everlasting snows of the Oberland and displaying their Romish merchandise in these most beautiful portions of Switzerland, they arrived in the neighborhood of Berne. The monk was at first forbidden to enter the city. But eventually, by means of certain friends he had there, he succeeded in gaining admission and set up his stall in St. Vincent's Church. Here he began to bawl out more lustily than before. "Here," said he to the rich, "are indulgences on parchment for a crown. There," said he to the poor, "are absolutions on common paper for two batz!" (A batz was worth about three cents.)

One day a celebrated knight, Jacques de Stein, appeared before him, prancing on a dapple-gray horse, which the monk admired very much. "Give me," said the knight, "an indulgence for myself, for my troop, five hundred strong, for all my vassals at Belp, and for all my ancestors, and you shall have my dapple-gray charger in exchange." This was asking a high price for a horse, but as it pleased the Franciscan, they soon came to terms. The charger was led to the monk's stable, and all those souls were declared forever exempt from hell. Another day, a citizen purchased of him for thirteen florins an indulgence empowering his confessor to absolve him, among other matters, from every kind of perjury. So much respect was felt for Samson that the councilor De May, an aged and enlightened man, who had spoken irreverently of him, was compelled to beg pardon of the haughty monk on his knees.

On the last day of his stay, the noisy sound of bells proclaimed the departure of the monk from Berne. Samson was in the church, standing on the steps of the high altar. The canon Henry Lupulus, formerly Zwingli's teacher, was the monk's interpreter. "When the wolf and the fox prowl about together," said the canon Anselm, turning to the schultheiss De Watteville, "your safest plan, my gracious lord, is to shut up your sheep and your geese."

But the monk cared little for such remarks, which, moreover, did not reach his ears. "Kneel down;" said he to the superstitious crowd; "recite three Paters, three Aves, and your souls will immediately be as pure as at the moment of your baptism." Upon this all the people fell on their knees.

Samson, desirous of surpassing himself, exclaimed, "I deliver from the torments of purgatory and of hell all the souls of the Bernese who are dead, whatever may have been the manner and the place of their death!" These mountebanks, like their brothers of the fairs, kept their best trick till the last.

Samson, laden with money, proceeded through Argovia and Baden toward Zurich. At every step, this monk, whose appearance had been so wretched when first he crossed the Alps, displayed greater haughtiness and splendor. The bishop of Constance (Hugo of Landenberg), who was irritated because Samson would not have his bulls legalized by him, had forbidden all the priests of his diocese to open their churches to him. At Baden, however, the priest of the parish dared not make any strenuous opposition to his traffic. The effrontery of the monk was redoubled. Heading a procession around the cemetery, he seemed to fix his eyes upon some object in the air while his acolytes were chanting the hymn for the dead and pretending to see the souls escaping from the cemetery to heaven, he exclaimed: "*Ecce volant!* See how they fly!"

One day a man went into the belfry and ascended to the top; erelong a cloud of white feathers, floating in the air, covered the astonished procession. "See how they fly!" exclaimed this wag, shaking a cushion on the summit of the tower. Many persons burst out laughing. Samson flew into a passion and was not to be appeased until he was told that the man's wits were sometimes disordered. He left Baden quite abashed.

He continued his journey, and about the end of February 1519, arrived at Bremgarten, which the schultheiss and junior priest of the town, who had seen him at Baden, had invited him to visit. In all that district no one enjoyed a better reputation than Dean Bullinger. This man, although ill informed in the Word of God and in the errors of the church, was frank, zealous, eloquent, charitable to the poor, and ever ready to do a kindness to the little ones of his flock, and was generally beloved.

In all Switzerland there was not a more hospitable house than his. He was fond of hunting and might often be seen with a pack of ten or twelve hounds and accompanied by the lords of Hallwyll, the abbot of Mury, and the patricians of Zurich, scouring the neighboring fields and forests. His table was free to all comers, and none of his guests was more festive than he. When the deputies to the diet were going to Baden by way of Bremgarten, they were always entertained by the dean. "Bullinger," said they, "holds a court like the most powerful lord."

Strangers had remarked that in this house lived a child with intelligent features. Henry, one of the dean's sons, had incurred many dangers from his earliest infancy. At one time he was attacked by the plague, and he was about to be buried when some feeble signs of life restored joy to his parent's hearts. At three years old, he knew the Lord's prayer and the Apostles' Creed, and, creeping into the church, he would go into his father's pulpit, gravely take his station, and repeat at the full strength of his voice: "I believe in God the Father," etc.

When he was twelve years of age, his parents sent him to the grammar school of Emmeric. Their hearts were filled with apprehension, for the times were dangerous for an inexperienced boy. When the regulations of a university appeared to them too severe, the students might often be seen quitting the school in troops, taking little children with them and encamping in the woods, whence they would send the youngest of their number to beg bread, or else, with arms in their hands, would fall upon travellers and rob them and then consume the fruits of their plunder in debauchery.

Fortunately, Henry was preserved from evil in this distant place. Like Luther, he gained his bread by singing from door to door, for his father wished him to learn to live on his own resources. He was sixteen years old when he opened a New Testament. "I there found," said he, "all that is necessary for man's salvation, and from that time I adhered to this principle, that we must follow the sacred Scriptures alone, and reject all human additions. I believe neither the Fathers nor myself, but explain Scripture by Scripture, without adding or taking away anything." Thus did God prepare this young man, who was one day to be Zwingli's successor.

About this time Samson arrived at Bremgarten with all his train. The bold dean, whom this little Italian army did not dismay, forbade the monk to sell his merchandise in his deanery. The schultheiss, the town-council, and the junior pastor—all friends to Samson—met together in a chamber of the inn where the latter had alighted, and, greatly disconcerted, had gathered round the impatient monk when the dean arrived. "Here are the papal bulls," said the monk; "open your church!"

The Dean: "I will not permit the purses of my parishioners to be drained by unauthenticated letters, for the bishop has not legalized them."

The Monk (solemnly): "The pope is above the bishop. I forbid you to deprive your flock of so signal a favor."

The Dean: "Should it cost me my life, I will not open my church."

The Monk (indignantly): "Rebellious priest! In the name of our most holy lord the pope, I pronounce against you the greater excommunication and will not absolve you until you have redeemed such unprecedented rashness by paying three hundred ducats."

The Dean (turning his back and quitting the room): "I shall know how to reply to my lawful judges. As for you and your excommunication, I care not for either."

The Monk (in a passion): "Impudent brute! I am going to Zurich, and I will there lay my complaint before the deputies of the Confederation."

The Dean: "I can appear there as well as you and will go thither immediately."

While these events were taking place at Bremgarten, Zwingli, who saw the enemy gradually approaching, preached energetically against the indulgences. The vicar, Faber of Constance, encouraged him, promising him the bishop's support. "I am aware," said Samson, as he was moving toward Zurich, "that Zwingli will speak against me, but I will stop his mouth."

In effect, Zwingli felt too deeply all the sweetness of Christ's forgiveness not to attack the paper indulgences of these foolish men. Like Luther, he often trembled because of his sinfulness, but he found in the Lord a deliverance from every fear. This modest but resolute man increased in the knowledge of God.

"When Satan frightens me," said he, "by crying out: 'You have not done this or that, which God commands!' forthwith the gentle voice of the gospel consoles me, by saying: 'What thou canst not do (and certainly thou canst do nothing), Christ has done and perfected.' Yes, when my heart is troubled because of my helplessness and the weakness of my flesh, my spirit is revived at the sound of these glad tidings: Christ is thy innocence! Christ is thy righteousness! Christ is thy salvation! Thou art nothing; thou canst do nothing! Christ is the Alpha and Omega; Christ is the First and the Last; Christ is all things; He can do all things. All created things will forsake and deceive thee. But Christ, the innocent and righteous one, will receive and justify thee. . . . Yes! it is He," exclaimed Zwingli, "who is our righteousness and the righteousness of all those who shall ever appear justified before the throne of God!"

In the presence of such truths, the indulgences fell of themselves. Zwingli accordingly feared not to attack them. "No man," said he, "can remit sins; Christ, who is very God and very man, alone has this power. Go! Buy indulgences . . . but be assured that you are not absolved. Those who sell remission of sins for money are the companions of Simon the magician, the friends of Balaam, and the ambassadors of Satan."

Dean Bullinger, still heated by his conversation with the monk, arrived at Zurich before him. He came to lay his complaints before the diet against this shameless merchant and his traffic. He found some envoys from the bishop who were there with the same motives and made common cause with them. All promised to support him. The spirit that animated Zwingli pervaded the city. The council of state resolved to oppose the monk's entry into Zurich.

Samson had reached the suburbs and alighted at an inn. He was preparing to mount his horse to make his solemn entry and had already one foot in the stirrup when deputies from the council appeared before him, offering him the honorary cup of wine as envoy from the pope and informing him that he might dispense with entering Zurich. "I have something to communicate to the diet in the name of his holiness," replied the monk. This was a mere trick. It was agreed, however, to receive him. But as he spoke of nothing but papal bulls, he was dismissed after being compelled to withdraw the excommunication pronounced against the dean of Bremgarten. He quitted the hall fuming with anger, and soon after the pope recalled him to Italy. A wagon, drawn by three horses and laden with the money that his falsehoods had wrung from the poor, preceded him on those steep paths of the St. Gothard that he had crossed eight months before, without money or parade, and burdened with only a few papers.

The Helvetic diet showed more resolution than the German. It was because neither bishops nor cardinals had a seat in it. And hence the pope, deprived of these supporters, acted more mildly toward Switzerland than toward Germany. But the affair of the indulgences, which played so important a part in the German Reformation, was merely an episode in that of the Swiss.

Chapter 7
Plague!

Zwingli did not spare himself. Such great and continued toil called for relaxation, and he was ordered to repair to the baths of Pfeffers. He departed, reaching Pfeffers through the frightful gorge formed by the impetuous torrent of the Jamina. He descended into that infernal gulf, as Daniel the hermit terms it, and arrived at those baths, perpetually shaken by the fall of the torrent, and moistened by the spray of its broken waters. Torches were required to be burned at noonday in the house where Zwingli lodged. It was even asserted by the inhabitants that frightful specters appeared sometimes amid the gloom.

And yet even here he found an opportunity of serving his Master. His affability won the hearts of many of the invalids. Among their number was the celebrated poet, Philip Ingentinus, professor at Friburg, in Brisgau, who from that time became a zealous supporter of the Reformation.

God was watching over His work and designed to accelerate it. Strong in frame, in character, and in talents, Zwingli, whose defect consisted in this strength, was destined to see it prostrated, that he might become such an instrument as God loves. He needed the baptism of adversity and infirmity, of weakness and pain. Zwingli was appointed to receive it by being brought into contact with sickness and death.

There is a moment in the history of the heroes of this world, of such as Charles XII or Napoleon, which decides their career and their renown. It is that in which their strength is suddenly revealed to them. An analogous moment exists in the life of God's heroes, but it is in a contrary direction. It is that in which they first recognize their helplessness and nothingness. From that hour they receive the strength of God from on high. A work like that of which Zwingli was to be the instrument is never accomplished by the natural strength of man. It would wither immediately, like a tree transplanted in all its maturity and vigor. A plant must be feeble or it will not take root, and a grain must die in the earth before it can become fruitful. God conducted Zwingli, and with him the work that depended on him, to the gates of the sepulchre. It is from among the dry bones, the darkness, and the dust of death, that God is pleased to select the instruments by means of which He designs to scatter over the earth His light, regeneration, and life.

Zwingli was hidden among those colossal rocks that encircle the furious torrent of the Jamina when he was suddenly informed that the plague, or the great death, as it was called, had broken out at Zurich. It appeared in all its terror in the month of August, on St. Lawrence's day, and lasted till Candlemas, sweeping off 2,500 inhabitants. The young men who resided in Zwingli's house had quitted it immediately, in accordance with the directions he had left behind him. His house was deserted, but it was His time to return to it.

He hastily quitted Pfeffers and reappeared in the midst of his flock, which the malady had decimated. His younger brother Andrew, who had waited for him, he immediately sent back to Wildhaus, and from that hour devoted himself entirely to the victims of this frightful scourge. Every day he proclaimed Christ and His consolations to the sick.

His friends, delighted to see him unharmed amid so many deadly arrows, experienced however a secret alarm. "Do your duty," said a letter from Basel, written by Conrad Brunner, who himself died of the plague a few months afterwards, "but at the same time remember to take care of your own life."

This caution came too late. Zwingli was attacked by the plague. The great preacher of Switzerland lay stretched on a bed from which he seemed likely never to rise. His thoughts were turned inward; his eyes were directed to heaven. He knew that God had given him a sure inheritance, and venting the feelings of his heart in a hymn overflowing with unction and simplicity, he exclaimed,

Lo! at the door
I hear death's knock!
Shield me, O Lord,
My strength and rock.

The hand once nailed
Upon the tree,
Jesus, uplift—
And shelter me.

Willest thou, then,
Death conquer me
In my noonday? . . .
So let it be!

Oh! may I die,
Since I am thine;
Thy home is made
For faith like mine.

Meantime, his disease increased in virulence. His despairing friends beheld this man, the hope of Switzerland and of the church, about to fall a prey to the tomb. His senses and his strength forsook him. His heart was dismayed, but he still found strength sufficient to turn toward God and to cry,

My pains increase:
Lord, stand thou near.
Body and soul
Dissolve with fear.

Now death is near,
My tongue is dumb;
Fight for me, Lord.
Mine hour is come!

See Satan's net
Is o'er me tost—
I feel his hand; . . .
Must I be lost?

His shafts, his voice
Alarm no more;
For here I lie
Thy cross before.

The city was filled with distress. The believers cried to God night and day, praying Him to restore their faithful pastor. The alarm had spread from Zurich to the mountains of the Tockenburg. The pestilence had made its appearance even on those lofty hills. Seven or eight persons had died in the village, among whom was a servant of Zwingli's brother Nicholas. No letter was received from the reformer. "Tell me," wrote young Andrew Zwingli, "in what state you are, my dear brother. The abbot and all our brothers salute thee." It would appear that Zwingli's parents were dead, since there was no mention of them.

The news of Zwingli's malady, and even the report of his death, was circulated through Switzerland and Germany. "Alas!" exclaimed Hedio, "the preserver of our country, the trumpet of the gospel, the magnanimous herald of truth, is cut down in the flower and springtide of his life!" When the news of Zwingli's decease reached Basel, the whole city resounded with lamentations and mourning.

Yet the spark of life that still remained began to burn more brightly. Although his frame was weak, his soul felt the unalterable conviction that God had called him to replace the candle of His Word on the empty candlestick of the church. The plague had forsaken its victim, and Zwingli exclaimed with emotion:

My God, my Sire,
Heal'd by thy hand,
Upon the earth
Once more I stand.

From guilt and sin
May I be free:
My mouth shall sing
Alone of thee.

The uncertain hour
For me will come, . . .
O'erwhelm'd perchance
With deeper gloom.

It matters not:
With joy I'll bear
My yoke, until
I reach heaven's sphere.

At the beginning of November, as soon as he could hold a pen, Zwingli wrote to his family. This gave unutterable joy to his friends, particularly to his young brother Andrew, who himself died of the plague in the following year. At Basel, Conrad Brunner, Zwingli's friend, and Bruno Amerbach, the celebrated printer, both young men, had died after three days' illness. It was believed in that city that Zwingli also had fallen. The university felt the deepest dejection. "Whom the gods love die young," said they. But who can describe their delight when Collins, a student from Lucerne, and after him a merchant from Zurich, brought intelligence that Zwingli had escaped from the jaws of death!

The vicar of the bishop of Constance, John Faber, that old friend of Zwingli's, who was subsequently his most violent antagonist, wrote to him: "Oh! my beloved Ulrich, what joy I feel at learning that you have been saved from the grasp of cruel death! When you are in danger the Christian commonwealth is threatened. The Lord has pleased to urge you by these trials to seek more earnestly for eternal life."

This was indeed the aim of the trials by which God had proved Zwingli, and this end was obtained, but in a different manner from that imagined by Faber. This pestilence of 1519, which committed such frightful ravages in the north of Switzerland, was in the hands of God a powerful means for the conversion of many souls. But on no one did it exercise so powerful an influence as on Zwingli. The gospel, which had hitherto been too much regarded by him as a mere doctrine, now became a great reality. He arose from the darkness of the sepulchre with a new heart. His zeal became more active; his life more holy; his preaching more free, more Christian, and more powerful. This was the epoch of Zwingli's complete emancipation. Henceforward he consecrated himself entirely to God.

Zwingli derived fresh strength, of which he stood so much in need, from communion with his friends. To Myconius especially he was united by the strongest affection. They walked in reliance on each other, like Luther and Melancthon.

Myconius was happy at Zurich. True, his position there was embarrassed, but tempered by the virtues of his modest wife. It was of her that Glarean said, "If I could meet with a young woman like her, I should prefer her to a king's daughter." Yet a faithful monitor often broke in upon the sweet affection of Zwingli and Myconius. It was the canon Xyloctect inviting Myconius to return to Lucerne, his native place. "Zurich is not your country," said he; "it is Lucerne! You tell me that the Zurichers are your friends; I do not deny it. But do you know what will be the end of it? Serve your country. This I would advise and entreat you, and, if I may, I would command you!"

Xyloctect, joining actions with words, procured his nomination as headmaster of the collegiate school at Lucerne. Myconius hesitated no longer; he saw the finger of God in this appointment, and however great the sacrifice, he resolved to make it. Who could tell that he might not be an instrument in the hand of the Lord to introduce the doctrine of peace in the warlike city of Lucerne?

But what a sad farewell was that of Zwingli and Myconius. They parted in tears. "Your departure," wrote Ulrich to his friend shortly after, "has inflicted a blow on the cause I am defending, like that suffered by an army in battle array when one of its wings is destroyed. Alas! now I feel all the value of my Myconius, and how often, without my knowing it, he has upheld the cause of Christ."

Zwingli felt the loss of his friend more deeply, as the plague had left him in a state of extreme weakness. "It has enfeebled my memory," wrote he on November 30, 1519, "and depressed my spirits." He was hardly convalescent before he resumed his duties. "But," said he, "when I am preaching, I often lose the thread of my discourse. All my limbs are oppressed with languor, and I am almost like a corpse."

Besides this, Zwingli's opposition to indulgences had aroused the hostility of their partisans. Myconius encouraged his friend by the letters he wrote from Lucerne. "What is your opinion," said Myconius to Zwingli, "of Luther's cause? As for me, I have no fear either for the gospel or for him. If God does not protect His truth, who shall protect it? All that I ask of the Lord is that He will not withdraw His hand from those who hold nothing dearer than His gospel. Continue as you have begun, and an abundant reward shall be conferred upon you in heaven!"

The arrival of an old friend consoled Zwingli for the departure of Myconius. Bunzli, who had been Ulrich's instructor at Basel, and who had succeeded the Dean of Wesen, the reformer's uncle, visited Zurich in the first week of the year 1520, and Zwingli and he formed a project of going to Basel to see their common friends. Zwingli's sojourn in that city was not fruitless. Capito, Hedio, and many others were electrified by his powerful language; and the former, commencing in Basel a work similar to that which Zwingli was carrying on in Zurich, began to explain the Gospel According to St. Matthew, before an ever-increasing audience. The doctrine of Christ penetrated and warmed their hearts. The people received it gladly and hailed with acclamations the revival of Christianity.

This was the dawn of the Reformation, and accordingly a conspiracy of priests and monks was soon formed against Capito. It was at this period that Albert, the youthful cardinal-archbishop of Mentz, desirous of attaching so great a scholar to his person, invited him to his court. Capito, seeing the difficulties that were opposed to him, accepted the invitation. The people were excited. Their indignation was roused against the priests, and a violent commotion broke out in the city. Hedio was thought of as his successor. But some objected to his youth, and others said, "He is Capito's disciple!"

"The truth stings," said Hedio; "it is not safe to wound tender ears by preaching it. But it matters not! Nothing shall make me swerve from the straight road."

The monks redoubled their efforts: "Do not believe those," exclaimed they from the pulpit, "who tell you that the sum of Christian doctrine is found in the Gospel and in St. Paul. Scotus has been more serviceable to Christianity than St. Paul himself. All the learned things that have been ever said or printed were stolen from Scotus. All that these hunters after glory have been able to do is merely to add a few Greek or Hebrew words to obscure the whole matter."

The disturbance increased, and there was cause to fear that, after Capito's departure, the opposition would become still more powerful. "I shall be almost alone," thought Hedio. "I, a weak and wretched man, to struggle unaided with these pestilent monsters." In these circumstances he called to God for succor and wrote to Zwingli, "Animate my courage by frequent letters. Learning and Christianity are now between the hammer and the anvil. Luther has just been condemned by the universities of Louvain and Cologne. If ever the church was in imminent danger, it is now."

Capito left Basel for Mentz on April 28 and was succeeded by Hedio. Not content with the public assemblies in the church, where he continued the explanation of St. Matthew, Hedio proposed in the month of June to have private meetings in his house for the more familiar communication of evangelical instruction to those who felt its necessity. This powerful means of edification in the truth and of exciting the interest and zeal of believers for divine things, could not fail, then as in all times, to arouse opposition among worldly minded people and domineering priests, both of which classes, though from different motives, are unwilling that God should be worshiped anywhere except within the boundary of certain walls. But Hedio was immovable.

Everything seemed to indicate that the battle between the gospel and popery was about to begin. "Let us stir up the temporizers," wrote Hedio to Zwingli. "The truce is broken. Let us put on our breastplates, for we shall have to fight against the most formidable enemies." Myconius wrote to Ulrich in the same strain, but the latter replied to these warlike appeals with admirable mildness: "I would allure these obstinate men," said he, "by kindness and friendly proceedings, rather than overthrow them by violent controversy. For if they call our doctrine (which is in truth not ours) a devilish doctrine, it is all very natural, and by this I know that we are really ambassadors from God. The devils cannot be silent in Christ's presence."

Chapter 8
The Preaching of Zwingli

Although Zwingli desired to follow a mild course, he did not remain inactive. After his illness, his preaching had become more profound and more vivifying. Upwards of two thousand persons in Zurich had received the Word of God in their hearts and confessed the evangelical doctrine and were already qualified to announce it themselves. Zwingli's doctrines have been so often misrepresented that it will not be irrelevant to glance at what he was then preaching to the people who daily thronged the cathedral of Zurich.

In the fall of the first man, Zwingli found a key to the history of the human race. "Before the fall," said he one day, "man had been created with a free will, so that, had he been willing, he might have kept the law. His nature was pure. The disease of sin had not yet reached him. His life was in his own hands. But having desired to be as God, he died . . . and not he alone, but all his posterity. Since then in Adam all men are dead, no one can recall them to life, until the Spirit, which is God himself, raises them from the dead."

The inhabitants of Zurich, who listened eagerly to this powerful orator, were overwhelmed with sorrow as he unfolded before their eyes that state of sin in which mankind is involved. But soon they heard the words of consolation, and the remedy was pointed out to them, which alone can restore man to life. "Christ, very man and very God," said the eloquent voice of this son of the Tockenburg herdsman, "has purchased for us a never-ending redemption. For since it was the eternal God who died for us, His passion is therefore an eternal sacrifice, and everlastingly effectual to heal; it satisfies the divine justice for ever in behalf of all those who rely upon it with firm and unshaken faith. Wherever sin is," exclaimed the reformer, "death of necessity follows.

Christ was without sin, and guile was not found in His mouth; and yet He died! . . . This death He suffered in our stead! He was willing to die that He might restore us to life; and as He had no sins of His own, the all-merciful Father laid ours upon Him. . . . Seeing that the will of man," said the Christian orator again, "had rebelled against the Most High, it was necessary for the reestablishment of eternal order and for the salvation of man, that the human will should submit in Christ's person to the divine will." He would often remark that the expiatory death of Jesus Christ had taken place in behalf of believers, of the people of God.

The souls that thirsted after salvation in the city of Zurich found repose at the sound of these glad tidings; but there still existed in their minds some long-established errors which it was necessary to eradicate. Starting from the great truth that salvation is the gift of God, Zwingli inveighed powerfully against the pretended merit of human works. "Since eternal salvation," said he, "proceeds solely from the merits and death of Jesus Christ, it follows that the merit of our own works is mere vanity and folly, not to say impiety and senseless impudence. If we could have been saved by our own works, it would not have been necessary for Christ to die. All who have ever come to God have come to Him through the death of Jesus Christ."

Zwingli foresaw the objections this doctrine would excite among some of his hearers. They waited on him and laid them before him. He replied to them from the pulpit: "Some people, perhaps more dainty than pious, object that this doctrine renders men careless and dissolute. But of what importance are the fears and objections that the daintiness of men may suggest? Whosoever believes in Jesus Christ is assured that all that cometh from God is necessarily good. If, therefore, the gospel is of God, it is good. And what other power besides could implant righteousness, truth, and love among men? . . . O God, most gracious, most righteous Father of all mercies," he exclaimed, "with what charity Thou hast embraced us, Thine enemies! . . . With what lofty and unfailing hopes hast Thou filled us, who deserved to feel nothing but despair! And to what glory hast Thou called, in Thy Son, our meanness and our nothingness! . . . Thou willest, by this unspeakable love, to constrain us to return Thee love for love!"

Following out this idea, he proceeded to show that love to the Redeemer is a law more powerful than the commandments. "The Christian," said he, "delivered from the law, depends entirely on Jesus Christ. Christ is his reason, his counsel, his righteousness, and his whole salvation. Christ lives and acts in him. Christ alone is his leader, and he needs no other guide." And then making use of a comparison within the range of his hearers' intelligence, he added, "If a government forbids its citizens under pain of death to receive any pension or largess from the hands of foreigners, how mild and easy is this law to those who, from love to their country and their liberty, voluntarily abstain from so culpable an action! But, on the contrary, how vexatious and oppressive it is to those who consult their own interest alone! Thus the righteous man lives free and joyful in the love of righteousness, and the unrighteous man walks murmuring under the heavy burden of the law that oppresses him!"

In the cathedral of Zurich there were many old soldiers who felt the truth of these words. Accordingly, Zwingli, growing bolder, proclaimed to the people of Zurich that love to the Redeemer was alone capable of impelling a man to perform works acceptable to God. "Works done out of Jesus Christ are worthless," said the Christian orator. "Since everything is done of Him, in Him, and by Him, what can we lay claim to for ourselves? Wherever there is faith in God, there God is; and wherever God abideth, there a zeal exists urging and impelling men to good works. Take care only that Christ is in thee, and that thou art in Christ, and doubt not that then He is at work with thee. The life of a Christian is one perpetual good work which God begins, continues, and completes."

Deeply affected by the greatness of that love of God, which is from everlasting, the herald of grace raised his voice in louder accents of invitation to irresolute and timid souls. "Are you afraid," said he, "to approach this tender Father who has elected you? Why has He chosen us of His grace? Why has He called us? Why has He drawn us to Him? Is it that we should fear to approach Him?"

Such was Zwingli's doctrine, the doctrine of Christ Himself. "If Luther preaches Christ, he does what I am doing," said the preacher of Zurich. "Those whom he has brought to Christ are more numerous than those whom I have led. But this matters not. I will bear no other name than that of Christ, whose soldier I am, and who alone is my chief. Never has one single word been written by me to Luther, nor by Luther to me. And why? . . . that it might be shown how much the Spirit of God is in unison with Himself, since both of us, without any collusion, teach the same doctrine of Christ with such uniformity."

Thus did Zwingli preach with courage and enthusiasm. The vast cathedral could not contain the multitude of his hearers. All praised God for the new life that was beginning to reanimate the lifeless body of the church. Many of the Swiss from every canton who came to Zurich either to attend the diet or for other motives, impressed by this new preaching, carried its precious seeds into all the valleys of their native country. A shout of rejoicing rose from every city and mountain. "Switzerland," wrote Nicholas Hageus from Lucerne to Zurich, "has hitherto given birth to such as Brutus, Scipio, and Caesar; but she has hardly produced a man who really knew Jesus Christ, and who nourished our souls, not with vain disputes, but with the Word of God. Now that divine Providence has given Switzerland a Zwingli for preacher and an Oswald Myconius for teacher, virtue and sacred learning are reviving among us. O fortunate Helvetia! If at last thou wouldst rest from war, and, already illustrious by thy arms, become more illustrious still by righteousness and peace!"

"There was a report," wrote Myconius to Zwingli, "that your voice could not be heard three paces off. But I see now that it was a falsehood, for all Switzerland hears you!"

"Thou hast armed thyself with an intrepid courage," wrote Hedio from Basel; "I will follow thee as far as I am able."

"I have heard thee," wrote Sebastian Hofmeister of Schaffhausen from Constance. "Would to God that Zurich, which is at the head of our happy Confederation, were healed of its disease, so that the whole body might be at length restored to health!"

But Zwingli met with adversaries as well as admirers. "Why," said some, "does he busy himself with the affairs of

Switzerland?" "Why," said others, "does he repeat the same things in every sermon?" In the midst of all this opposition, dejection often came over Zwingli's soul. Everything seemed in his eyes falling into confusion, and society to be on the eve of a general convulsion. He thought it impossible for any new truth to appear without its antagonistic error springing up immediately. If any hope arose in his heart, fear grew up by its side. He soon, however, threw off his dejection. "The life of man here below is a continual war," said he. "Whoever desires to obtain glory must face the world, and like David force this haughty Goliath, so proud of his stature, to bite the dust. The church," said he, as Luther had done, "was purchased by blood, and by blood must be restored. The more numerous are its impurities, the more men like Hercules must we call up to cleanse these Augean stables."

Zwingli's devotion was not unrewarded. The Word of Christ, preached with so much energy, was destined to bear fruit. Many magistrates were gained over. They had found in God's Word their consolation and their strength. Afflicted at seeing the priests, and above all the monks, uttering shamelessly from the pulpit whatever came into their heads, the council published a decree ordering them to preach nothing in their sermons "that they had not drawn from the sacred fountains of the Old and New Testaments."

It was in 1520 that the civil authority thus interfered for the first time in the work of the Reformation, acting as a Christian magistrate to defend the Word of God and to protect the dearest interests of the citizens—depriving the church of its liberty (in the opinion of others), subjecting it to the secular power, and giving the signal of that long train of evils which the union of church and state has since engendered. But there is still another thing to be pointed out: the act of these magistrates was of itself an effect of the preaching of the Word of God. The Reformation in Switzerland then emerged from simple individualities and became a national work. Born in the hearts of a few priests and learned men, it extended, rose up, and took its station on higher ground. Like the waters of the sea, it rose gradually, until it had covered a vast expanse.

The monks were confounded. They had been ordered to preach the Word of God only, and most of them had never read it.

One opposition provokes another. This decree became the signal of the most violent attacks against the Reformation. Plots began to be formed against the priest of Zurich; his life was in danger. One day, as Zwingli and his curates were quietly conversing in their house, some citizens entered hastily, saying, "Have you strong bolts to your doors? Be on your guard tonight."

"We often had such alarms as these," adds Staheli, "but we were well armed, and a patrol was stationed in the street to protect us."

In other places, recourse was had to still more violent measures. An aged man of Schaffhausen, named Galster, possessing a just spirit and a fervor rare at his age, and rejoicing in the light he had found in the gospel, endeavored to communicate it to his wife and children. In his zeal, which may have been indiscreet, he openly attacked the relics, priests, and superstition with which his canton abounded. He soon became an object of hatred and terror even to his own family. The old man, anticipating evil designs, left his house brokenhearted and fled to the neighboring forests. Here he remained some days, sustaining life upon what he could find, when suddenly, on the last night of the year 1520, torches flashed through the forest in every direction, and the shouts of men and the cry of savage dogs reechoed through its gloomy shades. The council had ordered a grand chase in the forest to discover the wretched man. The hounds caught their prey. The unhappy Galster was dragged before the magistrate and summoned to abjure his faith. As he continued steadfast, he was beheaded.

Chapter 9
Persecution and Expansion

The year thus inaugurated by this bloody execution had hardly begun, when Zwingli received a visit at Zurich from a young man about twenty-eight years of age, of tall stature, and whose exterior denoted candor, simplicity, and diffidence. He introduced himself as Berthold Haller, and on hearing his name, Zwingli embraced the celebrated preacher of Berne with that affability which imparted such a charm to his manners.

Haller was born at Aldingen in Württemberg. The Bernese had about that time resolved on attracting literary men to their republic, which had already become so famous by its feats of arms. Berthold, who was then only twenty-one years old, repaired thither. Subsequently Haller was named canon and shortly after preacher of the cathedral. The gospel taught by Zwingli had reached Berne. Haller believed, and from that hour desired to see the mighty man whom he already respected as a father. He went to Zurich, where Myconius had announced him.

Haller, a man of meek disposition, confided to Zwingli all his trials; and Zwingli, the strong man, inspired him with courage. "My soul," said Berthold to Zwingli one day, "is overwhelmed; . . . I cannot support such unjust treatment. I am determined to resign my pulpit and retire to Basel, to employ myself wholly, in Wittembach's society, with the study of sacred learning."

"Alas!" replied Zwingli, "I too feel discouragement creep over me when I see myself unjustly assailed. But Christ awakens my conscience by the powerful stimulus of His terrors and promises. He alarms me by saying, 'Whosoever shall be ashamed of me before men, of him shall I be ashamed before my Father,' and He restores me to tranquillity by adding, 'Whosoever shall confess me before men, him also will I confess before my Father.'

O my dear Berthold, take courage! Our names are written in imperishable characters in the annals of the citizens on high. I am ready to die for Christ. . . . Oh! that your fierce bear-cubs," added he, "would hear the doctrine of Jesus Christ, then would they grow tame." (A *bear* figures in the shield of Berne.) "But you must undertake this duty with great gentleness, lest they should turn round furiously, and rend you in pieces."

Haller's courage revived. "My soul," wrote he to Zwingli, "has awakened from its slumber. I must preach the gospel. Jesus Christ must be restored to this city, whence He has been so long exiled." Thus did the flame that glowed so brightly in Zwingli's bosom rekindle that of Berthold, and the timid Haller rushed into the midst of the savage bears, who, grinding their teeth (says Zwingli), sought to devour him.

It was in another quarter, however, that the persecution was to break out in Switzerland. The warlike Lucerne stood forward as an adversary. The military spirit prevailed in this canton, the advocate of foreign service, and the leading men of the capital knit their brows whenever they heard one word of peace calculated to restrain their warlike disposition. When Luther's works reached this city, some of the inhabitants began to read them and were struck with horror. Oswald Myconius never spoke of Luther, except to his most intimate friends, and was content simply to announce the gospel of Christ. Yet notwithstanding this moderation, loud cries were heard in the city: "We must burn Luther and the schoolmaster [Myconius]!"

"I am assailed by my adversary, like a ship in a hurricane at sea," said Myconius to one of his friends.

One day at the beginning of the year 1520, he was suddenly called before the council. "You are enjoined," said they, "never to read Luther's works to your pupils, never to mention him before them, and never even to think of him." The lords of Lucerne presumed, it will be seen, to extend their jurisdiction very widely. Shortly after this, a preacher declaimed from the pulpit against heresy. All the assembly was moved. Every eye was turned on Myconius, for who could the preacher have had in view but him? Myconius remained quietly in his place, as if the matter did not concern him. But on leaving the church, as he was walking with his friend the Canon Xyloctect, one of the councilors, who had not yet recovered from his agitation, passed near them. "Well! you disciples of Luther," said he angrily, "why do you not defend your master?" They made no reply.

"I live," said Myconius, "in the midst of savage wolves, but I have this consolation, that most of them have lost their teeth. They would bite if they could; but as they cannot, they merely howl."

The senate was called together, for the tumult among the people kept increasing. "He is a Lutheran!" said one of the councilors. "He is a teacher of novelties!" said another. "He is a seducer of youth," said a third. "Let him appear! Let him appear!" cried all. The poor schoolmaster came before them and heard fresh menaces and prohibitions. His simple spirit was wounded and depressed. His gentle wife could only console him by her tears.

"Everyone is against me," exclaimed he in his anguish. "Assailed by so many tempests, whither shall I turn, or how shall I escape them? . . . If Christ were not with me, I should long ago have fallen beneath their blows."

While the truth thus met with so many obstacles at Lucerne, it was triumphant at Zurich. Zwingli labored unceasingly. Desirous of meditating on the whole of Scripture in the original languages, he applied himself diligently to the study of Hebrew under the direction of John Boschenstein. But his object in studying the Scriptures was to preach them. On Fridays the peasants who came in crowds, bringing their produce to the market of the city, showed great eagerness for the Word of God. To satisfy their wants, Zwingli had begun, in the month of December 1520, to expound the Psalms every market day, preparing his sermon by previous meditation on each particular text.

With reference to his Sunday preaching, Zwingli, after having expounded the life of our Lord according to St. Matthew, proceeded to show, by explaining the Acts of the Apostles, how the doctrine of Christ had been propagated. He next set forth the rule of a Christian life, as inculcated in the Epistles to Timothy. He made use of the Epistle to the Galatians to combat doctrinal errors, and combined with it the two Epistles of Peter, to demonstrate to the condemners of St. Paul how the same Spirit animated both these apostles. He concluded with the Epistle to the Hebrews, that he might explain to their fullest extent all the blessings which flow from the gift of Jesus Christ, the great high priest of the Christian.

But Zwingli did not confine himself to adult men alone; he endeavoured to kindle in the young also a sacred fire by which they should be animated. One day in the year 1521, as he was engaged in his closet studying the Fathers of the church, extracting the most remarkable passages and carefully classifying them in a thick volume, he saw a young man enter whose features strongly interested him. It was Henry Bullinger, who, having returned from Germany, had come to see him, impatient to know that teacher of his native land whose name was already celebrated in Christendom. The handsome youth fixed his eyes successively on the reformer and his books and felt a call to follow Zwingli's example. The latter welcomed him with that cordiality which won every heart.

Another young man had also gained Zwingli's affection. This was Gerold Meyer von Knonau. His mother, Anna Reinhardt, who subsequently occupied an important place in the life of the reformer, had been a great beauty and was still distinguished by her virtues. A young man of noble family, John Meyer von Knonau, who had been brought up at the court of the bishop of Constance, to whom he was related, had conceived an ardent affection for Anna. But she belonged to a plebeian family. The elder Meyer von Knonau had refused his consent to their union and disinherited his son after the marriage.

In 1513 Anna was left a widow with one son and two daughters, and she now lived solely for the education of the poor orphans. Their grandfather was inexorable. One day, however, the widow's servant took young Gerold out with her, a lively and graceful boy, then only three years old, and as she stopped with him in the fish market, the elder Meyer, who chanced to be at the window, noticed him, watched every movement, and asked to whom this beautiful child, so buoyant with life and freshness, belonged. "It is your son's," was the reply. The old man's heart was touched—the ice was melted—everything was forgotten, and he clasped in his arms the wife and the children of his son.

Zwingli had become attached as if he were his own child to the young, noble, and courageous Gerold, who was destined to expire in the flower of his age at the reformer's side, his hand upon the sword, and surrounded by the dead bodies of his enemies. Thinking that Gerold could not find in Zurich sufficient resources for study, Zwingli in 1521 sent him to Basel.

The young Von Knonau did not find Hedio, Zwingli's friend, in that city. As Capito was obliged to accompany the Archbishop Albert to the coronation of Charles V, he had engaged Hedio to supply his place at Mentz. Basel thus successively lost her most faithful preachers. The church seemed abandoned, but other men appeared. Four thousand hearers crowded the church of William Rubli, priest of St. Alban's. He attacked the doctrine of the Mass, purgatory, and the invocation of saints. But this man, who was turbulent and greedy of public applause, inveighed against error rather than contend for the truth. On the festival of Corpus Christi he joined the great procession, but instead of the relics, which it was customary to parade through the streets, there was carried before him a copy of the Holy Scriptures, handsomely bound, and with this inscription in large letters: "*The Bible;* this is the true relic, all others are but dead men's bones."

Courage adorns the servant of God; ostentation disfigures him. The work of an evangelist is to preach the Bible and not to make a pompous display of it. The enraged priests accused Rubli before the council. A crowd immediately filled the square of the Cordeliers. "Protect our preacher," said the citizens to the council. Fifty ladies of distinction interposed in his favor, but Rubli was compelled to leave Basel. Somewhat later he was implicated in the fanatical disorders of the time. As the Reformation evolved, it everywhere rejected the chaff that was mixed up with the good grain.

At this time, from the lowliest of chapels was heard a humble voice distinctly proclaiming the gospel doctrines. It was that of the youthful Wolfgang Wissemburger, the son of a councilor of state and chaplain to the hospital. All the inhabitants of Basel who felt new desires experienced a deeper affection for the meek chaplain than they had for the haughty Rubli himself. Wolfgang began to read Mass in German.

The monks renewed their clamors, but this time they failed. Wissemburger was enabled to continue preaching the gospel, "for," says an old chronicler, "he was a citizen and his father a councilor." This first success of the Reformation at Basel was an omen of still greater. At the same time, it was of much importance to the progress of the work throughout the Confederation. Zurich was not alone. The learned Basel began to be charmed at the sound of the new doctrine. The foundations of the new temple were extending. The Reformation in Switzerland was attaining a higher stage of development.

Zurich was, however, the center of the movement. But in the year 1521, important political events grieved Zwingli's heart and in some measure diverted men's minds from the preaching of the gospel. Pope Leo X, who had offered his alliance simultaneously to Charles V and Francis I, had at length decided for the emperor. The war between these two rivals was about to burst forth in Italy. "The pope shall have nothing left but his ears," said the French general Lautrec. This ill-timed jest increased the pontiff's anger. The king of France claimed the support of the Swiss cantons, which, with the exception of Zurich, were in alliance with him. His call was obeyed. The pope flattered himself with the hope of engaging Zurich in his cause, and the Cardinal of Sion (Schinner), who was always intriguing, in full confidence in his dexterity and eloquence, hastened to this city to procure soldiers for his master.

But he met with a resolute opposition from his old friend Zwingli. The latter was indignant at the thought of seeing the Swiss sell their blood to the foreigner; his imagination already conjured up the sight of the Zurichers under the standards of the pope and the emperor crossing their swords in the plains of Italy with the confederates assembled under the banner of France. At this fratricidal picture, his patriotic and Christian soul thrilled with horror.

He thundered from the pulpit: "Will you," exclaimed he, "tear in pieces and destroy the Confederation? . . . We hunt down the wolves that ravage our flocks, but we make no resistance to those who prowl around us to devour men! . . . It is not without reason that the mantles and the hats they wear are red. Shake these garments, and down will fall ducats and crowns. But if you wring them, you will see them dripping with the blood of your brothers, your fathers, your sons, and your dearest friends!" In vain did Zwingli raise his voice. The cardinal with his red hat succeeded, and 2,700 Zurichers departed under the command of George Berguer. Zwingli's heart was wrung. His influence was not, however, lost. For many years after, the banners of Zurich were not unfolded and carried through the gates of the city in behalf of foreign princes.

Chapter 10
Dispute over Fasting

Wounded in his feelings as a citizen, Zwingli devoted himself with fresh zeal to the preaching of the gospel. His sermons increased in energy. "I will never cease laboring to restore the primitive unity of the church of Christ," said he. He began the year 1522 by showing the difference between the precepts of the gospel and those of men. When the season of Lent came round, he preached with still greater vigor. After having laid the foundations of the new building, he was desirous of sweeping away the rubbish of the old. "For four years," said he to the crowd assembled in the cathedral, "you have eagerly received the holy doctrine of the gospel. Glowing with the fire of charity, fed with the sweets of the heavenly manna, it is impossible you can now find any savor in the wretched nutriment of human traditions." And then attacking the compulsory abstinence from meat at certain seasons, he exclaimed with his artless eloquence, "There are some who maintain that to eat meat is a fault, and even a great sin, although God has never forbidden it, and yet they think it not a crime to sell human flesh to the foreigner, and drag it to slaughter!" At this daring language, the partisans of the military capitulations, who were present in the assembly, shuddered with indignation and anger and vowed never to forget it.

While Zwingli was preaching thus energetically, he still continued to say Mass. He observed the established usages of the church and even abstained from meat on the appointed days. But there were some turbulent persons who did not act so prudently. Rubli, who had taken refuge at Zurich, permitted himself to be led astray by an extravagant zeal. The former curate of Saint Alban's, a Bernese captain, and Conrad Huber, a member of the great council, were accustomed to meet at the house of the latter to eat meat on Friday and Saturday. On this they greatly prided themselves. The question of fasting engrossed every mind. An inhabitant of Lucerne, having come to Zurich, said to one of his friends in this city, "You worthy confederates of Zurich are wrong in eating meat during Lent."

The Zuricher replied, "You gentlemen of Lucerne, however, take the liberty to eat meat on the prohibited days."

"We have purchased it from the pope."

"And we, from the butcher. . . . If it be an affair of money, one is certainly as good as the other." The council, having received a complaint against the transgressors of the ecclesiastical ordinances, requested the opinion of the parish priest. Zwingli replied that the practice of eating meat every day was not blamable of itself, but that the people ought to abstain from doing it until a competent authority should have come to some decision on the matter. The other members of the clergy concurred in his sentiments.

The enemies of the truth took advantage of this fortunate circumstance. Their influence was declining. The victory would remain with Zwingli, unless they made haste to strike some vigorous blow. They importuned the bishop of Constance. "Zwingli," exclaimed they, "is the destroyer and not the keeper of the Lord's fold."

The ambitious Faber, Zwingli's old friend, had just returned from Rome full of fresh zeal for the papacy. From the inspirations of this haughty city were destined to proceed the first religious troubles in Switzerland. A decisive struggle between the evangelical truth and the representatives of the Roman pontiff was now to take place. Truth acquires its chief strength in the attacks that are made upon it. The priests then stood up, as in the days of the apostles, against the new doctrine. Without these attacks, it would probably have remained hidden and obscure in a few faithful souls. But God was watching the hour to manifest it to the world. The partisans of the papacy, seeing the fire already smoldering in Zurich, rushed forward to extinguish it, but they only made the conflagration fiercer and more extensive.

In the afternoon of April 7, 1522, three ecclesiastical deputies from the bishop of Constance entered Zurich. Two of them had an austere and angry look; the third appeared of milder disposition. They were Melchior Battli, Doctor Brendi, and John Vanner, preacher of the cathedral, an evangelical man who preserved silence during the whole of the business. It was already dark when Luti ran to Zwingli and said, "The bishop's commissioners have arrived. Some great blow is preparing. All the partisans of the old customs are stirring. A notary is summoning all the priests for an early meeting tomorrow in the hall of the chapter."

The assembly of the clergy accordingly took place on the following day when the coadjutor rose and delivered a speech which his opponents described as haughty and violent; he studiously refrained, however, from uttering Zwingli's name. A few priests, recently gained over to the gospel, were thunderstruck. Their pallid features, their silence, and their sighs betrayed their total loss of courage. Zwingli now stood up and answered in a manner that effectually silenced his adversaries.

At Zurich, as in the other cantons, the most violent enemies of the new doctrine were to be found in the Smaller Council. The deputation, worsted before the clergy, laid their complaints before the magistrates. Zwingli was absent, and accordingly they had no reply to fear. The result appeared decisive. They were about to condemn the gospel without its defenders being heard. Never had the Reformation of Switzerland been in greater danger. It was on the point of being stifled in its cradle. The councilors who were friendly to Zwingli then appealed to the jurisdiction of the Great Council. This was the only remaining chance of safety, and God made use of it to save the cause of the gospel.

The Two Hundred were convened. The partisans of the papacy made every exertion to prevent Zwingli's admission. He struggled hard to obtain a hearing, knocking at every door and leaving not a stone unturned, to use his own expression. "It is impossible," said the burgomasters. "The council has decided to the contrary."

"Upon this," says Zwingli, "I remained tranquil, and with deep sighs laid the matter before Him who heareth the groans of the captive, beseeching him to defend His gospel."

On April 9, the Two Hundred met. "We desire to have our pastors here," immediately said the friends of the Reformation who belonged to it. The Smaller Council resisted, but the Great Council decided that the pastors should be present at the accusation and even reply if they thought fit. The deputies of Constance were first introduced, and next the three priests of Zurich— Zwingli, Engelhard, and the aged Roeschli.

After these antagonists, thus brought face to face, had scrutinized each other's appearance, the coadjutor stood up. "If his heart and head had only been equal to his voice," says Zwingli, "he would have excelled Apollo and Orpheus in sweetness, and the Gracchi and Demosthenes in power."

"The civil constitution," said this champion of the papacy, "and the Christian faith itself are endangered. Men have recently appeared who teach novel, revolting, and seditious doctrines." At the end of a long speech, he fixed his eyes on the assembled senators, and said, "Remain in the church! . . . Out of it no one can be saved. Its ceremonies alone are capable of bringing the simple to a knowledge of salvation; and the shepherds of the flock have nothing more to do than explain their meaning to the people."

As soon as the coadjutor had finished his speech, he prepared to leave the council room with his colleagues, when Zwingli said earnestly, "Most worthy coadjutor, and you, his companions, stay, I entreat you, until I have vindicated myself."

The Coadjutor: "We have no commission to dispute with any one."

Zwingli: "I have no wish to dispute, but to state fearlessly what I have been teaching up to this hour."

The Burgomaster Roust (addressing the deputation from Constance): "I beseech you to listen to the reply the pastor desires to make."

The Coadjutor: "I know too well the man I have to deal with. Ulrich Zwingli is too violent for any discussion to be held with him."

Zwingli: "How long since has it been customary to accuse an innocent man with such violence and then refuse to hear his defense? In the name of our common faith, of the baptism we have both received, of Christ the author of salvation and of life, listen to me. If you cannot as deputies, at least do so as Christians."

After firing her guns in the air, Rome was hastily retreating from the field of battle. The reformer wanted only to be heard, and the agents of the papacy thought of nothing but running away. A cause thus pleaded was already gained by one side and lost by the other. The Two Hundred could no longer contain their indignation. A murmur was heard in the assembly; again the burgomaster entreated the deputies to remain. Abashed and speechless, they returned to their places.

Zwingli said, "The reverend coadjutor speaks of doctrines that are seditious and subversive of the civil laws. Let him learn that Zurich is more tranquil and more obedient to the laws than any other city of the Helvetians, a circumstance which all good citizens ascribe to the gospel. Is not Christianity the strongest bulwark of justice among a nation? What is the result of all ceremonies but shamefully to disguise the features of Christ and of His disciples? Yes! there is another way, besides these vain observances, to bring the unlearned people to the knowledge of the truth. It is that which Christ and His apostles followed . . . the gospel itself! Let us not fear that the people cannot understand it. He who believes, understands. The people can believe; they can therefore understand. This is a work of the Holy Ghost and not of mere human reason. As for that matter, let him who is not satisfied with forty days, fast all the year if he pleases. It is a matter of indifference to me. All that I require is, that no one should be compelled to fast, and that for so trivial an observance the Zurichers should not be accused of withdrawing from the communion of Christians."

"I did not say that," exclaimed the coadjutor. "No," said his colleague Dr. Brendi, "he did not say so." But all the senate confirmed Zwingli's assertion.

"Excellent citizens," continued the latter, "let not his charge alarm you! The foundation of the church is that rock, that Christ, who gave Peter his name because he confessed him faithfully. In every nation, whoever sincerely believes in the Lord Jesus is saved. It is out of this church that no one can have everlasting life. To explain the gospel and to follow it is our whole duty as ministers of Christ. Let those who live upon ceremonies undertake to explain them!"

The coadjutor blushed and remained silent. The council of the Two Hundred then broke up. On the same day they came to the resolution that the pope and the cardinals should be requested to explain the controverted point and that in the meanwhile the people should abstain from eating meat during Lent.

This discussion had forwarded the work of the Reformation. The champions of Rome and those of the new doctrine had met face to face, as it were, in the presence of the whole people, and the advantage had not remained on the side of the pope. This was the first skirmish in a campaign that promised to be long and severe and alternated with many vicissitudes of mourning and joy. But the first success at the beginning of a contest gives courage to the whole army and intimidates the enemy. The Reformation had seized upon a ground from which it was never to be dislodged. If the council thought themselves still obliged to act with caution, the people loudly proclaimed the defeat of Rome. "With the energy of St. Paul," said they to Zwingli, "you have attacked these false apostles and their Ananiahs—those whited walls. . . . The satellites of Antichrist can never do more than gnash their teeth at you!"

But at the same time, the enemies of the gospel were rallying their forces. There was no time to lose if they desired to suppress it, for it would soon be beyond the reach of their blows. Hoffmann laid before the chapter a voluminous accusation against the reformer. "Suppose," he said, "the priest could prove by witnesses what sins or what disorders had been committed by ecclesiastics in certain convents, streets, or taverns, he ought to name no one! Why would he have us understand (it is true I have scarcely ever heard of him myself) that he alone derives his doctrine from the fountainhead and that others seek it only in . . . puddles? Is it not impossible, considering the diversity of men's minds, that every preacher should preach alike?"

Zwingli answered this accusation in a full meeting of the chapter, scattering his adversaries' charges, "as a bull with his horns tosses straw in the air." The matter which had appeared so serious, ended in loud bursts of laughter at the canon's expense. But Zwingli did not stop there. On April 16 he published a treatise on the free use of meats.

Chapter 11
Progress of the Reform

Zwingli's firmness delighted the friends of truth. But adversaries were plotting against the friends of the Reformation. Not an hour passed in which the means of getting rid of Zwingli were not discussed. One day he received an anonymous letter, which he communicated immediately to his two curates. "Snares surround you on every side," wrote his secret friend. "A deadly poison has been prepared to take away your life. Never eat food but in your own house, and only what has been prepared by your own cook. The walls of Zurich contain men who are plotting your destruction. . . . I am your friend; you shall know me hereafter."

On the next day after that in which Zwingli had received this mysterious epistle, just as Staheli was entering church, a chaplain stopped him and said, "Leave Zwingli's house forthwith; a catastrophe is at hand!" Certain fanatics, who despaired of seeing the Reformation checked by words, were arming themselves. Whenever mighty revolutions are taking place in society, assassins ordinarily spring from the foul dregs of the agitated people. God watched over Zwingli.

While the murderers were beholding the failure of their plots, the legitimate organs of the papacy were again in commotion. The bishop and his councilors resolved to renew the war. Intelligence of this reached Zwingli from every quarter. The reformer, in full reliance on the Word of God, said, "I fear them . . . as a lofty rock fears the roaring waves . . . with the aid of God!" On May 2 the bishop of Constance (Hugo of Landenberg) published a mandate, in which, without naming either Zwingli or Zurich, he complained that speculative persons were reviving doctrines already condemned and that both learned and ignorant were in the habit of discussing in every place the deepest mysteries. John Vanner, preacher of the cathedral at Constance, was the first attacked: "I prefer," said he, "being a Christian with the hatred of many, to abandoning Christ for the friendship of the world."

But it was Zurich that the rising heresy required to be crushed. Faber and the bishop knew that Zwingli had many enemies among the canons. They resolved to take advantage of this enmity. Toward the end of May, a letter from the bishop arrived at Zurich. It was addressed to the provost and chapter. "Sons of the church," wrote the prelate, "let those perish who will perish! But let no one seduce you from the church." At the same time the bishop entreated the canons to prevent those culpable doctrines, which engendered pernicious sects, from being preached or discussed among them, either in private or in public. When this letter was read in the chapter, all eyes were fixed on Zwingli. The latter, understanding the meaning of this look, said to them, "I see that you think this letter refers to me. Please to give it me, and, God willing, I will answer it."

Zwingli replied in his *Archeteles* (a word which signifies the beginning and the end) "for," said he, "I hope this first answer will also be the last." In this work he spoke of the bishop in a very respectful manner and ascribed all the attacks of his enemies to a few intriguing men. "What have I done?" said he. "I have endeavoured to conduct them to the only true God and to Jesus Christ his Son. To this end, I have not made use of captious arguments, but plain and sincere language, such as the children of Switzerland can understand." And then, passing from a defensive to an offensive attitude, he added with great beauty, "When Julius Caesar felt the mortal wound, he folded his garments around him, that he might fall with dignity. The downfall of your ceremonies is at hand! See at least that they fall decently, and that light be everywhere promptly substituted for darkness."

This was the sole result of the bishop's letter to the chapter of Zurich. Since every friendly remonstrance had proved vain, it was necessary to strike a more vigorous blow. Upon this, Faber and Landenberg cast their eyes around them, fixing them at last on the diet, the supreme council of the Helvetic nation. Deputies from the bishop appeared before this body, stating that their master had issued a mandate forbidding the priests in his diocese to make any innovation in matters of doctrine; that his authority had been despised; and that he now invoked the support of the chiefs of the Confederation to aid him in reducing the rebels to obedience and in defending the true and ancient faith.

The enemies of the Reformation had the majority in this first assembly of the nation. Not long before, it had published a decree interdicting all those priests from preaching, whose sermons, in its opinion, were a cause of dissension among the people. This injunction of the diet, which then for the first time interfered with the Reformation, fell to the ground. But now, being resolved to act with severity, this assembly summoned before them Urban Weiss, pastor of Fislispach near Baden, whom the general report accused of preaching the new faith and rejecting the old. Weiss was set at liberty for a season at the intercession of several individuals and under bail of a hundred florins offered by his parishioners.

But the diet had taken its position. Everywhere the monks and priests began to recover their courage. At Zurich they had shown themselves more imperious immediately after the first decree of this assembly. Several members of the council were in the habit of visiting the three convents night and morning and even of taking their meals there. The monks tampered with these well-meaning guests and solicited them to procure an injunction from the government in their favor. "If Zwingli will not hold his tongue," said they, "we will bawl louder than he."

The diet had sided with the oppressors. The council of Zurich knew not what to do. On June 7 they voted an ordinance forbidding anyone to preach against the monks. Tranquillity was not restored; the battle that was fought from the pulpit every day grew hotter. The council nominated a deputation before which the pastors of Zurich and the readers and preachers of the convents were summoned to appear in the provost's house. After a lively debate, the burgomaster enjoined both parties to preach nothing that might endanger the public peace.

"I cannot comply with this injunction," said Zwingli; "I am resolved to preach the gospel freely and unconditionally, in conformity with the previous ordinance. I am bishop and pastor of

Zurich; to me has been confided the cure of souls. It is I who have taken oath, and not the monks. They ought to yield, and not I. If they preach lies, I will contradict them, even in the pulpits of their own convents. If I myself teach a doctrine contrary to the holy gospel, then I desire to be rebuked, not only by the chapter, but by any citizen whatsoever, and moreover to be punished by the council."

"We demand permission," said the monks, "to preach the doctrines of St. Thomas." The committed of the council determined, after proper deliberation, "that Thomas [Aquinas], Scotus, and the other doctors should be laid aside, and that nothing should be preached but the gospel." Thus did the truth once more prevail. But the anger of the papal partisans was augmented. The ultramontane canons could not conceal their rage. They stared insolently at Zwingli in the chapter.

These menaces did not check Zwingli. There was still one place in Zurich where, thanks to the Dominicans, the light had not yet penetrated. This was the nunnery of Oetenbach. Here the daughters of the first families of Zurich were accustomed to take the veil. It seemed unjust that these poor women, shut up within the walls of their convent, should be the only persons that did not hear the Word of God. The Great Council ordered Zwingli to visit them. The reformer went into that pulpit which had hitherto been confined to the Dominicans and preached "on the clearness and certainty of the Word of God." He subsequently published this remarkable discourse, which did not fall on barren ground and which still further exasperated the monks.

A circumstance now occurred that extended this hostility and communicated it to many other hearts. The Swiss, under the command of Stein and Winkelreid, had just suffered a bloody defeat at the Bicocca. They had made a desperate charge upon the enemy, but Pescara's artillery and the lansquenets of Freundsberg had overthrown both commanders and standards, while whole companies had been mown down and suddenly exterminated. Winkelreid and Stein, with members of the noble families of Mulinen, Diesbach, Bonstetten, Tschudi, and Pfyffer, had been left on the field of battle. Schwytz especially had been decimated. The bloody relics of this frightful combat had returned to

Switzerland, carrying mourning in their train. A cry of woe resounded from the Alps to the Jura and from the Rhône to the Rhine.

But no one felt so keen a pain as Zwingli. He immediately wrote an address to Schwytz dissuading the citizens of this canton from foreign service. "Your ancestors," said he with all the warmth of a patriot's heart, "fought with their enemies in defense of liberty; but they never put Christians to death for mere gain. These foreign wars bring innumerable calamities on our country. The scourge of God chastises our confederate nations, and Helvetian liberty is on the verge of expiring between the interested caresses and the deadly hatred of foreign princes." This address, having been presented to the assembly of the people of Schwytz, produced such an effect that they resolved to abstain provisionally from every foreign alliance for the next twenty-five years.

But erelong the French party procured the repeal of this generous resolution, and Schwytz, from that hour, became the canton most opposed to Zwingli and his work. Even the disgrace that the partisans of these foreign treaties brought upon their native land only served to increase the hatred of these men against the intrepid minister who was endeavoring to avert from his country so many misfortunes and such deep shame. An opposition, growing more violent every day, was formed in the Confederation against Zwingli and Zurich. The usages of the church and practices of the recruiting officers, as they were attacked conjointly, mutually supported each other in withstanding the impetuous blast of that reform which threatened to overthrow them both.

At the same time enemies from without were multiplying. It was not only the pope but also other foreign princes, who vowed a pitiless hostility to the Reformation. Did it not pretend to withdraw from their ranks those Helvetian halberds to which their ambition and pride had been indebted for so many triumphs? But on the side of the gospel there remained God and the most excellent of the people; this was enough.

Chapter 12
The Assembly at Einsidlen

Disorders of a revolting character hastened the time when Zurich and the neighboring cantons snapped asunder the Roman yoke. A married schoolmaster, desiring to enter holy orders, obtained his wife's consent with this view, and they separated. The new priest, finding it impossible to observe his vow of celibacy and unwilling to wound his wife's feelings, quitted the place where she lived and went into the see of Constance, where he formed a criminal connection. His wife heard of this and followed him. The poor priest had compassion on her, and dismissing the woman who had usurped her rights, took his lawful spouse into his house. The procurator-fiscal immediately drew up a complaint; the vicar-general was in a ferment; the councilors of the consistory deliberated and ordered the curate either to forsake his wife or his benefice. The poor wife left her husband's house in tears, and her rival reentered it in triumph. The church declared itself satisfied, and from that time the adulterous priest was left undisturbed.

Not long after, a parish priest of Lucerne seduced a married woman and lived with her. The husband, having returned to Lucerne, availed himself of the priest's absence to recover his wife. As he was taking her home, the seducer met them, fell upon the injured husband, and inflicted a wound of which the latter died.

All pious men felt the necessity of reestablishing the law of God, which declares marriage honorable in all. The evangelical ministers had discovered that the law of celibacy was of human origin, imposed by the pontiffs and contrary to the Word of God, which, describing a faithful bishop, represents him as a husband and father (I Tim. 3:2, 4). At the same time, they observed that of all abuses that had crept into the church, none had been a cause of more vice and scandal. They thought, therefore, that it was not only lawful, but also, even more, a duty to God to reject it. Many of them now returned to this ancient usage of apostolical times. Xyloctect was married. Zwingli also took a wife about this period.

No woman had been more respected in Zurich than Anna Reinhardt, the widow of Meyer von Knonau, Gerold's mother. From Zwingli's arrival, she had been one of his most attentive hearers. She lived near him, and he had noticed her piety, her modesty, and her affection for her children. The young Gerold, who had become, as it were, his adopted son, drew him still closer to the mother. The sufferings undergone by this Christian woman had communicated a seriousness that contributed to show forth her evangelical virtues more brightly. At this time she was about thirty-five years old, and her fortune only amounted to four hundred florins. It was on her that Zwingli fixed his eyes as a companion for life.

He comprehended all the sacredness and sympathy of the conjugal state. He entitled it "a most holy alliance." "In like manner," said he, "as Christ died for His followers, and gave Himself entirely for them, so should married persons do all and suffer all for one another." But Zwingli, when he took Anna Reinhardt to wife, did not make his marriage known. This is undoubtedly a blamable weakness in a man at other times so resolute. The light that he and his friends had acquired on the question of celibacy was not general. Weak minds might have been scandalized. He feared that his usefulness in the church would be paralyzed if his marriage were made public. He sacrificed a portion of his happiness to these fears, excusable perhaps, but which he ought to have shaken off.

But far higher interests than these occupied the minds of the friends of truth. The diet, as we have seen, pressed by the enemies of the Reformation, had enjoined the evangelical preachers to preach no doctrines likely to disturb the people. Zwingli felt that the moment for action had arrived, and with his characteristic energy he convened a meeting at Einsidlen of the ministers of the Lord who were friendly to the gospel. Toward the end of June and the beginning of July 1522, pious ministers were seen from every side journeying toward the celebrated chapel of Einsidlen on a new pilgrimage. Leo Juda, the priest of Einsidlen, joyfully received all these ministers of Jesus Christ into the old abbey. Subsequent to Zwingli's residence, this place had become the stronghold of truth and a dwelling place for the righteous.

Zwingli proposed that his friends should address an urgent petition to the cantons and the bishop, with a view of obtaining the free preaching of the gospel, and at the same time the abolition of compulsory celibacy, the source of such criminal disorders. All concurred in his opinion. Ulrich had himself prepared the address. The petition to the bishop was read first; this was on July 2. A cordial affection knit together the preachers of the gospel truth in Switzerland. There were many others who sympathized with the men who had met at Einsidlen; such were Haller, Myconius, Hedio, Capito, Oecolampadius, Sebastian Meyer, Hoffmeister, and Vanner. This harmony is one of the most beautiful features of the Swiss Reformation. These excellent persons ever acted as one man and remained friends until death.

The men of Einsidlen felt that it was only by the power of faith that the members of the Confederation, divided by the foreign capitulations, could become a single body. But their eyes were directed to heaven. "The heavenly teaching," said they to their ecclesiastical superior in the address of July 2, "that truth which God the Creator has manifested by His Son to the human race immersed in sin, has been long veiled from our eyes by the ignorance, not to say the wickedness, of a few men. But this same Almighty God has resolved to reestablish it in its primitive estate. Unite, then, with those who desire the whole body of Christians should return to their Head, which is Christ. . . . On our part, we are determined to proclaim His gospel with indefatigable perseverance, and at the same time with such discretion that no one shall complain of it. Favor this, astonishing it may be, but not rash undertaking. Be like Moses, in the way, at the head of the people when they went out of Egypt, and with your own hands overthrow every obstacle that opposes the triumphant progress of the truth."

After this spirited appeal, the evangelists assembled at Einsidlen came to the question of celibacy. Zwingli had nothing to ask in this respect. He had such a wife as, according to Saint Paul's description, the wife of a minister of Christ should be—

grave, sober, faithful in all things (I Tim. 3:11). But he thought of his brethren, whose consciences were not as yet, like his own, emancipated from human ordinances. He longed, moreover, for that time when all the servants of God might live openly and fearlessly in the bosom of their families, having their children in subjection with all gravity (I Tim. 3:4).

"You cannot be ignorant," said the men of Einsidlen, "how deplorably the laws of chastity have hitherto been violated by the priests. When in the consecration of the ministers of the Lord, they ask of him who speaks for all the rest, 'Are those whom you present to us righteous men?'—he answers, 'They are righteous.' 'Are they learned?'—'They are learned.' But when he is asked, 'Are they chaste?' then he replies, 'As far as human weakness permits.' The New Testament everywhere condemns licentious intercourse; everywhere it sanctions marriage." Here follows a great number of quotations.

"It is for this reason," continued they, "we entreat you, by the love of Christ, by the liberty he has purchased for us, by the wretchedness of so many feeble and wavering souls, by the wounds of so many ulcerated consciences, by all divine and human motives . . . to permit what has been rashly enacted to be wisely repealed; for fear the majestic edifice of the church should fall with a frightful crash, and spread destruction far and wide. Behold with what storms the world is threatened! If wisdom does not interfere, the ruin of the priestly order is certain."

The petition to the Confederation was longer still. "Excellent sirs," thus spoke the allies of Einsidlen to the confederates at the end of their appeal, "we are all Swiss, and you are our fathers. There are some among us who have been faithful in the field of battle, in the chambers of pestilence, and in the midst of other calamities. It is in the name of sincere chastity that we address you. Who is unaware that we should better satisfy the lust of the flesh by not submitting to the regulations of lawful wedlock? But we must put an end to the scandals that afflict the church of Christ. If the tyranny of the Roman pontiff is resolved to oppress us, fear nothing, brave heroes! The authority of the Word of God, the rights of Christian liberty, and the sovereign power of grace will surround and protect us. We have all the same country, the same faith; we are Swiss, and the virtue of our illustrious ancestors has always displayed its power by an invincible defense of those who are unjustly oppressed."

Thus in Einsidlen itself, in that ancient stronghold of superstition, did Zwingli and his friends boldly uplift the banner of truth and liberty. They appealed to the heads of the state and of the church. The band of friends at Einsidlen separated calm, rejoicing, and full of hope in that God in whose hands they had placed their cause.

"It was something really sublime for those times," says Henry Bullinger, "that these men should have thus dared stand forth and, rallying round the gospel, expose themselves to every danger. But God preserved them all, so that no harm befell them, for God always preserves His own." It was indeed sublime. It was a bold step in the progress of the Reformation, one of the brightest days of the religious regeneration of Switzerland. A holy confederation was formed at Einsidlen. Humble but intrepid men had grasped the sword of the Spirit, which is the Word of God, and the shield of faith. The gauntlet was thrown down—the challenge was given—not only by one man but also by men of different cantons, prepared to sacrifice their lives: they must await the struggle.

It was in the convents especially that the indignation was greatest. Every meeting that was held in them either for discussion or amusement saw some new attack burst forth. One day there was a great banquet at the convent of Fraubrunn, and as the wine had got into the heads of the guests, they began to launch the most envenomed darts against the gospel. What most incensed the priests and monks was the evangelical doctrine that in the Christian church there ought not be any sacerdotal caste raised above the believers.

One single friend of the Reformation was present, Macrinus, a layman, and master of the school at Soleure. At first he avoided the discussion, passing from one table to the other. But at length, unable to endure the violent language of the guests, he rose boldly and said aloud, "Yes! all true Christians are priests and sacrificers, as St. Peter says, 'Ye are priests and kings.'"

At these words, one of the loudest bawlers, the dean of Burgdorff, a tall, strong man with a voice of thunder, burst out laughing. "So then, you Greeklings and pedagogues are the royal priesthood? . . . a pretty priesthood, forsooth! . . . beggarly kings . . . priests without prebends or livings!" And at the very instant, priests and monks with one accord fell on the imprudent layman.

It was in Lucerne, however, that the bold step of the men of Einsidlen was destined to produce the greatest commotion. The diet had met in this city, and complaints arrived from every quarter against these daring preachers who would prevent Helvetia from quietly selling the blood of her children to the stranger. On July 22, 1522, as Oswald Myconius was at dinner in his own house with the canon Kilchmeyer and others favorably disposed to the gospel, a youth sent by Zwingli stood at the door. He brought the two famous petitions of Einsidlen and a letter from Zwingli calling upon Myconius to circulate them in Lucerne. "It is my advice," added the reformer, "that this should be done quietly, gradually, rather than all at once, for we must learn to give up everything—even one's wife—for Christ's sake."

The critical moment was approaching in Lucerne. The shell had fallen in the midst of the city and was about to explode. Myconius's guests read the petitions. "May God prosper this beginning!" exclaimed Myconius, adding immediately, "From this very hour this prayer should be the constant occupation of our hearts." The petitions were circulated immediately, perhaps with more ardor than Zwingli had required. But the moment was extraordinary. Eleven men, the flower of the clergy, had placed themselves in the breach; it was desirable to enlighten men's minds, to decide the wavering, and to win over the most influential members of the diet.

Myconius, in the midst of his exertions, did not forget his friends. The youthful messenger had told him of the attacks Zwingli had to put up with on the part of the monks of Zurich. "The truth of the Holy Ghost is invincible," wrote Myconius to him on the same day. "Shielded with the buckler of Scripture, you have conquered not only in one contest, nor in two, but in three, and the fourth is now beginning. . . . Grasp those powerful arms which are harder than adamant! Christ, to protect His followers, requires nothing but his Word. Your struggles impart unflinching courage to all who have devoted themselves to Jesus Christ."

The two petitions did not produce the desired effect in Lucerne. Some pious men approved of them, but their numbers were few. Many, fearing to compromise themselves, would neither praise nor blame them. "These folks," said others, "will never succeed in this business!" All the priests murmured and whispered against them, and the people became violent against the gospel. The passion for a military life had been revived in Lucerne after the bloody defeat of the Bicocca, and war alone filled every mind. Myconius, who watched attentively these different impressions, felt his courage sinking. The gospel future that he had pictured in Lucerne and Switzerland seemed to vanish. "Our countrymen are blind as regards heavenly things," said he with a deep sigh. "We can hope nothing from the Swiss which concerns the glory of Christ."

In the council and the diet, the irritation was greatest. The pope, France, England, the empire—all were in commotion around Switzerland after the defeat of the Bicocca and the evacuation of Lombardy by the French. Were not the political affairs complicated enough, that these eleven men should come with their petitions and add mere religious questions? The deputies of Zurich alone inclined in favor of the gospel. The canon Xyloctect, fearing for the safety of himself and his wife (for he had married a daughter of one of the first families in the country), had shed tears of regret, as he refused to go to Einsidlen and sign the addresses. The canon Kilchmeyer was bolder, and he had everything to fear. On August 13 he wrote to Zwingli, "Sentence threatens me, but I await it with courage." As his pen was tracing these words, the usher of the council entered his room and summoned him to appear on the morrow. "If they throw me into prison," said he, continuing his letter, "I shall claim your help, but it will be easier to transport a rock from our Alps than to remove me a finger's breadth from the Word of Jesus Christ." The respect due to his family, and the determination of the council to make the storm burst on Oswald Myconius, saved the canon.

Berthold Haller had not signed the petitions, perhaps because he was not a Swiss. But with unyielding courage he explained the

Gospel of St. Matthew, after Zwingli's example. A great crowd filled the cathedral of Berne. The Word of God operated more powerfully on the people than Manuel's dramas.

Haller was summoned to the town hall; the people escorted this meek man thither and remained assembled in the square in front. The council were divided in their sentiments. "It is a matter that concerns the bishop," said the most influential members. "We must give him up to Monseigneur of Lausanne." Haller's friends trembled at these words and besought him to withdraw as soon as possible. The people surrounded him and accompanied him home, and a great body of armed citizens remained before his house, determined to form a rampart for their humble pastor with their bodies. The bishop and council shrank back at this spirited demonstration, and Haller was saved.

He did not, however, combat alone in Berne. Sebastian Meyer refuted the pastoral letter of the bishop of Constance and especially the hackneyed charge "that the disciples of the gospel teach a new doctrine and that the old is the true one." "To have been a thousand years wrong," said he, "will not make us right for one single hour, or else the pagans should have kept to their creed. If the most ancient doctrines ought to be preferred, fifteen hundred years are more than five hundred, and the gospel is older than the decrees of the pope."

John Vannius, a chorister of the cathedral, soon declared in favor of the evangelical doctrine, for in this war no soldier fell whose place was not immediately filled by another. "How can the muddy water of the Tiber," said Vannius, "subsist beside the pure stream that Luther has drawn from the springs of St. Paul?" But the mouth of the chorister also was shut. "In all Switzerland you will hardly find men more unfavorably disposed toward sound doctrine than the Friburgers," wrote Myconius to Zwingli.

An exception must, however, be made as regards Lucerne, and this Myconius knew well. He had not signed the famous petitions, but if he did not, his friends did, and a victim was wanted. The ancient literature of Greece and Rome was beginning, through his exertions, to shed its light upon Lucerne. Students resorted thither from various quarters to hear the learned professor, and the friends of peace listened with delight to milder sounds than the clash of halberds, swords, and breastplates that as yet had echoed alone in this warlike city.

Myconius had sacrificed everything for his country. He had quitted Zurich and Zwingli; he had lost his health; his wife was ailing; his child was young. Should Lucerne once cast him forth, he could nowhere look for an asylum. But this they heeded not. Factions are pitiless, and what should excite their compassion does but inflame their anger. Hertenstein, burgomaster of Lucerne, an old and valiant warrior who had become celebrated in the Swabian and Burgundian wars, proposed the school-master's dismissal and wished to drive him from the canton with his Greek, his Latin, and his gospel. He succeeded.

As he left the meeting of the council in which Myconius had been deprived of his post, Hertenstein met Berguer, the Zurich deputy: "We send you back your schoolmaster," said he ironically. "Prepare a comfortable lodging for him."

"We will not let him sleep in the open air," immediately replied the courageous deputy. But Berguer promised more than he could perform.

The burgomaster's tidings were but too true, and they were soon made known to the unhappy Myconius. He was stripped of his appointment, banished. The only crime with which he was reproached was being Luther's disciple. He turned his eyes around him and nowhere found a shelter.

"Here," said he then to Zwingli, "is your poor Myconius banished by the council of Lucerne. . . . Whither shall I go? . . . I know not. . . . Assailed yourself by such furious storms, how can you shelter me? In my tribulation I cry to that God who is my chief hope. Ever rich, ever kind, He does not permit any who call upon Him to turn away unheard. May He provide for my wants!"

He had not long to wait for the word of consolation. There was one man in Switzerland inured to the battles of faith. Zwingli drew nigh to his friend and raised him up. "So rude are the blows by which men strive to overthrow the house of God," said Zwingli, "and so frequent are their attacks, that it is not only the wind and rain that burst upon it, as our Lord predicts (Matt. 7:27), but also the hail and the thunder. If I did not see that the Lord kept watch over the ship, I should long since have abandoned the helm. But I see Him, through the storm, strengthening the tackling, handing the yards, spreading the sails; nay more, commanding the very winds. . . . Should I not be a coward and unworthy the name of a man if I abandoned my post and sought a disgraceful death in flight? I confide entirely in His sovereign goodness. Let Him govern, let Him carry us forward, let Him hasten or delay, let Him plunge us even to the bottom of the deep. . . . We will fear nothing. We are vessels that belong to Him. He can make use of us as he pleases, for honor or dishonor.

"As for yourself, this is my advice. Appear before the council and deliver an address worthy of you and of Christ; that is to say, calculated to melt and not irritate their feelings. Deny that you are Luther's disciple; confess that you are Christ's. Let your pupils surround you and speak too, and if this does not succeed, then come to your friend—come to Zwingli—and look upon our city as your home!"

Encouraged by this language, Myconius followed the advice of the reformer. But all his efforts were unavailing. This witness to the truth was compelled to leave his country, and the people of Lucerne decried him so much that in every quarter the magistrates prevented his finding an asylum. "Nothing remains for me but to beg my bread from door to door," exclaimed this confessor of Christ, whose heart was crushed at the sight of so much hostility.

But erelong, the friend of Zwingli was with his sick wife and infant child compelled to leave that ungrateful city, where, of all his family, one only of his sisters had received the gospel. He crossed its ancient bridge; he bade farewell to those mountains which appear to rise from the bosom of the Walstatter lake into the clouds. The canons Xyloctect and Kilchmeyer, the only friends whom the Reformation yet counted among his fellow countrymen, followed him not long after. The Gospel itself departed from Lucerne.

"It was thus," says Bullinger's chronicle, "that the persecutions of the confederates against the gospel began: and this took place at the instigation of the clergy, who in every age have dragged Jesus Christ before the judgment seat of Herod and of Pilate."

Nor did Zwingli himself escape trial. About this time, he was wounded in his tenderest point. The rumor of his doctrines and of his struggles had passed the Sentis, penetrated the Tockenburg, and reached the heights of Wildhaus. The family of herdsmen from which the reformer had sprung was deeply moved. Of Zwingli's five brothers, some had continued their peaceful mountain labors; others, to their brother's great regret, had taken up arms, quitted their herds, and served a foreign prince. Both were alike astonished at the reports that reached their chalets. Already they pictured to themselves their brother dragged to Constance before the bishop and a pile erected for his destruction on the same spot where John Huss had perished in the flames. These proud herdsmen could not endure the idea of being called the brothers of a heretic. They wrote to Zwingli, describing their pain and their fears.

Zwingli replied to them as follows: "So long as God shall permit me, I will execute the task, which he has confided to me, without fearing the world and its haughty tyrants. I know every thing that can befall me. There is no danger, no misfortune that I have not carefully weighed long ago. My own strength is nothingness itself, and I know the power of my enemies. But I know also that I can do every thing in Christ, who strengthens me. Though I should be silent, another would be constrained to do what God is now doing through me, and I should be punished by the Almighty. Banish all anxiety, my dear brothers. If I have any fear, it is lest I have been milder and gentler than suits our times. What reproach (say you) will be cast upon our family, if you are burnt, or put to death in any other way! Oh, my beloved brothers, the gospel derives from the blood of Christ this remarkable property, that the most violent persecutions, far from checking its progress, serve but to accelerate it. Those alone are the true soldiers of Christ who do not fear to bear in their body the wounds of their Master. All my labors have no other aim than to proclaim to men the treasures of happiness that Christ hath purchased for us, that all might take refuge in the Father through the death of his

Son. If this doctrine scandalizes you, your anger cannot stop me. You are my brothers—yes!—my own brothers, sons of the same father, fruit of the same womb; . . . but if you were not my brothers in Christ and in the work of faith, then my grief would be so violent that nothing could equal it. Farewell. I shall never cease to be your affectionate brother, if only you will not cease yourselves to be the brethren of Jesus Christ."

The confederates appeared to rise, like one man, against the gospel. The addresses of Einsidlen had given the signal. Zwingli, agitated at the fate of Myconius, saw, in his misfortunes, the beginning of calamities. Enemies in Zurich, enemies without; a man's own relatives becoming his opponents; a furious opposition on the part of the monks and priests; violent measures in the diet and councils; coarse and perhaps bloody attacks from the partisans of foreign service; the highest valleys of Switzerland, that cradle of the Confederation, pouring forth its invincible phalanxes, to save Rome, and annihilate at the cost of their lives the rising faith of the sons of the Reformation—such was the picture the penetrating eye of the reformer discovered in the distance, and he shuddered at the prospect.

On August 22, 1522, Zwingli, thoughtful and agitated, laid all his anguish before the throne of God. "O Jesus," said he, "Thou seest how the wicked and the blasphemers stun Thy people's ears with their clamors. Thou knowest how from my childhood I have hated all dispute, and yet, in despite of myself, Thou hast not ceased to impel me to the conflict. . . . Therefore do I call upon Thee with confidence to complete what Thou hast begun. If I have built up anything wrongly, do Thou throw it down with thy mighty hand. If I have laid any other foundation than Thee, let Thy powerful arm destroy it. O Vine abounding in sweetness, whose husbandman is the Father, and whose branches we are, do not abandon Thy shoots! For Thou hast promised to be with us until the end of the world!"

Chapter 13
Victory for
the Preaching of the Gospel

Zwingli was advancing in the Christian life. Tearing him from his thoughtless and worldly life, the gospel had imprinted a seriousness on his character that was not natural to him. This seriousness was very necessary to him. We have seen how toward the close of the year 1522 numerous enemies appeared, rising up against the Reformation. Zwingli was overwhelmed with reproaches from every quarter, and disputes would often take place even in the churches.

Leo Juda, who was a man of small stature but full of love for the poor and zeal against false teachers, had arrived at Zurich about the end of the year 1522 to occupy the station of pastor of St. Peter's Church. He had been replaced at Einsidlen by Oswald Myconius. This was a valuable acquisition for Zwingli and for the Reformation.

One day, not long after his arrival, as he was in the church of which he had been appointed pastor, Leo heard an Augustinian monk asserting forcibly that man is able of himself to satisfy the righteousness of God. "Reverend father prior," said Leo, "listen to me for an instant, and you, my dear citizens, keep still. I will speak as becomes a Christian."

He then proved to the people the falseness of the doctrine to which he had been listening. Upon this, a great disturbance arose in the church, and immediately several persons angrily fell upon "the little priest" from Einsidlen. Zwingli appeared before the Great Council, requiring permission to give an account of his doctrine in the presence of the deputies of the bishop; the council, desirous of putting an end to these disturbances, convened a conference for January 29, 1523.

The news spread rapidly through the whole of Switzerland. His adversaries exclaimed in their vexation, "A diet of vagabonds is to be held at Zurich. All the beggars from the highways will be there."

Zwingli, desiring to prepare for the struggle, published sixty-seven theses. The mountaineer of the Tockenburg boldly assailed the pope in the eyes of all Switzerland:

> All those who maintain that the gospel is nothing without the confirmation of the church, blaspheme God.

> Jesus Christ is the only way of salvation for all those who have been, who are, or who shall be.

> All Christians are Christ's brethren, and brethren of one another, and they have no father upon earth: thus orders, sects, and parties fall to the ground.

> We should not constrain those who will not acknowledge their error, unless they disturb the public peace by their seditious behavior.

Such were some of Zwingli's propositions.

Early in the morning of Thursday, January 29, more than six hundred persons had collected in the hall of the Great Council at Zurich. Citizens and strangers, scholars, men of rank and the clergy had responded to the call of the council. "What will be the end of all this?" asked they of one another. No one ventured to reply, but the attention, emotion, and agitation prevailing in this assembly clearly manifested that they were expecting some extraordinary result.

The burgomaster Roust, who had fought at Marignan, presided at the conference. The chevalier James d'Anwyl, grand master of the episcopal court at Constance, the vicar-general Faber, and many other doctors were present as the bishop's representatives. Sebastian Hofmeister had been sent by Schaffhausen, and he was the only deputy from the cantons: such was still the weakness of the Reformation in Switzerland. On a table in the middle of the hall lay a Bible; in front of it sat Zwingli. "I am agitated and tormented on every side," he had said, "and yet I stand firm, relying not on my own strength, but on Christ the rock, with whose help I can do all things."

Zwingli stood up and said, "I have preached that salvation is found in Jesus Christ alone, and for this reason I am stigmatized throughout Switzerland as a heretic, a seducer of the people, a rebel. . . . Now, then, in the name of God, here I stand!"

Upon this all eyes were turned toward Faber, who rose and made answer: "I was not sent here to dispute, but merely to listen!" The assembly, in surprise, began to laugh. "The Diet of Nuremberg," continued Faber, "has promised a council within a year. We must wait until it meets."

"What!" said Zwingli, "is not this vast and learned meeting as good as any council?" Then turning to the presidents, he added, "Gracious lords, defend the Word of God."

A deep silence followed this appeal; it was interrupted by the burgomaster, who said: "If there is any one here who has anything to say, let him do so." There was another pause.

"I call upon all those who have accused me, and I know that there are several here," said Zwingli, "to come forward and reprove me for the love of truth." No one said a word.

Zwingli repeated his request a second and third time, but to no purpose. Faber, thus closely pressed, dropped for an instant the reserve he had imposed on himself to declare that he had convicted the pastor of Filispach of his error and that man was now confined in prison. But immediately after, Faber resumed his character as a spectator. It was in vain that he was urged to set forth the reasons by which he had convicted this pastor. He obstinately refused.

This silence on the part of the Catholic doctors tried the patience of the meeting. A voice was heard exclaiming from the farther part of the hall: "Where are now these valiant fellows, who talk so loudly in the streets? Come along, step forward, there's your man!" No one moved. Upon this, the burgomaster said with a smile: "It would appear that this famous sword with which you smote the pastor of Filispach will not come out of its sheath today"; and he then broke up the meeting.

When the assembly met again in the afternoon, the council declared that Master Ulrich Zwingli, not being reproved by anyone, might continue to preach the holy gospel and that the rest of the clergy in the canton should teach nothing that they could not substantiate by Scripture.

"Praised be God, who will cause his holy Word to prevail in heaven and earth!" exclaimed Zwingli.

Upon this, Faber could not restrain his indignation. "The theses of Master Ulrich," said he, "are contrary to the honor of the church and the doctrine of Christ, and I will prove it."

"Do so," replied Zwingli.

But Faber declined his challenge, except it should be at Paris, Cologne, or Friburg. "I will have no other judge than the gospel," said Zwingli. "Sooner than you can shake one of its words, the earth will open before you."

"The gospel!" sneered Faber, "always the gospel! . . . Men might live in holiness, peace, and charity, even if there were no gospel."

At these words the spectators rose indignantly from their seats. Thus terminated the disputation.

The Reformation had gained the day; it was now to accelerate its conquests. After his battle of Zurich, in which the most skillful champions of the papacy were dumb, who would be bold enough to oppose the new doctrine? But weapons of a different kind were tried. Zwingli's firmness and republican bearing overawed his adversaries; accordingly they had recourse to peculiar measures to subdue him. While Rome was pursuing Luther with her anathemas, she endeavored to win over the reformer of Zurich by gentleness.

The dispute was scarcely ended when Zwingli received a visit from the captain of the pope's guard—the son of the burgomaster Roust. He was accompanied by the legate Einsius, the bearer of a papal brief in which Adrian VI called Zwingli his beloved son and assured him of "his special favor." At the same time the pope urged the chaplain Zink to gain over Zwingli.

"And what has the pope commissioned you to offer him?" asked Oswald Myconius.

"Everything," replied Zink, "except the papal chair."

There was no mitre or crozier or cardinal's hat that the pope would not have given to bribe the reformer of Zurich. But Rome was strangely mistaken in this respect; all her proposals were unavailing. In Zwingli, the Catholic Church had a still more pitiless enemy than Luther. He cared far less than the Saxon reformer for the ideas and ceremonies of former ages. It was enough for him that any custom, however innocent in itself, was connected with some abuse; he fell violently upon it. The Word of God (thought he) should stand alone.

But if Rome understood so imperfectly what was then taking place in Christendom, she found councilors who endeavoured to put her in the way.

Faber, exasperated at seeing the pope thus humble himself before his adversary, hastened to enlighten him. He was a courtier with a constant smile upon his lips and honied words in his mouth. To judge from his own language, he was everybody's friend, even of those whom he accused of heresy. But his hatred was mortal.

While the pope was complimenting Zwingli on his eminent virtues and the special confidence he placed in him, the enemies of the reformer were increasing in number throughout Switzerland. The veteran soldiers, the great families, the herdsmen of the mountains combined their hatred against this doctrine which thwarted their tastes. At Lucerne, the magnificent representation of Zwingli's passion was announced; the people dragged the reformer's effigy to the scaffold, shouting out that they were going to put the heretic to death; and laying hands on some Zurichers who happened to be at Lucerne, compelled them to be spectators of this mock execution.

"They shall not trouble my repose," said Zwingli. "Christ will never be wanting to his followers." Even the diet reechoed with threats against him. "My dear confederates," said the councilor of Mullinen to the cantons, "make a timely resistance to the

Lutheran cause. . . . At Zurich a man is no longer master in his own house!"

This agitation among the enemy announced what was passing in Zurich more loudly than any proclamations could have done. The victory was indeed bearing fruit. The conquerors were gradually taking possession of the country, and every day the gospel made fresh progress. Twenty-four canons and a great number of chaplains voluntarily petitioned the council to reform their statutes. It was decided to replace these sluggish priests by pious and learned men, with commission to give the Zurich youth a Christian and liberal education, and to establish in the place of their vespers and Latin masses, a daily explanation of a chapter in the Bible, according to the Hebrew and Greek texts, first for the learned and afterwards for the people.

There are unfortunately in every army a number of those desperate heroes who leave their ranks and make unseasonable attacks on points that ought still to be respected. A young priest, Louis Hetzer, had published a treatise in German titled *The Judgment of God Against Images,* which produced a great sensation, and the images wholly engrossed the thoughts of a part of the people. It is only to the detriment of those essentials that ought to occupy his mind that man can fix his attention on secondary matters.

At a place called Stadelhofen, outside the city gates, stood a crucifix elaborately carved and richly ornamented. The most zealous partisans of the Reformation, shocked at the superstitions to which this image gave rise, could not pass by without giving vent to their indignation. A citizen named Claude Hottinger, "a worthy man," says Bullinger, "and well read in the Holy Scriptures," having fallen in with the miller of Stadelhofen, to whom the crucifix belonged, asked him when he intended to throw down his idols. "No one compels you to worship them," replied the miller.

"But do you not know," retorted Hottinger, "that the Word of God forbids us to have any graven images?"

"Well then," said the miller, "if you are authorized to remove them, I abandon them to you." Hottinger thought himself empowered to act, and shortly after, about the end of September, he was seen to pass the gates with a body of citizens. On arriving at the crucifix, they deliberately dug round it, until the image, yielding to their efforts, fell to the earth with a loud crash.

This daring action spread dismay on every side. One might have thought that religion itself had fallen with the crucifix of Stadelhofen. "They are guilty of sacrilege! They deserve to be put to death!" exclaimed the friends of Rome. The council caused the image breakers to be apprehended.

"No!" cried Zwingli and his colleagues from their pulpits, "Hottinger and his friends are not guilty in the sight of God and worthy of death. But they may be punished for having acted with violence and without the sanction of the magistrates."

Meantime, acts of a similar nature were continually taking place. A curate of Saint Peter's, one day noticing in front of the church a number of poor people ill fed and with tattered garments, said to one of his colleagues, as he turned his eyes on the costly ornaments of the saints, "I should like to strip these idols of wood to procure clothing for these poor members of Jesus Christ." A few days later, at three o'clock in the morning, the saints and all their ornaments disappeared.

The council flung the curate into prison, notwithstanding he protested his innocence of this proceeding. "What!" exclaimed the people. "Is it these logs of wood that Jesus ordered us to clothe? Is it on account of these images that he will say to the righteous: 'I was naked, and ye clothed me'?"

Thus, the greater the resistance, the higher soared the Reformation; and the more it was compressed, the more energetically did it spring forward and threaten to overthrow all that withstood it.

Chapter 14
"Forward in the Name of God"

Even these excesses were destined to be salutary. A new combat was needed to secure fresh triumphs, for in the things of the Spirit, as in the affairs of the world, there is no conquest without a struggle. And as the soldiers of Rome stood motionless, the conflict was to be brought on by the undisciplined sons of the Reformation. In fact, the magistrates were embarrassed and agitated. They felt the necessity of having their consciences enlightened, and with this view they resolved to appoint another public disputation in the German language, in which the question of idols should be examined according to Scripture.

The bishops of Coire, Constance, and Basel, the university of the latter city, and the twelve cantons were accordingly requested to send deputies to Zurich. But the bishops declined the invitation, and calling to mind the wretched figure their deputies had made at the former disputation, they had little inclination to repeat such humiliating scenes. Let the evangelicals dispute if they please, but let them dispute alone.

On the first occasion, the Roman party had kept silence; on the second, they were resolved not to appear. Rome may possibly have imagined that the great combat would cease for want of combatants. The bishops were not alone in refusing to attend. The men of Unterwalden replied that they had no scholars among them but only worthy and pious priests who explained the gospel as their fathers had done, that they would send no deputy to Zwingli "and his fellows," but that, if he fell into their hands, they would treat him in such a manner as to deprive him of all wish to relapse into the same faults. Schaffhausen and St. Gall alone sent representatives.

On October 26, after the sermon, an assembly of more than nine hundred persons, composed of members of the Great Council and of three hundred and fifty priests, filled the large hall of the townhouse. Zwingli and Leo Juda were seated at a table, on which lay the Old and New Testaments in the original languages. Zwingli spoke first, and overthrowing with a vigorous arm the authority of the hierarchy and of its councils, established the rights of every Christian church and claimed the liberty of the primitive ages—of those times when the church knew neither general nor provincial councils.

"The universal church," said he, "is spread over the whole world, wherever there is faith in Christ, in India as well as at Zurich. . . . And as for particular churches, we have them at Berne, at Schaffhausen, and even here. But the popes, with their cardinals and their councils, form neither the universal church nor a particular church. The assembly before which I now speak," continued he with energy, "is the church of Zurich. It desires to hear the Word of God, and it has the right of ordering all that may appear to it conformable with the Holy Scriptures."

Thus did Zwingli rely on the church, but on the true church; not on the clergy alone, but on the assembly of Christians, on the people. All that the Scriptures say of the church in general, he applied to particular churches. He did not think that any church could err which listened with docility to the Word of God. In his eyes, the church was represented politically and ecclesiastically by the Great Council. At first he explained every question from the pulpit, and when his hearers' minds were convinced of the truth, he carried the matter before the Great Council, who, in harmony with the ministers of the church, formed such decisions as the church called for.

In the absence of the bishop's deputies, Conrad Hoffmann, the same aged canon who had procured Zwingli's election to Zurich, undertook the defense of the pope. He maintained that the church, the flock, the "third estate," had no right to discuss such matters. "I was thirteen years at Heidelberg," said he, "living in the house of a very great scholar, whose name was Doctor Joss, a worthy and pious man, with whom I long ate and drank and led a merry life. But I always heard him say that it was not proper to discuss such matters, so you see. . . ." All were ready to burst into laughter; but the burgomaster checked them. "Let us therefore wait for a council," continued Hoffmann. "For the present, I shall not dispute, but obey the bishop's orders, even should he be a knave!"

"Wait for a council!" replied Zwingli. "And who will attend a council? The pope with some sluggish and ignorant bishops who will do nothing but what suits their fancy. No! the Church is not there! Hong and Kussnacht [two Zurich villages] are certainly more of a church than all the bishops and popes put together!"

Thus did Zwingli vindicate the rights of the Christian people, whom Rome had deprived of their privileges. The assembly before which he was speaking was not, in his judgment, the church of Zurich, but its first representative. This is the beginning of the Presbyterian system in the age of the Reformation. Zwingli was withdrawing Zurich from the jurisdiction of the bishop of Constance, separating it from the Latin hierarchy, and founding on this idea of the flock, of the Christian assembly, a new ecclesiastical constitution, to which other countries were afterwards to adhere.

The disputation continued. Many priests having risen to defend the images, but without having recourse to Holy Writ; Zwingli and the other reformers confuted them by the Bible. "If no one stands forward to defend the use of images by arguments derived from Scripture," said one of the presidents, "we shall call upon some of their advocates by name."

As no one arose, the priest of Wadischwyl was called. "He is asleep," answered one of the spectators. The priest of Horgen was next called. "He has sent me in his place," replied the curate, "but I will not answer for him."

Evidently the power of God's Word was making itself felt in this assembly. The partisans of the Reformation were full of energy, liberty, and joy. Their adversaries appeared speechless, uneasy, and dejected. They summoned, one after another, the parish priests of Laufen, Glattfelden, and Wetzikon; the rector and priest of Pfaffikon; the dean of Elgg; and the priest of Baretschwyl, with the Dominicans and Gray friars (notorious for their preaching in defense of images, the virgin, the saints, and the Mass). All made answer that they could say nothing in their favor, and that henceforward they would apply themselves to the study of the truth. "Hitherto," said one of them, "I have put my trust in the old doctors. Now, I will believe in the new."

"You should believe not in us, but in God's Word," exclaimed Zwingli. "It is Scripture alone that can never err!"

The sitting had been long, and night was approaching. The president, Hofmeister of Schaffhausen, stood up and said, "Blessed be the Almighty and Everlasting God for that in all things he has vouchsafed us the victory." He then exhorted the councilors of Zurich to pull down all the images.

On Tuesday, the assembly met again in order to discuss the doctrine of the Mass. Vadian was in the chair. "My brethren in Christ," said Zwingli, "far from us be the thought that there is any deception or falsehood in the body and blood of Christ. Our only aim is to show that the Mass is not a sacrifice that one man can offer to God for another, unless anyone should maintain also that a man can eat and drink for his friend."

Vadian having twice demanded if any there present desired to uphold by Scripture the doctrine impugned, and no one having replied, the canons of Zurich, the chaplains, and many other ecclesiastics declared that they agreed with Zwingli.

But scarcely had the reformers thus vanquished the partisans of the old doctrines than they had to contend against those impatient spirits who call for sudden and violent innovations and not for wise and gradual reforms. The senator Grebel, a man highly respected in Zurich, had a son named Conrad, a youth of remarkable talents, a violent enemy of ignorance and superstition, which he attacked with the most cutting satire. Conrad Grebel was blustering and passionate, caustic and ill-natured in his speech, void of natural affection, dissipated, speaking loudly and frequently of his own innocence and seeing nothing but evil in his neighbors. He rose and said: "It is not enough to have disputed about the Mass. We must put an end to its abuses."

"The council will draw up an edict on the subject," replied Zwingli. Upon this Simon Stumpf exclaimed, "The Spirit of God has already decided. Why refer to the decision of the council?"

The commander Schmidt of Kussnacht arose gravely, and in language full of wisdom said, "Let us teach Christians to receive Christ in their hearts. Until this hour, ye have all gone after idols. The dwellers in the plain have run to the mountains, and those of the mountains have gone to the plain; the French to Germany, and the Germans to France. Now ye know whither ye ought to go. God has combined all things in Christ. Ye noble citizens of Zurich! Go to the true source, and may Christ at length reenter your territory and there resume His ancient empire."

This discourse made a deep impression, and no one stood up to reply to it. Zwingli rose with emotion and said, "Gracious lords, God is with us. . . . He will defend His cause. Now, then, forward in the name of God." Here Zwingli's agitation became so great that he could not proceed. He wept, and many joined their tears with his.

Thus ended the disputation. The presidents rose, the burgomaster thanked them, and the aged warrior, turning to the council, said gravely, with that voice which had so often been heard on the field of battle, "Now, then, . . . let us grasp the sword of God's Word, and may the Lord prosper His work."

This dispute, which took place in October 1523, was decisive. The majority of the priests, who had been present at it, returned full of zeal to the different parts of the canton, and the effect of these two days was felt throughout Switzerland. The church of Zurich, that had always preserved a certain independence with respect to the see of Constance, was then entirely emancipated. Instead of resting on the pope through the bishop, it rested henceforward through the people on the Word of God. Zurich recovered the privileges that Rome had taken from her. Town and country vied with each other in interest for the work of the Reformation, and the Great Council did but follow the movements of the people. On all important occasions the city and the villages made known their opinions. Luther had restored the Bible to the Christian world. Zwingli went further; he restored their rights. This is a characteristic feature of the Swiss Reformation. The maintenance of sound doctrine was thus confided, under God, to the people.

Zwingli did not allow himself to be elated by victory. On the contrary, the Reformation, according to his wish, was carried on with great moderation. "God knows my heart," said he, when the council asked his advice. "He knows that I am inclined to build up, and not to throw down. I am aware that there are timid souls who ought to be conciliated. Let the Mass, therefore, for some time longer be read on Sunday in all the churches, and let us avoid insulting the priests who celebrate it." The council drew up an edict to this purport.

The Reformation at Zurich followed a prudent and Christian course. Daily raising this city more and more, it surrounded her with glory in the eyes of all the friends of the Word of God. Accordingly, those in Switzerland who had saluted the new light that was dawning upon the church felt themselves powerfully attracted toward Zurich. Oswald Myconius, expelled from Lucerne, had been residing for six months at Einsidlen, when, as he was returning one day from a journey he had made to Glaris, oppressed by fatigue and by the heat of the sun, he saw his little boy Felix running to meet him and to tell him that he had been invited to Zurich to superintend one of the schools.

Myconius could not believe such joyful tidings. He hesitated between fear and hope. "I am thine," wrote he at last to Zwingli. Geroldsek saw him depart with regret; gloomy thoughts filled his mind. "Alas!" said he to Myconius, "all those who confess Christ are going to Zurich. I fear that one day we shall all perish there together." A melancholy presentiment, which by the death of Geroldsek himself and of so many other friends of the gospel, was but too soon fulfilled on the plains of Kappel.

At Zurich, Myconius found at last a safe retreat. His predecessor, who from his stature had been nicknamed at Paris "the great devil," had neglected his duties. Myconius devoted all his heart and strength to their fulfillment. He explained the Greek and Latin classics and taught rhetoric and logic, and the youth of the city listened to him with delight. Myconius was destined to become for the rising generation what Zwingli was to those of riper years.

At first Myconius was alarmed at the advanced age of the scholars under his care. But he had gradually resumed his courage and was not long in distinguishing among his pupils a young man, twenty-four years of age, from whose eyes beamed forth a love of study. Thomas Plater, for such was his name, was a native of the Valais. At the age of nine years, he had been placed under the care of a priest who was his relation, by whom the little peasant was often so cruelly beaten that he cried (as he tells us himself) like a kid under the knife. He was taken by one of his cousins to attend the German schools. But he had already attained the age of twenty years, and yet, through running from school to school, he scarcely knew how to read.

When he arrived at Zurich, he came to the determination of gaining knowledge, and having taken his place in Myconius's school, he said to himself, "There shalt thou learn or die." The light of the gospel shone into his heart. One very cold morning, when he had no fuel for the schoolroom stove, which it was his duty to keep up, he thought to himself, "Why should you want wood, while there are many idols in the church!" There was no one as yet in the church, although Zwingli was to preach, and the bells were already summoning the congregation. Plater entered very softly, laid hold of an image of St. John that stood upon an altar, and thrust it into the stove, saying, "Down with you, for in you must go." Most assuredly neither Myconius nor Zwingli would have sanctioned such a proceeding.

It was in truth by better arms than these that incredulity and superstition were to be combated. Zwingli and his colleagues had given the hand of fellowship to Myconius, and the latter daily expounded the New Testament in the Church of Our Lady before an eager and attentive crowd. Another public disputation, held on January 13 and 14, 1524, had again proved fatal to Rome; and in vain did the canon Koch exclaim: "Popes, cardinals, bishops, councils—these are my church!"

Everything was making progress in Zurich; men's minds were becoming more enlightened and their hearts more decided, and the Reformation was increasing in strength. Zurich was a fortress gained by the new doctrine, and from her walls it was about to spread over the whole Confederation.

Chapter 15
Baptized with Blood

The adversaries were aware of what might be the consequences of these changes in Zurich. They felt that they must now decide upon striking a vigorous blow. They had been silent spectators long enough. The ironclad warriors of Switzerland determined to rise at last, and whenever they arose, the field of battle had been dyed with blood.

The diet had met at Lucerne. The clergy were endeavoring to excite the chief council of the nation in their favor. Friburg and the Forest Cantons proved their docile instruments. Berne, Basel, Soleure, Glaris, and Appenzell were undecided. Schaffhausen was inclining toward the gospel, but Zurich alone stood forward boldly in its defense. The partisans of Rome urged the assembly to yield to their demands and prejudices. "Let the people be forbidden," said they, "to preach or repeat any new or Lutheran doctrine in private or in public, and to talk or dispute about such things in taverns and over their wine." Such was the ecclesiastical law they were desirous of establishing in the Confederation.

Nineteen articles were drawn up to this effect, approved of by all the states except Zurich, on January 26, 1523, and sent to all the bailiffs with orders to see that they were strictly observed, "which caused great joy among the priests," says Bullinger, "and great sorrow among believers." A persecution, regularly organized by the supreme authority of the Confederation, was about to begin.

One of the first who received the mandate of the diet was Henry Flackenstein of Lucerne, bailiff of Baden. Hottinger, banished from Zurich for pulling down the crucifix of Stadelhofen, had retired to this bailiwick, where he had not concealed his opinions. One day, as he chanced to be dining at the Angel Tavern in

Zurzach, he had said that the priests wrongly interpreted Holy Scripture and that man should put his trust in God alone. The landlord, who was continually going in and out to bring bread and wine, listened to what appeared to him such very extraordinary language. Another day, Hottinger paid a visit to his friend John Schütz of Schneyssingen. After they had eaten and drunk together, Schütz asked him, "What is this new faith that the Zurich pastors are preaching?"

"They preach," replied Hottinger, "that Christ was sacrificed once for all Christians; that by this one sacrifice He has purified and redeemed them from all their sins; and they show by Holy Scripture that the Mass is a lie."

After this (in February 1523), Hottinger had quitted Switzerland, and gone on business to Waldshut, on the other side of the Rhine. Measures were taken to seize his person, and about the end of the same month, the poor unsuspecting Zuricher, having recrossed the river, had scarcely reached Koblenz, a village on the left bank of the Rhine, before he was arrested. He was taken to Klingenau, and as he there frankly confessed his faith, the exasperated Flackenstein said, "I will take you to a place where you will find people to make you a suitable answer."

The bailiff conducted him successively before the judges of Klingenau, before the superior tribunal of Baden, and, since he could find no one who would declare him guilty, before the diet sitting at Lucerne. He was firmly resolved to seek judges who would condemn his prisoner.

The diet lost no time and condemned Hottinger to be beheaded. When informed of his sentence, he gave glory to God. "That will do," said James Troger, one of his judges, "we do not sit here to listen to sermons. You can have your talk some other time."

"He must have his head taken off this once," said the bailiff Am Ort, with a laugh. "If he should ever get it on again, we will all embrace his faith."

"May God forgive all those who have condemned me," said the prisoner. A monk then presented a crucifix to his lips, but he put it away, saying, "It is in the heart that we must receive Jesus Christ."

When he was led out to execution, many of the spectators could not refrain from tears. "I am going to eternal happiness," said he, turning toward them. On reaching the place where he was to die, he raised his hands to heaven, exclaiming, "Into thy hands, O my Redeemer, I commit my spirit!" In another minute his head rolled upon the scaffold.

The blood of Hottinger was hardly cold before the enemies of the Reformation seized the opportunity of still further inflaming the anger of the confederates. It was in Zurich itself that the mischief should be crushed. The terrible example that had just been given must have filled Zwingli and his partisans with terror. Another vigorous effort, and the death of Hottinger would be followed by that of the reform. The diet immediately resolved that a deputation should be sent to Zurich, calling upon the councils and the citizens to renounce their faith.

The deputation received an audience on March 21. "The ancient Christian unity is broken," said the deputies. "The disease is gaining ground; already have the clergy of the four Forest Cantons declared that unless the magistrates come to their aid, they must discontinue their functions. Confederates of Zurich, join your efforts to ours. Stifle this new faith. Dismiss Zwingli and his disciples, and then let us all unite to remedy the injuries that have been inflicted on the popes and their courtiers."

Zurich did not leave her friends or enemies long in suspense. The council announced calmly and nobly that they could make no concessions in what concerned the Word of God, and then proceeded to make a still more forcible reply.

Since the year 1351, it had been customary for a numerous procession, each member of which bore a cross, to go on Whitmonday on a pilgrimage to Einsidlen to worship the virgin. This festival, which had been established in commemoration of the battle of Tatwyll, was attended with great disorder. The procession should have taken place on May 7. On the petition of the three pastors, it was prohibited by the council, and all the other processions were reformed in their turn.

They did not stop here. The relics, that source of innumerable superstitions, were honorably interred. Then, at the request of the three pastors, the council published a decree, to the effect that honor being due to God alone, the images should be removed from all the churches of the canton, and their ornaments sold for the benefit of the poor. Twelve councilors, one from each guild, the three pastors, the city architect, blacksmiths, carpenters, builders, and masons, went into the various churches, and, having closed the doors, took down the crosses, defaced the frescoes, whitewashed the walls, and took away the images, to the great delight of the believers, who regarded this proceeding as a striking homage paid to the true God. In some of the country churches, the ornaments were burnt "to the honor and glory of God." Erelong the organs were taken down, on account of their connection with many superstitious practices, and a baptismal service was drawn up, from which everything unscriptural was excluded.

But while Zwingli was thus advancing with mighty strides to the head of the Confederation, the disposition of the cantons became daily more hostile. The Zurich government felt the necessity of relying on the people. Moreover, the people, that is to say the assembly of believers, was, according to Zwingli's principles, the highest power to which there could be any appeal on earth. It was resolved to test the state of public opinion, and the bailiffs were enjoined to demand of all the parishes whether they were ready to suffer everything for our Lord Jesus Christ, "who," said the council, "gave His life and His blood for us sinners." The whole canton had carefully followed the progress of the Reformation in the city, and in many places, the cottages of the peasants had become Christian schools, wherein the Holy Scriptures were read.

The proclamation of the council was read and enthusiastically received in every parish. "Let our lords," answered they, "remain fearlessly attached to the Word of God: we will aid them in upholding it; and if any one seeks to molest them, we will come to their support like brave and loyal fellow citizens." The peasantry of Zurich showed then that the strength of the church is in the Christian people.

The Word of God could not thus invade extensive countries without its triumphs exasperating the pope in his palace, the priest in his presbytery, and the Swiss magistrates in their councils. Their terror increased from day to day. The people had been consulted. The Christian people became of consequence in the Christian church, and appeals were made to their sympathy and faith and not to the decrees of the Roman chancery. So formidable an attack required a still more formidable resistance. On April 18, the pope addressed a brief to the confederates. The diet, which met at Zug in the month of July, yielding to the urgent exhortations of the pontiff, sent a deputation to Zurich, Schaffhausen, and Appenzell, commissioned to acquaint these states with the firm resolve of the diet to crush the new doctrine and to prosecute its adherents to the forfeiture of their goods, their honors, and even their lives.

Zurich did not hear this warning without emotion. But a firm reply was made, that, in matters of faith, the Word of God alone must be obeyed. On receiving this answer Lucerne, Schwytz, Uri, Unterwalden, Friburg, and Zug trembled with rage. Unmindful of the reputation and strength the accession of Zurich had formerly given to the infant Confederation, forgetting the precedence that had been immediately accorded to her, the simple and solemn oaths that had been made to her, and the many victories and reverses they had shared with her—these states declared that they would no longer sit in diet with Zurich. But threats and the rupture of alliances were not enough. The fanaticism of the cantons called for blood, and it was soon seen with what arms Rome intended to combat the Word of God.

One of Zwingli's friends, the worthy Oexlin, was pastor of Burg upon the Rhine, in the neighborhood of Stein. The bailiff Am-Berg, who had appeared to listen to the gospel with delight, being desirous of obtaining that bailiwick, had promised the leading men of Schwytz to root out the new faith. Oexlin, although not within his jurisdiction, was the first upon whom he exercised his severity.

About midnight, on July 7, 1524, some persons knocked at the pastor's door. They were the bailiff's soldiers, who entered the house, seized Oexlin, and carried him away prisoner, in defiance of his cries. Thinking they meant to assassinate him, he cried "Murder!" The inhabitants started from their beds in affright, and the village soon became the scene of a frightful tumult, which was heard as far as Stein. The sentinel on guard at the castle of Hohenklingen fired the alarm gun, the tocsin was rung, and the inhabitants of Stein, Stammheim, and the adjoining places were soon moving and inquiring of one another in the darkness what was the matter.

At Stammheim lived the deputy bailiff Wirth, whose two eldest sons, Adrian and John, both young priests full of piety and courage, were preaching the gospel with great unction. John especially abounded in faith and was ready to sacrifice his life for his Savior. Hannah, the mother, who had borne the bailiff many children and had brought them up in the fear of the Lord, was revered for her virtues throughout the whole district. At the noise of the tumult in Burg, the father and the two eldest sons went out like their neighbors. The father was indignant that the bailiff of Frauenfeld should have exercised his authority in a manner contrary to the laws of the country. The sons learned with sorrow that their brother, their friend, the man whose good example they were delighted to follow, had been dragged away like a criminal. Each of them seized a halberd, and in spite of the fears of a tender wife and mother, the father and his two sons joined the band of citizens of Stein with the determination of rescuing their pastor. Unhappily, a number of those miscreants who make their appearance in every disorder had joined the expedition. They pursued the bailiff's officers. The latter, hearing the tocsin and the shouts of alarm, redoubled their speed, dragging their victim after them, and soon placed the river Thur between themselves and their pursuers.

When the people of Stein and Stammheim reached the bank of the river and found no means of crossing, they halted and resolved to send a deputation to Frauenfeld. The populace, finding themselves near the Carthusian convent of Ittingen, whose inmates were believed to have encouraged the tyranny of the bailiff Am-Berg, entered the building and took possession of the refectory. These miserable wretches soon became intoxicated, and shameful disorders were the consequence. Wirth vainly entreated them to leave the convent. He was in danger of being maltreated by them. His son Adrian remained outside the cloister. John entered but soon came out again, distressed at what he had seen. The drunken peasants proceeded to ransack the wine cellars and the store rooms, to break the furniture, and to burn the books.

When the news of these disorders reached Zurich, some deputies from the council hastened to the spot and ordered all persons under the jurisdiction of the canton to return to their homes. They did so immediately. But a body of Thurgovians, attracted by the disturbance, established themselves in the convent, for the sake of its good cheer. On a sudden a fire broke out, though no one knew how, and the monastery was burnt to the ground.

Five days after this, the deputies of the cantons met at Zug. Nothing was heard in the assembly but threats of vengeance and death. "Let us march with banners flying on Stein and Stammheim," said they, "and put the inhabitants to the sword." The deputy bailiff and his two sons had long been objects of especial dislike on account of their faith. "If any one is guilty," said the deputy of Zurich, "he must be punished, but according to the laws of justice and not by violence." Vadian, deputy of St. Gall, supported this opinion.

Upon this, the avoyer John Hug of Lucerne, unable to contain himself any longer, exclaimed with frightful imprecations, "The heretic Zwingli is the father of all these insurrections, and you too, doctor of St. Gall, are favorable to his infamous cause, and aid him in securing its triumphs. . . . You ought no longer to have a seat among us." The deputy of Zug endeavoured to restore peace, but in vain. Vadian left the hall, and as the populace had designs upon his life, he quitted the town secretly and reached the convent of Kappel by a circuitous route.

Zurich, intent on suppressing every disorder, resolved to apprehend provisionally those persons who were marked out by the rage of the confederates. Wirth and his two sons were living quietly at Stammheim. "Never will the enemies of God be able to vanquish His friends," said Adrian Wirth from the pulpit. The father was warned of the fate impending over him and was entreated to flee with his two sons. "No," answered he, "I will wait for the officers, putting my trust in God." And when the soldiers made their appearance at his house, he said, "My lords of Zurich might have spared themselves all this trouble. If they had only sent a child I should have obeyed their summons." The three Wirths were taken to Zurich and put in prison. Rutiman, bailiff of Nussbaum, shared their fate. They were strictly examined, but nothing reprehensible was found in their conduct.

As soon as the deputies of the cantons had heard of the imprisonment of these four citizens, they required them to be sent to Baden and ordered that in case of refusal their troops should march upon Zurich and carry them off by force.

"To Zurich belongs the right of ascertaining whether these men are guilty or not," said the deputies of that state, "and we have found no fault in them." On this, the deputies of the cantons exclaimed, "Will you surrender them to us? Answer yes or no, and not a word more." Two deputies of Zurich mounted their horses and rode off with all haste to their constituents.

On their arrival, the whole town was in agitation. If the prisoners were refused, the confederates would come and seek them with an armed force. To give them up was consenting to their death. Opinions were divided. Zwingli declared for their refusal. "Zurich," said he, "ought to remain faithful to its constitution."

At last it was supposed a middle course had been found. "We will deliver the prisoners into your hands," said they to the diet, "but on condition that you will examine them solely with regard to the affair of Ittingen and not on their faith." The diet acceded to this proposition, and on the Friday before St. Bartholomew's Day (August 18, 1524) the three Wirths and their friend, accompanied by four councilors of state and several armed men, quitted Zurich.

On Friday evening, the accused arrived at Baden, where an immense crowd was waiting for them. At first they were taken to an inn, and thence to prison. They could scarcely advance, the crowd so pressed around to catch a sight of them. The father, who walked in front, turned toward his two sons and observed to them meekly, "See, my dear children, we are (as the apostle says) men 'appointed to death: for we are made a spectacle unto the world, and to angels, and to men'" (I Cor. 4:9).

Then, as he saw among the crowd his deadly enemy, Amberg, the cause of all his misfortunes, he went up to him and held out his hand, although the bailiff would have turned away. "There is a God in heaven who knows all things," said he calmly as he grasped his adversary's hand.

The examination began on the following day. The bailiff Wirth was first brought in.

He was put to the torture, without any regard to his character or his age, but he persisted in declaring his innocence of the pillage and burning of Ittingen. He was then accused of having destroyed an image representing St. Anne. Nothing could be substantiated against the other prisoners, except that Adrian Wirth was married and preached after the manner of Zwingli and Luther and that John Wirth had given the sacrament to a sick man without bell and taper.

But the more apparent their innocence, the greater was the fury of their adversaries. From morning until noon they inflicted the cruelest tortures on the old man. His tears could not soften his judges. John Wirth was treated with still greater barbarity. "Tell us," they asked him in the midst of his anguish, "whence did you learn this heretical faith? From Zwingli or from any other person?" And when he exclaimed, "O merciful and everlasting God, help and comfort me!" "Where is your Christ now?" said one of the deputies.

When Adrian appeared, Sebastian of Stein, the Bernese deputy, said to him, "Young man, tell us the truth, for if you refuse to do so, I swear by the knighthood that I gained on the very spot where the Lord suffered martyrdom, that we will open your veins one after another." They then fastened the young man to a rope and hoisted him into the air. "There, my little master," said Stein with a devilish sneer, "there is your wedding present," alluding to the marriage of this youthful servant of the Lord.

When the examination was ended, the deputies returned to their cantons to deliver their report and did not meet again till four weeks after. The bailiff's wife, the mother of the two priests, repaired to Baden, carrying an infant child in her arms, to inter-cede with the judges. John Escher of Zurich accompanied her as her advocate. Among the judges he saw Jerome Stocker, lan-damman of Zug, who had been twice bailiff of Frauenfeld. "Landamman!" said he, "you know the bailiff Wirth. You know that he has always been an upright man."

"You say the truth, my dear Escher," replied Stocker; "he has never injured anybody. Fellow citizens and strangers were always kindly welcomed to his table. His house was a convent, an inn, and an hospital, and so, if he had committed robbery or murder, I would have made every exertion to obtain his pardon. But see-ing that he has burnt Saint Anne, Christ's grandmother, he must die!"

"The Lord have mercy upon us," exclaimed Escher.

The gates were now shut. It was September 28, and the deputies of Berne, Lucerne, Uri, Schwytz, Unterwalden, Zug, Glaris, Friburg, and Soleure, having proceeded to deliberate on their judgment with closed doors, as was customary, passed sen-tence of death on the bailiff Wirth, on his son John, who was the firmest in his faith and who appeared to have led away the others, and on the bailiff Rutiman. Adrian, the second son, was granted to his mother's tears.

The officers proceeded to the tower to fetch the prisoners. "My son," said the father to Adrian, "never avenge our death, al-though we have not deserved punishment."

Adrian burst into tears. "Brother," said John, "the cross of Christ must always follow His Word."

After the sentence was read, the three Christians were led back to prison, John Wirth walking first, the two vice-bailiffs next, and a priest behind them. As they were crossing the castle bridge, on which was a chapel dedicated to St. Joseph, the priest called out to the two old men, "Fall down and call upon the saints."

John Wirth, who was in front, turned round at these words and said, "Father, be firm. You know that there is only one Mediator between God and man, the Lord Jesus Christ."

"Assuredly, my son," replied the old man, "and by the help of His grace I will continue faithful even to the end." Upon this they all three began to repeat the Lord's Prayer and so crossed the bridge.

They were next conducted to the scaffold. John Wirth, whose heart was filled with the tenderest anxiety for his parent, bade him farewell. "My dearly beloved father," said he, "henceforward thou art no longer my father, and I am no longer thy son, but we are brothers in Christ our Lord, for whose name we must suffer death. Today, if it be God's pleasure, my beloved brother, we shall go to Him who is the Father of us all. Fear nothing."

"Amen!" replied the old man, "and may God Almighty bless thee, my beloved son and brother in Christ!"

The bailiff Rutiman prayed in silence.

All three then knelt down "in Christ's name," and their heads rolled upon the scaffold.

The crowd, observing the marks of torture upon their bodies, gave loud utterance to their grief. The two bailiffs left twenty-two children and forty-five grandchildren.

Hannah was obliged to pay twelve golden crowns to the executioner who had deprived her husband and her son of life.

Thus blood, innocent blood, had been shed. Switzerland and the Reformation were baptized with the blood of the martyrs. The great enemy of the gospel had done his work, but in doing it, his power was broken. The death of the Wirths was to accelerate the triumphs of the Reformation.

Chapter 16
Abolition of the Mass

It was not thought desirable to proceed to the abolition of the Mass in Zurich immediately after the suppression of images, but now the proper moment seemed to have arrived.

Not only had the light of the gospel diffused among the people but the violence of the blows struck by the enemy also called upon the friends of God to reply to them by some impressive demonstration of their unalterable fidelity.

Every time Rome erected a scaffold and heads fell upon it, the Reformation exalted the holy Word of the Lord and threw down some abuses. When Hottinger was executed, Zurich suppressed images; and now that the heads of the Wirths had rolled on the ground, Zurich would reply by the abolition of the Mass. The more Rome increased her cruelties, the more the Reformation increased in strength.

On April 11, 1525, the three pastors of Zurich, accompanied by Megander and Oswald Myconius, appeared before the Great Council and demanded the reestablishment of the Lord's Supper. Their language was solemn. All minds were absorbed in meditation. Every man felt the importance of the resolution which the council was called upon to take. The Mass, that mystery which for more than three centuries had been the very soul of the religious service of the Latin Church, was to be abolished, the corporeal presence of Christ to be declared an illusion, and the illusion itself removed from the minds of the people.

Courage was needed to arrive at such a resolution, and there were men in the council who shuddered at this daring thought. Joachim Am-Grutt, undersecretary of state, alarmed at the bold demand of the pastors, opposed it with all his might. "These words, 'This is my body,'" said he, "unquestionably prove that the bread is the body of Christ Himself."

Zwingli observed that *esti* ("is") is the proper word in the Greek language to express "signifies," and he quoted several instances in which this word is employed in a figurative sense. The Great Council were convinced and did not hesitate; the gospel doctrines had penetrated their hearts. Besides, as they were separating from the Church of Rome, there was a certain satisfaction in making that separation as complete as possible and in digging a gulf between it and the Reformation. The council, therefore, ordered the Mass to be suppressed and decreed that on the next day, Holy Thursday, the Lord's Supper should be celebrated in conformity with the apostolic usages.

The altars had disappeared. Plain tables bearing the sacramental bread and wine were substituted in their place, and an attentive crowd pressed round them. There was something particularly solemn in this multitude. On Holy Thursday, the young people; on Friday, the day of the Passion, the adult men and women; and on Easter Sunday, the aged; all celebrated in turn the death of the Lord.

The deacons read aloud the passages of Scripture that relate to this sacrament. The pastors addressed the flock in an earnest exhortation, calling upon those to retire from this sacred feast who, by persevering in their sin, would pollute the body of Jesus Christ. The people knelt down, the bread was carried round on large platters or wooden plates, and each one broke off a morsel. The wine was next distributed in wooden goblets. In this manner it was thought they made a nearer approach to the simplicity of the primitive Supper. Emotions of surprise or joy filled every heart.

Thus was the reform carried on in Zurich. The simple celebration of the Lord's Supper appeared to have shed anew over the church the love of God and of the brethren. The words of Jesus Christ were once more spirit and life. While the different orders and parties in the Church of Rome were incessantly disputing among themselves, the first effect of the gospel was to restore charity among the brethren. The love of the first ages was then revived in Christendom. Enemies were seen renouncing their long-cherished and inveterate enmities and embracing one another after having partaken of the sacramental bread.

Zwingli, delighted at these affecting manifestations, returned thanks to God that the Lord's Supper was again working those miracles of charity which the sacrifice of the Mass had long ceased to accomplish.

"Peace dwells in our city," exclaimed he. "Among us there is no fraud, no dissension, no envying, no strife. Whence can proceed such harmony except from the Lord, and that the doctrine we preach inclines us to innocence and peace?"

Charity and unity then prevailed. But while the celebration of the Lord's Supper at Zurich was attended by a return to Christian brotherhood, Zwingli and his friends had to support a severer struggle against their adversaries from without. Zwingli was not only a Christian teacher but he was also a true patriot, and we know how zealously he contended against the foreign capitulations, pensions, and alliances. He felt convinced that these external influences must tend to destroy piety, blind the reason, and scatter discord on every side. But his bold protests were destined to prejudice the advancement of the Reformation.

In almost every canton, the chiefs who received the pensions of the foreigner and the officers who led the youth of Helvetia to battle formed powerful factions, formidable oligarchies, that attacked the Reformation, not so much on behalf of the church as on account of the injury it would inflict on their interests and honors. They had already gained the victory in Schwytz; and that canton, where Zwingli, Leo Juda, and Oswald Myconius had taught, and which seemed as if it would walk in the footsteps of Zurich, had suddenly reverted to the mercenary capitulations and shut its gates against the Reformation.

Even in Zurich, some wretches, instigated by foreign intrigues, attacked Zwingli during the night, flung stones at his house, broke the windows, and called with loud cries for "the red-haired Uli, the vulture of Glaris," so that Zwingli awoke from his sleep and ran to his sword. This action is very characteristic of the man.

But these isolated attacks could not paralyze the movement by which Zurich was carried onward and which was beginning to shake all Switzerland. They were pebbles thrown into a torrent to check its course. Everywhere its waters were swelling, threatening to sweep away the most formidable obstacles.

The Bernese informed the people of Zurich that several states had refused to sit with them in future in the diet. "Well, then," replied these men of Zurich with calmness, "we have the firm assurance that God, the Father, Son, and Holy Ghost, in whose name the Confederation was formed, will not desert us, and will at last, of His great mercy, make us sit at the right hand of His sovereign majesty." Possessing such faith, the Reformation had nothing to fear.

Chapter 17
The Anabaptists

But the battle fought by the Reformation in the great day of the sixteenth century, under the standard of the Word of God, was not one and single, but manifold. The Reformation had many enemies to contend with at once. After having first protested against the decretals and the supremacy of the pope and then against rationalists, philosophers, or schoolmen, it had equally to struggle with the reveries of enthusiasm and the hallucinations of mysticism. It opposed alike these three powers with the shield and the sword of Divine revelation.

It must be admitted that there is a great similarity, a striking unity, between these three powerful adversaries. The false systems that in every age have been the most opposed to evangelical Christianity have always been distinguished by their making religious knowledge proceed from within the man himself. Rationalism makes it proceed from reason; mysticism from certain inner lights; and Roman Catholicism from an illumination of the pope. These three errors look for truth in man; evangelical Christianity looks for it wholly in God. While mysticism, rationalism, and Roman Catholicism admit a permanent inspiration in certain of our fellow men and thus open a door to every extravagance and diversity, evangelical Christianity recognizes this inspiration solely in the writings of the apostles and prophets and alone presents that great, beautiful, and living unity which is ever the same in all ages. The task of the Reformation was to reestablish the rights of the Word of God, in opposition not only to Roman Catholicism but also to mysticism and rationalism.

The fanaticism of some of the Anabaptists (a term applied to them by their opponents, but which they never admitted as applicable to themselves) appeared in full vigor in Switzerland and threatened the edifice that Zwingli, Haller, and Oecolampadius had built on the Word of God. Conrad Grebel, whose restless and ardent disposition we have already noticed; Felix Manz, a canon's son; and several other Zurichers endeavoured to gain over Zwingli. In vain the latter had gone further than Luther. He saw a party springing up which desired to proceed further still. "Let us form a community to true believers," said Grebel to him, "for to them alone the promise belongs, and let us found a church in which there shall be no sin."

"We cannot make a heaven upon earth," replied Zwingli, "and Christ has taught us that we must let the tares grow up along with the wheat."

Grebel, having failed with the reformer, would have desired to appeal to the people. "The whole community of Zurich," said he, "ought to have the final decision in matters of faith." But Zwingli feared the influence these radical enthusiasts might exercise over a large assembly. He thought that, except on extraordinary occasions when the people might be called upon to express their accordance, it was better to confide the interests of religion to a college, which might be considered the chosen representatives of the church. Accordingly, the Council of Two Hundred, which exercised the supreme political authority in Zurich, was also entrusted with the ecclesiastical power, on the express condition that they should conform in all things to the Holy Scriptures.

No doubt it would have been better to have thoroughly organized the church and called on it to appoint its own representatives, who should be entrusted solely with the religious interests of the people. For a man may be very capable of administering the interests of the state and yet very unskillful in those of the church, just as the reverse of this is true also. Nevertheless, the inconvenience was not then so serious as it would have been in these days, since the members of the Great Council had frankly entered into the religious movement. But, however this may be, Zwingli, while appealing to the church, was careful not to make it too prominent, and he preferred the representative system to the actual sovereignty of the people.

Being rejected by Zwingli, Grebel turned to another quarter. Rubli, formerly pastor at Basel; Brodtlein, pastor at Zollikon; and Louis Hetzer received him with eagerness. They resolved to form an independent congregation in the midst of the great congregation, a church within the church. The baptism of adult believers only was to be their means of assembling their congregation. "Infant baptism," said they, "is a horrible abomination, a flagrant impiety, invented by the wicked spirit, and by Nicholas II, pope of Rome."

The council of Zurich was alarmed and ordered a public discussion to be held. As they still refused to abjure their opinions, some of the Zurichers among their number were thrown into prison, and several foreigners were banished. But persecution only inflamed their zeal. "Not by words alone," cried they, "but with our blood, we are ready to bear testimony to the truth of our cause." Some of them, girding themselves with cords or ozier twigs, ran through the streets, exclaiming, "Yet a few days, and Zurich will be destroyed! Woe to thee, Zurich! Woe! Woe!" The simple-minded and pious were agitated and alarmed. Fourteen men, among whom was Felix Manz, and seven women were apprehended, in spite of Zwingli's intercession, and put on bread and water in the heretic's tower. After being confined a fortnight, they managed to loosen some planks in the night, and aiding one another, effected their escape.

A monk who had escaped from his convent, George Jacob of Coire, surnamed Blaurock, joined their sect, and from his eloquence was denominated a second Paul. This daring monk travelled from place to place, constraining many, by his imposing fervor, to receive his baptism. One Sunday, when at Zollikon, the impetuous monk interrupted the deacon as he was preaching, calling out in a voice of thunder, "It is written, 'My house is a house of prayer, but ye have made it a den of thieves.'" Then raising the staff he carried in his hand, he struck four violent blows.

"I am a door," exclaimed he. "Whosoever entereth by me shall find pasture. I am a good shepherd. My body I give to the prison; my life I give to the sword, the stake, or the wheel. I am the beginning of the baptism and of the bread of the Lord."

While Zwingli was opposing this torrent in Zurich, St. Gall was soon inundated with it. Grebel arrived there and was received by the brethren with acclamations, and on Palm Sunday he proceeded to the banks of the Sitter with a great number of his adherents, whom he there baptized.

The news quickly spread through the adjoining cantons, and a great crowd flocked from Zurich, Appenzell, and several other places to the "Little Jerusalem."

Zwingli's heart was wrung at the sight of this agitation. He saw a storm bursting on these districts where the seed of the gospel was just beginning to spring up. Resolving to oppose these sentiments on baptism, he wrote a treatise on that subject, which the council of St. Gall, to whom it was addressed, ordered to be read in the church before all the people.

"My dear brethren in the Lord," said Zwingli, "the water of the torrents that issue from our rocks carries with it everything within its reach. At first it is only small stones; but these dash violently against larger ones, until at last the torrent becomes so strong that it carries away all it meets and leaves in its track wailing and vain regrets, and fertile meadows changed into a wilderness. The spirit of strife and self-righteousness acts in a similar manner. It excites discord, destroys charity, and where it found beautiful and flourishing churches, leaves behind it nothing but flocks plunged into mourning and desolation."

"Give us the Word of God," exclaimed one who was present in the church, "and not the word of Zwingli." Immediately confused voices were heard. "Away with the book! Away with the book!" shouted the multitude. After this they rose and quitted the church, crying out, "You may keep the doctrine of Zwingli. As for us, we will keep the Word of God."

The fanaticism now broke forth into the most lamentable disorders. Maintaining that the Lord had exhorted us to become like children, these unhappy creatures began to clap their hands and skip about in the streets, to dance in a ring, sit on the ground, and tumble each other about in the dust. Some burnt the New Testament, saying, "The letter killeth, the Spirit giveth life."

Others, falling into convulsions, pretended to have revelations from the Holy Ghost.

In a solitary house on the Mullegg near St. Gall, lived an aged farmer, John Schucker, with his five sons. They had all of them, including the domestics, received the new religion, and two of the sons, Thomas and Leonard, were distinguished for their fanaticism. On Shrove Tuesday (February 7, 1526), they invited a large party to their house, and their father killed a calf for the feast. The viands, the wine, and this numerous assembly heated their imaginations. The whole night was passed in fanatical conversation and gesticulations, convulsions, visions, and revelations.

In the morning, Thomas, still agitated by this night of disorder, and having, as it would seem, lost his reason, took the calf's bladder, and placing in it part of the gall, intending thus to imitate the symbolical language of the prophets, approached his brother Leonard, saying with a gloomy voice, "Thus bitter is the death thou art to suffer!" He then added: "Brother, Leonard, kneel down!" Leonard fell on his knees; shortly after, "Brother Leonard, arise!" Leonard stood up.

The father, brothers, and others of the company looked on with astonishment, asking themselves what God would do. Thomas soon resumed: "Leonard, kneel down again!" He did so.

The spectators, alarmed at the gloomy countenance of the wretched man, said to him, "Think of what you are about, and take care that no mischief happens."

"Fear not," replied Thomas, "nothing will happen but the will of the Father." At the same time he hastily caught up a sword and striking a violent blow at his brother, kneeling before him as a criminal before the executioner, he cut off his head, exclaiming, "Now the will of the Father is accomplished."

All the bystanders recoiled with horror at the deed, and the farm resounded with groans and lamentations. Thomas, who had nothing on but a shirt and trousers, rushed barefooted and bareheaded out of the house, ran to St. Gall with frenzied gestures, entered the house of the burgomaster Joachim Vadian, and said to him with haggard looks and wild cries, "I proclaim to thee the day of the Lord!"

The frightful news soon spread through St. Gall. "He has slain his brother, as Cain slew Abel," said the people.

The culprit was seized. "It is true I did it," he continually repeated, "but it is God who did it through me."

On February 16, this unhappy creature lost his head by the sword of the executioner. Fanaticism had made its last effort. Men's eyes were opened, and, according to an old historian, the same blow took off the head of Thomas Schucker and of fanaticism of St. Gall.

Fanaticism still prevailed at Zurich. On November 6 in the preceding year, a public discussion on the subject of infant baptism had been held in the council hall, when Zwingli and his friends proposed the following theses:

> Children born of believing parents are children of God, like those who were born under the Old Testament, and consequently may receive baptism.

> Baptism under the New Testament is what circumcision was under the Old; consequently, baptism ought now to be administered to children, as circumcision was formerly.

> We cannot prove the custom of rebaptizing either by examples, texts, or arguments drawn from Scripture; and those who are rebaptized crucify Jesus Christ afresh.

But the dispute was not confined to religious questions. They called for the abolition of tithes on the ground that they were not of divine appointment. Zwingli replied that the maintenance of the schools and churches depended on the tithes. He desired a complete religious reform but was decided not to permit the public order or political institutions to be in the least degree shaken. This was the limit at which he perceived that word from heaven, written by the hand of God, "Hitherto shalt thou come, and no farther." It was necessary to stop somewhere, and here Zwingli and the reformers halted, in spite of those headstrong men who endeavoured to hurry them farther still.

But if the reformers halted, they could not stop the enthusiasts, who seemed placed at their sides as if in contrast with their discretion and prudence. It was not enough for them to have formed a church. This church in their eyes was the state. When they were summoned before the tribunals, they declared they did not recognize the civil authority, that it was only a remnant of paganism, and that they would obey no other power than God. They taught that it was not lawful for Christians to fill public offices or to carry the sword. Resembling in this respect certain irreligious enthusiasts that have sprung up in our days, they looked upon a community of goods as the perfection of humanity.

Thus the danger was increasing; the existence of civil society was threatened. It rose up to reject from its bosom these destructive elements. The government, in alarm, suffered itself to be hurried into strange measures. Being resolved to make an example, it condemned Manz to be drowned. On January 5, 1527, he was placed in a boat. His mother (the aged concubine of the canon) and his brother were among the crowd that followed him to the water's edge. "Persevere unto the end," exclaimed they. When the executioner prepared to throw Manz into the lake, his brother burst into tears, but his mother, calm and resolute, witnessed with dry and burning eyes the martyrdom of her son.

On the same day Blaurock was scourged with rods. As they were leading him outside of the city, he shook his blue cloak and the dust from off his feet against the city of Zurich. It would appear that two years later this unhappy creature was burnt alive by the Roman Catholics of the Tyrol.

Undoubtedly a spirit of rebellion existed. No doubt the old ecclesiastical law, condemning heretics to death, was still in force, and the Reformation could not in one or two years reform every error. Further, there is no question that the Catholic states would have accused the Protestant states of encouraging disorder if they had not punished these enthusiasts. These considerations may explain, although they cannot justify, the severity of the magistrates. They might have taken measures against everything that infringed the civil authority. But religious errors, being combated by the teachers, should have enjoyed complete liberty before the civil tribunals. Such opinions are not to be expelled by the scourge. They are not drowned by throwing their professors into the water. They float up again from the depth of the abyss, and fire but serves to kindle in their adherents a fiercer enthusiasm and thirst for martyrdom. Zwingli, with whose sentiments on this subject we are acquainted, took no part in these severities.

Chapter 18

Condemnation

Thus the Reformation had struggles to maintain in every quarter, having contended with the fanaticism of some of the Anabaptists. But its great conflict was always with Catholicism.

The victories of the Reformation could not remain unnoticed. Monks, priests, and prelates, in distraction, felt that the ground was everywhere slipping from beneath their feet and that the Roman Church was on the point of sinking under unprecedented dangers. The oligarchs of the cantons, the advocates of foreign pensions and capitulations, saw that they could delay no longer if they wished to preserve their privileges. At the very moment when the Roman church was frightened and beginning to sink, they stretched out their mailed hands to save it. A Stein and a John Hug of Lucerne united with a John Faber, and the civil authority rushed to the support of that hierarchical power which openeth its mouth to blaspheme and maketh war upon the saints.

Their first efforts were directed against Berne. The seven Roman Catholic cantons, in collusion with the Bernese oligarchs, sent a deputation to that city, who laid their complaints before the council on Whitmonday 1526. "All order is destroyed in the church," said the schultheiss (chief magistrate) of Lucerne, "God is blasphemed; the sacraments, the mother of God, and the saints are despised; and imminent and terrible calamities threaten to dissolve our praiseworthy Confederation." At the same time the Bernese partisans of Rome, in harmony with the Forest cantons, had summoned to Berne the deputies of the country, chosen from those who were devoted to the papacy. Some of them had the courage to pronounce in favor of the gospel. The sitting was stormy.

"Berne must renounce the evangelical faith and walk with us," said the Forest cantons. The Bernese councils decreed that they would maintain "the ancient Christian faith, the holy sacraments, the mother of God, the saints, and the ornaments of the churches." Thus Rome triumphed, and the mandate of 1526 was about to annul that of 1523. In effect, all the married priests not born in the canton were compelled to leave it. They drove from their borders all who were suspected of Lutheranism. They exercised a vigilant censorship over every work sold by the booksellers, and certain books were publicly burnt. Even John Faber, with audacious falsehood, said publicly that Haller had bound himself before the council to perform mass again and to preach the doctrine of Rome. It was resolved to take advantage of so favorable an opportunity to crush the new faith.

For a long while public opinion had been demanding a discussion. This was the only means left of quieting the people. "Convince us by the Holy Scriptures," said the council of Zurich to the diet, "and we will comply with your wishes."

"The Zurichers," it was everywhere said, "have made you a promise. If you can convince them by the Bible, why not do so? If you cannot, why do you not conform to the Bible?"

The conferences held at Zurich had exercised an immense influence, and it was felt necessary to oppose them by a conference held in a Roman Catholic city, with all necessary precautions to secure the victory to the pope's party.

True, these discussions had been pronounced unlawful, but means were found to evade this difficulty. "It is only intended," said they, "to check and condemn the pestilent doctrines of Zwingli." This being settled, they looked about for a vigorous champion, and Doctor Eck offered himself. He feared nothing. "Zwingli no doubt has milked more cows than he has read books," said he, by Hofmeister's account.

The Great Council of Zurich sent Doctor Eck a safe-conduct to go direct to Zurich; but Eck replied that he would wait for the answer of the Confederation. Zwingli then offered to dispute at St. Gall or Schaffhausen, but the council, acting on an article of the federal compact, which provided "that every accused person should be tried in the place of his abode," ordered Zwingli to withdraw his offer.

At last the diet fixed that the conference should take place at Baden on May 16, 1526. This meeting promised to be important, for it was the result and the seal of the alliance which had just been concluded between the clergy and the oligarchs of the Confederation. "See," said Zwingli to Vadian, "what Faber and the oligarchs now venture to attempt."

Accordingly, the decision of the diet produced a great sensation in Switzerland. It was not doubted that a conference held under such auspices would be unfavorable to the Reformation. Are not the five cantons the most devoted to the pope supreme in Baden, said the Zurichers? Have they not already declared Zwingli's doctrine heretical and pursued it with fire and sword? Was not Zwingli burnt in effigy at Lucerne, with every mark of ignominy? At Friburg, were not his writings committed to the flames? Do they not everywhere call for his death? Have not the cantons that exercise sovereign rights in Baden declared that in whatever part of their territory Zwingli made his appearance, he should be apprehended? Did not Uberlinger, one of their chiefs, say that the only thing in the world that he desired was to hang Zwingli, though he should be called a hangman all the rest of his days? And has not Doctor Eck himself, for years past, been crying out that the heretics must be attacked with fire and sword? What then will be the end of this conference? What other result can it have, but the death of the reformer?

Such were the fears that agitated the commission appointed at Zurich to examine into the affair. Zwingli, an eyewitness of their agitation, rose and said, "You know what happened at Baden to the valiant men of Stammheim and how the blood of the Wirths dyed the scaffold . . . and it is to the very place of their execution that they challenge us! . . . Let Zurich, Berne, St. Gall, or even Basel, Constance, or Schaffhausen, be selected for the conference. Let it be agreed to discuss essential points only, employing nothing else than the Word of God. Let no judge be set above it. And then I am ready to appear."

Meanwhile, fanaticism was already bestirring itself and striking down its victims. A consistory, headed by that same Faber who had challenged Zwingli, on May 10, 1526, about a week before the discussion at Baden, condemned to the flames, as a heretic, an evangelical minister named John Hugel, pastor of Lindau. At the same time, another minister, Peter Spengler, was drowned at Friburg by order of the bishop of Constance.

Sinister rumors reached Zwingli from all quarters. His brother-in-law, Leonard Tremp, wrote to him from Berne, "I entreat you, as you regard your life, not to repair to Baden. I know that they will not respect your safe-conduct."

It was affirmed that a plan had been formed to seize and gag him, throw him into a boat, and carry him off to some secret place. With these threats and persecutions before them, the council of Zurich decreed that Zwingli should not go to Baden.

The discussion being fixed for May 19, the disputants and the representatives of the cantons and bishops began to arrive gradually. On the side of the Roman Catholics appeared in the foremost place the warlike and vainglorious Doctor Eck; on the side of the Protestants, the retiring and gentle Oecolampadius. The latter was well aware of the perils attending this discussion. "He had long hesitated, like a timid stag worried by furious dogs," says a historian. At length he decided on going to Baden, previously making this solemn declaration: "I acknowledge no other standard of judgment than the Word of God." At first, he had earnestly desired that Zwingli should share his danger, but he soon became convinced that, if the intrepid doctor had appeared in that fanatical city, the anger of the Catholics, kindling at his sight, would have caused the death of both of them.

They began by determining the regulations of the conference. Doctor Eck proposed that the deputies of the Forest Cantons should be empowered to pronounce the final judgment, which was, in truth, anticipating the condemnation of the reformed doctrines. Thomas Plater, who had come from Zurich to attend the colloquy, was despatched by Oecolampadius to ask Zwingli's advice.

Arriving during the night, he was with difficulty admitted into the reformer's house. "Unlucky disturber," said Zwingli to him, as he rubbed his eyes, "for six weeks I have not gone to bed, owing to this discussion. . . . What are your tidings?" Plater stated Eck's demands. "And who can make those peasants understand such things?" replied Zwingli. "They would be much more at home in milking their cows."

On May 21 the conference opened. Eck and Faber, accompanied by prelates, magistrates, and doctors, robed in garments of damask and silk, and adorned with rings, chains, and crosses, repaired to the church. Eck haughtily ascended a pulpit splendidly decorated, while the humble Oecolampadius, meanly clothed, was forced to take his seat in front of his opponent on a rudely carved stool. "All the time the conference lasted," said the chronicler Bullinger, "Eck and his friends were lodged at the Baden parsonage, faring sumptuously, living gaily and scandalously, and drinking much wine, with which the abbot of Wettingen provided them. Eck took the baths at Baden (it was said) but . . . in wine. The evangelicals, on the contrary, made a sorry appearance, and the people laughed at them as at a troop of mendicants. Their way of living was in strong contrast to that of the papal champions. The landlord of the Pike, the inn at which Oecolampadius lodged, being curious to know what the latter did in his room, reported that every time he peeped in, he found him reading or praying. 'It must be confessed,' said he, 'that he is a very pious heretic.'"

The disputation lasted eighteen days, and during the whole time the clergy walked daily in solemn procession, chanting litanies in order to ensure victory. Eck alone spoke in defense of the Catholic doctrines. According to his usual custom he disputed with great violence, seeking to gall his adversaries by sarcasm, and from time to time slipping out an oath. But the president never called him to order.

> Eck stamps with his feet, and thumps with his hands,
> He blusters, he swears, and he scolds;
> Whatever the pope and the cardinals teach,
> Is the faith, he declares, that he holds.

Oecolampadius, on the contrary, with his calm features and noble and patriarchal air, spoke with so much mildness, and at the

VERA IMAGO IOHANNIS ECKII.
THEOLOGIÆ·D. ÆTATIS·
SVÆ· XLIII·

ECK EIN GROSSER FEIND CHRISTI WAR
HAT SEHR VERFOLGT DIE CHRISTLICH SCHAR
MIT SCHREIBEN VND VNNVCZEM GSCHWECZ
BRACHT ER DIE EINFELTIGEN INS NECZ
EIFRIG VND BÖS WAR ALL SEIN SIINN
VERGEBS IM GOTER IST LANG HIINN.

Catholic theologian John Eck was a leading opponent
of both Martin Luther and Ulrich Zwingli.

same time with such courage and ability that even his adversaries, affected and impressed, said one to another, "Oh! that the tall, sallow man were on our side." At times, however, he was moved when he saw the hatred and violence of his auditors. "How impatiently they listen to me!" said he. "But God will not forsake His glory, and that is all we seek."

Oecolampadius having combated Doctor Eck's first thesis on the real presence, Haller, who had come to Baden after the opening of the conference, entered the lists against the second. But little used to such conferences, possessed a timid character, tied down by the orders of his government, and embarrassed by the looks of his avoyer Gaspard of Mullinen, a great enemy to the Reformation, Haller possessed not the haughty confidence of his opponent. But he had more real strength. When Haller had finished, Oecolampadius returned to the combat and pressed Eck so closely that the latter was compelled to fall back on the customs of the church. "Custom," replied Oecolampadius, "has no force in our Switzerland, unless it be according to the constitution. Now, in matters of faith, the Bible is our constitution."

The third thesis on the invocation of saints; the fourth, on images; the fifth, on purgatory, were successively discussed. No one rose to contest the truth of the last two, which turned on original sin and baptism.

Zwingli took an active part in the whole of the discussion. The Catholic party, which had appointed four secretaries, had forbidden all other persons to take notes under pain of death. But Jerome Walsch, a student from the Valais, who possessed an excellent memory, impressed on his mind all that he heard and on returning home hastened to commit it to writing. Thomas Plater and Zimmerman of Winterthur carried these notes to Zwingli every day, with letters from Oecolampadius, and brought back the reformer's answers. Soldiers armed with halberds were posted at all the gates of Baden, and it was only by inventing different excuses that these two messengers evaded the inquiries of the sentinels, who could not understand why they were so frequently passing to and fro.

Plater said in his autobiography, "When they asked me, 'What are you going to do?' I replied, 'I am carrying chickens to sell to the gentlemen at the baths'; for they gave me some chickens at Zurich, and the sentries could not make out how I procured them always, and in so short a time." Thus Zwingli, though absent from Baden in body, was present in spirit.

He advised and strengthened his friends and refuted his adversaries. "Zwingli," said Oswald Myconius, "has labored more by his meditations, his sleepless nights, and the advice which he transmitted to Baden, than he would have done by discussing in person in the midst of his enemies."

During the whole conference, the Roman Catholics were in commotion, sending letters in every direction and loudly boasting of their victory. "Oecolampadius," exclaimed they, "vanquished by Doctor Eck and laid prostrate in the lists, has sung his recantation. The dominion of the pope will be everywhere restored." These statements were circulated through the cantons, and the people, prompt to believe everything they hear, gave credit to all the vaunts of the Catholic partisans.

When the dispute was finished, the monk Murner of Lucerne, nicknamed "the tomcat," stepped forward and read forty charges against Zwingli. "I thought," said he, "that the coward would come and reply to them, but he has not appeared. Well, then, by every law, both human and divine, I declare forty times that the tyrant of Zurich and all his partisans are traitors, liars, perjurers, adulterers, infidels, robbers, sacrilegers, gallows-birds, and such that every honest man must blush at having any intercourse whatever with them." Such was the abuse which at this time was honored with the name of "Christian controversy," by doctors whom the Roman church should herself disavow.

Great agitation prevailed in Baden. The general impression was that the Roman champions had talked the loudest but argued the weakest. Only Oecolampadius and ten of his friends voted against Eck's theses, while eighty persons, including the presidents of the debate and all the monks of Wittingen, adopted them. Haller had quitted Baden before the end of the conference.

The majority of the diet then decreed that, as Zwingli, the chief of this pestilent doctrine, had refused to appear, and as the ministers who had come to Baden had resisted all conviction, they were all together cast out from the bosom of the Catholic Church.

But this famous conference, owing to the zeal of the oligarchs and clergy, was destined to be fatal to both. Those who had combated for the gospel were, on their return home, to fill their countrymen with enthusiasm for the cause they had defended, and two of the most important cantons in the Helvetic alliance, Berne and Basel, were thenceforth to begin their separation from the papacy.

The first blows were to fall on Oecolampadius, a stranger in Switzerland, and he did not return to Basel without apprehension. But his anxiety was soon dissipated. The mildness of his language had struck all impartial witnesses, much more than the clamors of Doctor Eck, and all pious men received him with acclamation. The adversaries made, in truth, every exertion to drive him from the pulpit, but in vain. He taught and preached with greater energy than before, and the people had never shown such thirst for the Word.

Similar results followed at Berne. The conference at Baden, intended to crush the Reformation, gave it a new impulse in this canton, the most powerful of all the Swiss league. Haller had no sooner arrived in the capital than the Smaller Council had summoned him before them and ordered him to celebrate the Mass. Haller demanded permission to reply before the Great Council, and the people, thinking it their duty to defend their pastor, hastened to the spot. Haller in alarm declared that he would rather leave the city than be the occasion of any disturbance.

Upon tranquility being restored, the reformer said, "If I am required to perform this ceremony, I must resign my office. The honor of God and the truth of his Holy Word are dearer to me than any care about what I shall eat or wherewithal I shall be clothed." Haller uttered these words with emotion. The members of the council were affected; even some of his opponents burst into tears.

Once more it was found that moderation was stronger than power. To satisfy Rome in some degree, Haller was deprived of his canonry, but nominated preacher. His most violent enemies, Lewis and Anthony Diesbach and Anthony d'Erlach, incensed at this resolution, immediately withdrew from the council and the city and renounced their citizenship. "Berne stumbled," said Haller, "but has risen up again with greater strength than ever." This firmness in the Bernese made a deep impression in Switzerland.

But the results of the conference at Baden were not limited to Basel and Berne. While these events were taking place in these powerful cities, a movement, more or less similar, was going on in several other states of the Confederation. The preachers of St. Gall, on their return from Baden, proclaimed the gospel. The images were removed from the parochial church of St. Lawrence after a conference, and the inhabitants sold their costly garments, their jewels, rings, and gold chains to found almshouses. The Reformation despoiled, but it was to clothe the poor, and the spoils were those of the reformed themselves.

At Mulhausen the gospel was preached with fresh courage. Thurgovia and the Rheinthal daily approximated more and more to Zurich. Immediately after the disputation, Zurzach removed the images from its churches, and almost the whole district of Baden received the gospel.

Nothing was better calculated to show which party had really triumphed, and hence Zwingli, as he looked around him, gave glory to God. "We have been attacked in many ways," said he, "but the Lord is not only above their threats but also the wars themselves. In the city and canton of Zurich there is an admirable agreement in favor of the gospel. We shall overcome all things by prayers offered up with faith." And shortly after, addressing Haller, Zwingli said: "Everything here below has its course. The rude north wind is followed by the gentle breeze. After the scorching heat of summer, autumn pours forth its treasures. And now, after severe contests, the Creator of all things, whom we serve, has opened a way for us into the camp of our adversaries. At last we may welcome among us the Christian doctrine, that dove so long repulsed, and which ceased not to watch for the hour of her return. Be thou the Noah to receive and save her."

Martin Luther, a portrait by Lucas Cranach

Chapter 19
Luther, Zwingli, and the Lord's Supper

The movements in Switzerland and Germany, which had till this time grown independently, began to come into contact with each other and in so doing, realized the diversity which was to be one of the characteristics of Protestantism. We shall there behold men perfectly agreed on all the great doctrines of faith and yet differing on certain secondary points. Passion, indeed, entered into these discussions. But while deploring such a melancholy intermixture, Protestantism, far from seeking to conceal her diversity, publishes and proclaims it. Its path to unity is long and difficult, but this unity is the real unity.

Zwingli and Luther, who had each been developed separately, the one in Switzerland and the other in Saxony, were to meet face to face. The same spirit, and in many respects the same character, animated both. Both alike were filled with love for the truth and hatred of injustice. Both were naturally violent, and this violence was moderated in each by a sincere piety. Both were ardently attached to their own convictions. Both resolved to defend them, and, little habituated to yield to the convictions of another, they were now to meet, like two proud warhorses which, rushing through the contending ranks, suddenly encounter each other in the hottest of the strife.

This difference is explained by the different lights in which the two reformers viewed the same object. Luther desired to maintain in the church all that was not expressly contrary to the Scriptures, and Zwingli to abolish all that could not be proved by them. The German reformer wished to remain united to the church of the preceding ages and was content to purify it of all that was opposed to the Word of God. The Zurich reformer passed over these ages, returned to the apostolic times, and, carrying out an entire transformation of the church, endeavored to restore it to its primitive condition.

Zwingli's Reformation was therefore the more complete. The work that Providence had confided to Luther, the restoration of the doctrine of justification by faith, was doubtless the great work of the Reformation. But when this was accomplished, others remained to be done, which, although secondary, were still important. To these Zwingli's exertions were more especially directed. Luther laid the foundation of the building; Zwingli raised its crowning stone.

A practical tendency predominated in the character of Zwingli and in the Reformation of which he was the author, and this tendency was directed to two great objects—simplicity of worship and sanctification of life. To harmonize the worship with the necessities of the mind that seeks not external pomp but invisible things—this was Zwingli's first aim. The idea of the corporeal presence of Christ in the Lord's Supper, the origin of so many ceremonies and superstitions of the church, must therefore be abolished. But another desire of the Swiss reformer led to the same results. He found that the Roman doctrine of the Eucharist, and even that of Luther, presupposed a certain magical influence prejudicial to sanctification. He feared lest Christians, imagining they received Jesus Christ in the consecrated bread, should henceforward less earnestly seek to be united to him by faith in the heart. "Faith," said he, "is not knowledge, opinion, imagination; it is a reality. It leads to a real union with divine things."

The union of all the disciples of the Word of God seemed a necessary condition to the success of the Reformation. How could the Protestants resist the power of Rome and of the empire if they were divided? Unfortunately, this union of minds that was now to be sought after above all things, was a very difficult task. Luther in 1519 had at first appeared not only to reform but also entirely to renovate the doctrine of the Lord's Supper, as the Swiss did somewhat later. "I go to the sacrament of the Lord's Supper," he had said, "and I there receive a sign from God that Christ's righteousness and passion justify me: such is the use of the sacrament." Luther in fact was never Zwinglian as regards the

Communion. While, according to Zwingli, the bread and wine are signs of the body and blood of Christ; according to Luther, the very body and blood of Jesus Christ are signs of God's grace. These opinions are widely different from one another.

Philip of Hesse, who was the most enterprising of all the evangelical princes, comprehended that religion was at length acquiring its due importance. Far from opposing the great development that was agitating the people, he put himself in harmony with the new ideas. Philip, who was afflicted at hearing the Catholics continually repeating, "You boast of your attachment to the pure Word of God, and yet you are nevertheless disunited," had made overtures to Zwingli in writing. He now went further and invited the theologians of the different parties to meet at Marburg.

Zwingli arrived safely at Basel and embarked on the river on September 6 with Oecolampadius and several merchants. In thirteen hours they reached Strasbourg, where the two reformers lodged in the house of Matthew Zell, the cathedral preacher. Catherine, the pastor's wife, prepared the dishes in the kitchen, waited on table, according to the ancient German manners, and then sitting down near Zwingli, listened attentively and spoke with so much piety and knowledge that the latter soon ranked her above many doctors. Zwingli quitted Strasbourg, and he and his friends, conducted along byroads, through forests, over mountains and valleys, by secret but sure paths, at length reached Marburg, escorted by forty Hessian cavaliers.

Luther, on his side, accompanied by Philipp Melancthon, Kaspar Cruciger, and Justus Jonas, had stopped on the Hessian frontier, declaring that nothing should induce him to cross it without a safe-conduct from the landgrave (Philip of Hesse). This document being obtained, Luther arrived at Alsfeld, where the scholars, kneeling under the reformer's windows, chanted their pious hymns. He entered Marburg on September 30, a day after the arrival of the Swiss.

Both parties went to inns, but they had scarcely alighted before the landgrave invited them to come and lodge in the castle, thinking by this means to bring the opposing bodies closer together. Philip entertained them in a manner truly royal. "Ah!" said the pious Jonas, as he wandered through the halls of the palace, "it is not in honor of the Muses, but in honor of God and of his Christ that we are so munificently treated in these forests of Hesse!" After dinner, on the first day, Oecolampadius, Caspar Hedio, and Martin Bucer, desirous of entering into the prince's views, went and saluted Luther. The latter conversed affectionately with Oecolampadius in the castle court. But Bucer, to whom Luther had once been very close and who was now on Zwingli's side, approached him. Then Luther said to him, smiling, "As for you, you are a good-for-nothing fellow and a knave!"

Philip of Hesse desired that, previously to the public conference, the theologians should have a private interview. It was however considered dangerous, says a contemporary, for Zwingli and Luther, who were both naturally violent, to contend with one another at the very beginning, and as Oecolampadius and Melancthon were the mildest, they were apportioned to the roughest champions. On Friday, October 1, Luther and Oecolampadius were conducted into one chamber, and Zwingli and Melancthon into another. The combatants were then left to struggle two and two.

The principal contest took place in the room of Zwingli and Melancthon. "It is affirmed," said Melancthon to Zwingli, "that some among you speak of God after the manner of the Jews, as if Christ was not essentially God."

"I think on the Holy Trinity," replied Zwingli, "with the Council of Nicea and the Athanasian creed."

"Councils! Creeds! What does that mean?" asked Melancthon. "Have you not continually repeated that you recognize no other authority than that of Scripture?"

"We have never rejected the councils," replied the Swiss reformer, "when they are based on the authority of the Word of God. The four first councils are truly sacred as regards doctrine, and none of the faithful have ever rejected them."

"But you teach," resumed Melancthon, "like Thomas Munster, that the Holy Ghost acts quite alone, independently of the sacraments and of the Word of God."

Philipp Melancthon, a portrait by Albrecht Dürer

"The Holy Ghost," replied Zwingli, "works in us justification by the Word, but by the Word preached and understood, by the soul and the marrow of the Word, by the mind and will of God clothed in human language."

Luther had pursued the same method with Oecolampadius as Melancthon with Zwingli. The discussion had in particular turned on baptism. Luther complained that the Swiss would not acknowledge that by this simple sacrament a man became a member of the church. "It is true," said Oecolampadius, "that we require faith—either an actual or a future faith. Why should we deny it? Who is a Christian, if it be not he who believes in Christ? However, I should be unwilling to deny that the water of baptism is in a certain sense a water of regeneration, for by it he, whom the church knew not, becomes its child."

These four theologians were in the very heat of their discussions when domestics came to inform them that the prince's dinner was on the table. It does not appear that the conference between Luther and Oecolampadius was resumed after dinner. Luther's manner held out very little hope, but Melancthon and Zwingli returned to the discussion, and the Zurich doctor, finding the Wittenberg professor escape him like an eel, as he said, and take "like Proteus a thousand different forms," seized a pen in order to fix his antagonist. Zwingli committed to writing whatever Melancthon dictated and then wrote his reply, giving it to the other to read. In this manner they spent six hours, three in the morning and three in the afternoon. They prepared for the general conference.

Zwingli requested that it should be an open one; this Luther resisted. It was eventually resolved that the princes, nobles, deputies, and theologians should be admitted. But a great crowd of citizens, and even many scholars and gentlemen, who had come from Frankfurt, from the Rhine districts, from Strasbourg, from Basel and other Swiss towns, were excluded. Brentz speaks of fifty or sixty hearers; Zwingli of twenty-four only.

On a gentle elevation, watered by the Lahn, is situated an old castle, overlooking the city of Marburg. In the distance may be seen the beautiful valley of the Lahn, and beyond, the mountaintops rising one above another, until they are lost in the horizon. It was beneath the vaults and Gothic arches of an antique chamber in this castle, known as the Knights Hall, that the conference was to take place.

On Saturday morning, October 2, the landgrave took his seat in the hall, surrounded by his court, but in so plain a dress that no one would have taken him for a prince. He wished to avoid all appearance of acting the part of a Constantine in the affairs of the church. Before him was a table which Luther, Zwingli, Melancthon, and Oecolampadius approached. Luther, taking a piece of chalk, bent over the velvet cloth which covered it and steadily wrote four words in large characters. All eyes followed the movement of his hand, and soon they read *Hoc est corpus meum* ("This is my body"). Luther wished to have this declaration continually before him, that it might strengthen his own faith and be a sign to his adversaries.

The landgrave's chancellor, John Feige, reminded them in the prince's name that the object of this colloquy was the reestablishment of union. "I protest," said Luther, "that I differ from my adversaries with regard to the doctrine of the Lord's Supper, and that I shall always differ from them. Christ has said, 'This is my body.' Let them show me that a body is not a body. I reject reason, common sense, carnal arguments, and mathematical proofs. God is above mathematics. We have the Word of God; we must adore it and perform it!"

"It cannot be denied," said Oecolampadius, "that there are figures of speech in the Word of God; as 'John is Elias,' 'the rock was Christ,' 'I am the vine.' The expression 'This is my body' is a figure of the same kind." Luther granted that there were figures in the Bible but denied that this last expression was figurative.

In order to prove it, Oecolampadius employed this syllogism:

"What Christ rejected in the sixth chapter of St. John, He could not admit in the words of the Eucharist.

"Now Christ, who said to the people of Capernaum, the flesh profiteth nothing, rejected by those very words the oral manducation [physical eating] of His body.

"Therefore He did not establish it at the institution of His Supper."

Luther: "I deny the minor [the second of these propositions]. Christ has not rejected all oral manducation, but only a material manducation, like that of the flesh of oxen or of swine."

Oecolampadius: "There is danger in attributing too much to mere matter."

Luther: "Everything that God commands becomes spirit and life. If we lift up a straw, by the Lord's order, in that very action we perform a spiritual work. We must pay attention to Him who speaks, and not to what He says. God speaks: Men, worms, listen! God commands: Let the world obey! And let us all together fall down and humbly kiss the Word."

Oecolampadius: "But since we have the spiritual eating, what need of the bodily one?"

Luther: "I do not ask what need we have of it, but I see it written, 'Eat, this is my body.' We must therefore believe and do. . . . If God should order me to eat dung, I would do it, with the assurance that it would be salutary."

At this point Zwingli interfered in the discussion. "We must explain Scripture by Scripture," said he. "Jesus says that to eat his flesh corporeally profiteth nothing (John 6:63); whence it would result that he had given us in the Supper a thing that would be useless to us. Besides, there are certain words that seem to me rather childish—dung, for instance. The oracles of the demons were obscure; not so are those of Jesus Christ."

Luther: "When Christ says the flesh profiteth nothing, He speaks not of His own flesh, but of ours."

Zwingli: "The soul is fed with the Spirit and not with the flesh."

Luther: "It is with the mouth that we eat the body; the soul does not eat it."

Zwingli: "Christ's body is therefore a corporeal nourishment, and not a spiritual."

Luther: "You are captious."

Zwingli: "Not so; but you utter contradictory things."

Luther: "If God should present me wild apples, I should eat them spiritually. In the Eucharist, the mouth receives the body of Christ, and the soul believes in His words."

Zwingli then quoted a great number of passages from the Holy Scripture, in which the sign is described by the very thing signified; and thence concluded that, considering our Lord's declaration in St. John, "The flesh profiteth nothing," we must explain the words of the Eucharist in a similar manner.

Yet Luther was by no means shaken. "'This is my body,'" repeated he, pointing with his finger to the words written before him. "'This is my body'": the Devil himself shall not drive me from that. To seek to understand it is to fall away from the faith."

"But, doctor," said Zwingli, "St. John explains how Christ's body is eaten, and you will be obliged at last to leave off singing always the same song."

"You make use of unmannerly expressions," replied Luther. The Wittenbergers themselves called Zwingli's argument "his old song." Zwingli continued without being disconcerted, "I ask you, doctor, whether Christ in the sixth chapter of St. John did not wish to reply to the question that had been put to Him?"

Luther: "Master Zwingli, you wish to stop my mouth by the arrogancy of your language. That passage has nothing to do here."

Zwingli (hastily): "Pardon me, doctor, that passage breaks your neck."

Luther: "Do not boast so much. You are in Hesse and not in Switzerland. In this country we do not break people's necks."

Then turning toward his friends, Luther complained bitterly of Zwingli, as if the latter had really wished to break his neck. "He makes use of camp terms and blood-stained words," said he.

Zwingli resumed: "In Switzerland also there is strict justice, and we break no man's neck without trial. That expression signifies merely that your cause is lost and hopeless."

Great agitation prevailed in the Knight's Hall. The roughness of the Swiss and obstinacy of the Saxon had come into collision. The landgrave, fearing to behold the failure of his project on conciliation, nodded assent to Zwingli's explanation. "Doctor," said he to Luther, "you should not be offended at such common expressions." It was in vain; the agitated sea could not again be calmed. The prince therefore arose, and they all repaired to the banqueting hall. After dinner they resumed their tasks.

"I believe," said Luther, "that Christ's body is in heaven, but I also believe that it is in the sacrament. It concerns me little whether it be against nature, provided that it be not against faith. Christ is substantially in the sacrament, such as He was born of the Virgin."

Oecolampadius (quoting a passage from St. Paul): "We know not Jesus Christ after the flesh" (II Cor. 5:16).

Luther: "'After the flesh' means, in this passage, after our carnal affections."

The struggle continued.

"I oppose you," said Zwingli, "with this article of our faith: *Ascendit in coelum*—'He ascended into heaven.' If Christ is in heaven as regards His body, how can He be in the bread? The Word of God teaches us that He was like His brethren in all things (Hebrews 2:17). He therefore cannot be in several places at once."

Luther: "Were I desirous of reasoning thus, I would undertake to prove that Jesus Christ had a wife; that He had black eyes, and lived in our good country of Germany. I care little about mathematics. . . . *(pointing to the words written before him)* Most dear sirs, since my Lord Jesus Christ says, *Hoc est corpus meum,* I believe that His body is really there."

Zwingli started from his chair, sprung toward Luther, and said, striking the table before him. "You maintain then, doctor, that Christ's body is locally in the Eucharist, for you say Christ's body is really *there, there, there,*" repeated Zwingli. "*There* is an adverb of place. Christ's body is then of such a nature as to exist in a place. If it is in a place, it is in heaven, whence it follows that it is not in the bread."

Luther: "I repeat that I have nothing to do with mathematical proofs. As soon as the words of consecration are pronounced over the bread, the body is there, however wicked be the priest who pronounces them."

Zwingli: "You are thus reestablishing popery."

Luther: "This is not done through the priest's merits, but because of Christ's ordinance. I will not, when Christ's body is in question, hear speak of a particular place. I absolutely will not."

Zwingli: "Must everything, then, exist precisely as you will it?"

The landgrave perceived that the discussion was growing hot, and, as the repast was waiting, he broke off the contest.

The conference was continued on the next day, Sunday, October 3, perhaps because of an epidemic (the Sweating Sickness) that had just broken out at Marburg and which did not allow any great prolongation of the colloquy. Luther, returning to the discussion of the previous evening, said, "Christ's body is in the sacrament, but it is not there as in a place."

Zwingli: "Then it is not there at all."

Luther: "Sophists say that a body may very well be in several places at once. The universe is a body, and yet we cannot assert that it is in a particular place."

Zwingli: "Ah! you speak of sophists, doctor. Are you really after all obliged to return to the onions and fleshpots of Egypt? As for what you say, that the universe is in no particular place, I beg all intelligent men to weigh this proof."

There was no reason, in fact, for prolonging the conference. A breach was inevitable. The chancellor, alarmed at such a termination of the colloquy, exhorted the theologians to come to some understanding. "I know but one means for that," said Luther; "and this it is: Let our adversaries believe as we do."

"We cannot," answered the Swiss.

"Well then," rejoined Luther, "I abandon you to God's judgment and pray that He will enlighten you."

"We will do the same," added Oecolampadius.

At Marburg, Luther and Zwingli clashed over several issues,
most notably the nature of the Lord's Supper.

While these words were passing, Zwingli sat silent, motionless, and deeply moved, and the liveliness of his affections, of
which he had given more than one proof during the conference,
was then manifested in a very different manner. He burst into
tears in the presence of all.

The conference was ended. It had been in reality more tranquil than the documents seem to show, or perhaps the chroniclers
appreciated such matters differently from ourselves. "With the
exception of a few sallies, all had passed off quietly, in a courte-
ous manner, and with very great gentleness," says an eyewitness.
"During the colloquy no other words than these were heard: 'Sir,
and very dear friend, your charity,' or other similar expressions.
Not a word of schism or of heresy. It might have been said that
Luther and Zwingli were brothers, and not adversaries." This is
the testimony of Brentz. But these flowers concealed an abyss,
and Jonas, also an eyewitness, styles the conference "a very sharp
contest."

The contagion that had suddenly broken out in Marburg was
creating frightful ravages and filled everybody with alarm. All

were anxious to leave the city. "Sirs," remarked the landgrave, "you cannot separate thus." Desirous of giving the doctors an opportunity of meeting one another with minds unoccupied by theological debates, he invited them to his table. This was Sunday night.

The time of departure drew near, and nothing had been done. The landgrave toiled earnestly at the union, as Luther wrote to his wife. He invited the theologians one after another into his closet. He pressed, entreated, warned, exhorted, and conjured them. "Think," said he, "of the salvation of the Christian republic, and remove all discord from its bosom." Never had a general at the head of an army taken such pains to win a battle.

A final meeting took place, and undoubtedly the church has seldom witnessed one of greater solemnity. Luther and Zwingli, Saxony and Switzerland, met for the last time. "Let us confess our union in all things in which we agree," said Zwingli, "and as for the rest, let us remember that we are brothers. There will never be peace between the churches if, while we maintain the grand doctrine of salvation by faith, we cannot differ on secondary points."

"Yes, yes!" exclaimed the landgrave; "you agree! Give then a testimony of your unity, and recognize one another as brothers."

"There is no one upon earth with whom I more desire to be united, than with you," said Zwingli, approaching the Wittenberg doctors. Oecolampadius, Bucer, and Hedio said the same.

"Acknowledge them! Acknowledge them as brothers!" continued the landgrave. Their hearts were moved; they were on the eve of unity. Zwingli, in the presence of the prince, the courtiers, and divines (it is Luther himself who records this), approached Luther and held out his hand. The two families of the Reformation were about to be united. Long quarrels were about to be stifled in their cradle. But Luther rejected the hand that was offered him. "You have a different spirit from ours," said he. These words communicated to the Swiss an electric shock. Their hearts sunk each time Luther repeated them, and he did so frequently. He himself is our informant.

A brief consultation took place among the Wittenberg doctors. Convinced that their peculiar doctrine on the Eucharist was essential to salvation, they considered all those who rejected it as without the pale of the faith. Turning toward Zwingli and his friends, the Wittenbergers said, "You do not belong to the communion of the Christian church; we cannot acknowledge you as brethren."

The Swiss were far from partaking of this sectarian spirit. "We think," said Bucer, "that your doctrine strikes at the glory of Jesus Christ, who now reigns at the right hand of the Father. But seeing that in all things you acknowledge your dependence on the Lord, we look at your conscience, which compels you to receive the doctrine you profess, and we do not doubt that you belong to Christ."

"And we," said Luther, "declare to you once more that our conscience opposes our receiving you as brethren."

"If such is the case," replied Bucer, "it would be folly to ask it."

"I am exceedingly astonished that you wish to consider me as your brother," pursued Luther. "It shows clearly that you do not attach much importance to your own doctrine."

"Take your choice," said Bucer, proposing a dilemma to the reformer. "Either you should not acknowledge as brethren those who differ from you in any point—and if so, you will not find a single brother in your own ranks—or else you will receive some of those who differ from you, and then you ought to receive us."

The Swiss had exhausted their solicitations. "We are conscious," said they, "of having acted as if in the presence of God. Posterity will be our witness." They were on the point of retiring. Luther remained like a rock, to the landgrave's great indignation.

Luther conferred anew with his colleagues. "Let us beware," said he to his friends, "of wiping our noses too roughly, lest blood should come."

Then turning to Zwingli and Oecolampadius, they said: "We acknowledge you as friends. We do not consider you as brothers and members of Christ's church. But we do not exclude you from that universal charity which we owe even to our enemies."

The hearts of Zwingli, Oecolampadius, and Bucer were ready to burst, for this concession was almost a new insult. "Let us carefully avoid all harsh and violent words and writings," said they, "and let each one defend himself without railing."

Luther then advanced toward the Swiss, and said, "We consent, and I offer you the hand of peace and charity." The Swiss rushed in great emotion toward the Wittenbergers and all shook hands. Luther himself was softened. Christian charity resumed her rights in his heart. "Assuredly," said he, "a great portion of the scandal is taken away by the suppression of our fierce debates. We could not have hoped for so much. May Christ's hand remove the last obstacle that separates us. There is now a friendly concord between us, and if we persevere in prayer, brotherhood will come."

It was desirable to confirm this important result by a report. "We must let the Christian world know," said the landgrave, "that, except the manner of the presence of the body and blood in the Eucharist, you are agreed in all the articles of faith." This was resolved on, but who should be charged with drawing up the paper? All eyes were turned upon Luther. The Swiss themselves appealed to his impartiality.

Luther retired to his closet, lost in thought, uneasy, and finding the task very difficult. "On the one hand," said he, "I should like to spare their weakness, but, on the other, I would not in the least degree strike at the holy doctrine of Christ." He did not know how to set about it, and his anguish increased. He got free at last. "I will draw up the articles," said he, "in the most accurate manner. Do I not know that whatever I may write, they will never sign them?" Erelong fifteen articles were committed to paper, and Luther, holding them in his hand, repaired to the theologians of the two parties.

These articles are of importance. The two doctrines that were evolved in Switzerland and in Saxony, independently of each other, were brought together and compared. A great unity was found between the German and the Swiss Reformations, for they both proceeded from the same divine teaching; and they both had a diversity on secondary points, for it was by man's instrumentality that God had effected them.

Luther took his paper, and reading the first article, said, "First, we believe that there is one sole, true, and natural God, creator of heaven and earth and of all creatures; and that this same God, one in essence and in nature, is threefold in person, that is to say, Father, Son, and Holy Ghost, as was declared in the Nicene Council, and as all the Christian church professes."

To this the Swiss gave their assent.

They were agreed also on the divinity and humanity of Jesus Christ, on His death and resurrection, on original sin, justification by faith, the operation of the Holy Ghost and of the Word of God, baptism, good works, confession, civil order, and tradition.

Thus far all were united. The Wittenbergers could not recover from their astonishment. The two parties had rejected, on the one hand, the errors of the Catholics who make religion little more than an outward form, and, on the other, those who speak exclusively of internal feelings; and they were found drawn up under the same banners between these two camps. But the moment was come that would separate them. Luther had kept till the last the article on the Eucharist.

The reformer resumed. "We all believe with regard to the Lord's Supper, that it ought to be celebrated in both kinds, according to the primitive institution; that the Mass is not a work by which a Christian obtains pardon for another man, whether dead or alive; that the sacrament of the altar is the sacrament of the very body and very blood of Jesus Christ; and that the spiritual manducation of this body and blood is specially necessary to every true Christian."

It was now the turn of the Swiss to be astonished. Luther continued: "In like manner, as to the use of the sacrament, we are agreed that, like the Word, it was ordained of Almighty God, in order that weak consciences might be excited by the Holy Ghost to faith and charity."

The joy of the Swiss was redoubled. Luther continued: "And although at present we are not agreed on the question whether the real body and blood of Christ are corporeally present in the bread and wine, yet both the interested parties shall cherish more and more a truly Christian charity for one another, so far as conscience permits, and we will all earnestly implore the Lord to condescend by his Spirit to confirm us in the sound doctrine."

The Swiss obtained what they had asked: unity in diversity. It was immediately resolved to hold a solemn meeting for the signature of the articles. They were read over again. Both parties then subscribed the copy of their adversaries, and this important document was sent to the press.

Thus the Reformation had made a sensible step at Marburg. After the Marburg conference, the controversy became more moderate. It was not, then, in vain that Philip of Hesse endeavored, at Marburg, to bring together the friends of the gospel. The landgrave having collected all the doctors at his table on the last day, they shook hands in a friendly manner, and each one thought of leaving the town.

On Tuesday, October 5, Philip of Hesse quitted Marburg early, and in the afternoon of the same day Luther departed, accompanied by his colleagues, but Luther did not go forth as a conqueror. A spirit of dejection and alarm had taken possession of his mind. He writhed in the dust, like a worm, according to his own expression.

As for Zwingli, he quitted Marburg in alarm at Luther's intolerance. "Lutheranism," wrote he to the landgrave, "will lie as heavy upon us as popery." He reached Zurich on October 19. "The truth," said he to his friends, "has prevailed so manifestly, that if ever any one has been defeated before all the world, it is Luther, although he constantly exclaimed that he was invincible." On his side, Luther spoke in a similar strain. "It is through fear of their fellow citizens," added he, "that the Swiss, although vanquished, are unwilling to retract."

If it should be asked on which side the victory really was, perhaps we ought to say that Luther assumed the air of a conqueror, but Zwingli was so in reality. The conference propagated through all Germany the doctrine of the Swiss, which had been little known there until then, and it was adopted by an immense number of persons.

Still the dominant principle at this celebrated epoch was unity. The adversaries are the best judges. The Roman Catholics were exasperated that the Lutherans and Zwinglians had agreed on all the essential points of faith. "They have a fellow feeling against the Catholic Church," said they, "as Herod and Pilate against Jesus Christ."

Chapter 20
Reformation at Berne

The divisions which the Reformation disclosed within its bosom humbled it and compromised its existence, but we must not forget that the cause of these divisions was one of the conditions of the existence of the regenerated church. No doubt it would have been desirable for Germany and Switzerland to have agreed, but it was of still greater importance that Germany and Switzerland should have each its original reform. If the Swiss Reformation had been only a feeble copy of the German, there would have been uniformity, but no duration. The tree, transplanted into Switzerland, without having taken deep root, would soon have been torn up by the vigorous hand that was erelong about to seize upon it.

The regeneration of Christianity in these mountains proceeded from forces peculiar to the Helvetic church and received an organization in conformity with the ecclesiastical and political condition of that country. By this very originality it communicated a particular energy to the principles of the Reformation, of much greater consequence to the common cause than a servile uniformity. The strength of an army arises in great measure from its being composed of soldiers of different arms.

The military and political influence of Switzerland was declining. The new developments of the European nations, subsequent to the sixteenth century, were about to banish to their native mountains those proud Helvetians who for so long a period had placed their two-handed swords in the balance in which the destinies of nations were weighed. The Reformation communicated a new influence in exchange for that which was departing. Switzerland, where the gospel appeared in its simplest and purest form, was destined to give in these new times to many nations of the two worlds a more salutary and glorious impulse than that which had hitherto proceeded from its halberds and its arquebuses.

The history of the Swiss Reformation is divided into three periods, in which the light of the gospel is seen spreading successively over three different zones. From 1519 to 1526 Zurich was the center of the Reformation, which was then entirely German and was propagated in the eastern and northern parts of the Confederation. Between 1526 and 1532 the movement was communicated from Berne; it was at once German and French and extended to the center of Switzerland from the gorges of the Jura to the deepest valleys of the Alps. In 1532, Geneva became the focus of the light, and the Reformation, which was here essentially French, was established on the shores of the Leman lake and gained strength in every quarter. It is the second of these periods—that of Berne—of which we are now to treat.

Of all the Swiss cantons, Berne appeared the least disposed to the Reformation. A military state may be zealous for religion, but it will be for an external and a disciplined religion. It requires an ecclesiastical organization that it can see, and touch, and manage at its will. It fears the innovations and the free movements of the Word of God; it loves the form and not the life. Such was the case with Berne. Its government, besides, was absorbed in political interests, and, although it had little regard for the pope, it cared still less to see a reformer put himself, as Zwingli did, at the head of public affairs. As for the people, feasting on the "butter of their kine and milk of their sheep, with fat of lambs," they remained closely shut up within the narrow circle of their material wants. Religious questions were not to the taste either of the rulers or of their fellow citizens.

The Bernese government, being without experience in religious matters, had proposed to check the movement of the reform by its edict of 1523. As soon as it discovered its mistake, it moved toward the cantons that adhered to the ancient faith. While that portion of the people whence the Great Council was recruited listened to the voice of the reformers, most of the patrician families, who composed the Smaller Council, believing their power, their interests, and their honor menaced, attached themselves to the old order of things. From this opposition of the two councils there arose a general uneasiness, but no violent shocks. Sudden movements and repeated starts announced from time to time that incongruous matters were fermenting in the nation. It was like an indistinct earthquake, which raises the whole surface without causing any rents; then anon all returns to apparent tranquillity. Berne, which was always decided in its politics, turned in religious matters at one time to the right, and at another to the left, and declared that it would be neither popish nor reformed. To gain time was, for the new faith, to gain everything.

What was done to turn aside Berne from the Reformation was the very cause of precipitating it into the new way. The haughtiness with which the five primitive cantons appropriated the guardianship of their confederates, the secret conferences to which Berne was not even invited, and the threat of addressing the people in a direct manner deeply offended the Bernese oligarchs.

Thomas Murner, a Carmelite of Lucerne, one of those rude men who act upon the populace but who inspire disgust in elevated minds, made the cup run over. Furious against the Zurich calendar, in which the names of the saints had been purposely omitted, he published in opposition to it the "Almanac of Heretics and Church Robbers," a tract filled with lampoons and invectives, in which the portraits of the reformers and their adherents, among whom were many of the most considerable men of Berne, were coupled with the most brutal inscriptions. Zurich and Berne in conjunction demanded satisfaction, and from this time the union of these two states daily became closer.

Zwingli, whose eye nothing escaped, saw that a favorable hour for Berne was coming and immediately gave the signal. "The dove commissioned to examine the state of the waters is returning with an olive branch into the ark," wrote he to the reformer Haller in Berne. "Come forth now, thou second Noah, and take possession of the land. Enforce, be earnest, and fix deeply in the hearts of men the hooks and grapnels of the Word of God, so that they can never again be rid of them."

Haller and his friends were on the point of replying to this appeal when their situation became complicated. Some of the radicals, arriving at Berne in 1527, led away the people from the evangelical preachers "on account of the presence of idols." Haller had a useless conference with them. "To what dangers is not Christianity exposed," cried he, "wherever these furies have crept in!" There has never been any revival in the church without the hierarchical or radical sects immediately endeavouring to disturb it. Haller, although alarmed, still maintained his unalterable meekness. "The magistrates are desirous of banishing them," said he, "but it is our duty to drive out their errors, and not their persons. Let us employ no other weapons than the sword of the Spirit." It was not from Catholicism that the reformers had learned these principles. A public disputation took place. Six of the radicals declared themselves convinced, and two others were sent out of the country.

The decisive moment was drawing near. The two great powers of the age, the gospel and the papacy, were stirring with equal energy. The Bernese councils were to speak out. They saw on the one hand the five primitive cantons taking daily a more threatening attitude and announcing that the Austrian would soon reappear in Helvetia to reduce it once more into subjection to Rome. On the other, they beheld the gospel everyday gaining ground in the Confederation. Which was destined to prevail in Switzerland—the lances of Austria or the Word of God? In the uncertainty in which the councils were placed, they resolved to side with the majority. Where could they discover a firm footing, if not there? "No one," said they, "can make any change of his own private authority. The consent of all is necessary."

The government of Berne had to decide between two mandates, both emanating from its authority: that of 1523, in favor of the free preaching of the gospel, and that of 1526, in favor "of the sacraments, the saints, the mother of God, and the ornaments of the churches." State messengers set out and traversed every parish. The people gave their votes against every law contrary to liberty, and the councils, supported by the nation, decreed that "the Word of God should be preached publicly and freely, even if it should be in opposition to the statutes and doctrines of men." Such was the victory of the gospel and of the people over the oligarchy and the priests.

Contentions immediately arose throughout the canton, and every parish became a battlefield. The peasants began to dispute with the priests and monks, in reliance on the Holy Scriptures. "If the mandate of our lords," said many, "accords to our pastors the liberty of preaching, why should it not grant the flock the liberty of acting?"

"Peace, peace!" cried the councils, alarmed at their own boldness. But the flocks resolutely declared that they would send away the Mass and keep their pastors and the Bible. Upon this, the papal partisans grew violent. The banneret Kuttler called the good people of Emmenthal "heretics, rascals, wantons," but these peasants obliged him to make an apology. The bailiff of Trachselwald was more cunning. Seeing the inhabitants of Rudersweil listening with eagerness to the Word of God, which a pious minister was preaching to them, he came with fifers and trumpeters and interrupted the sermon, inviting the village girls by words and by lively tunes to quit the church for the dance.

These singular provocations did not check the reform. Six of the city companies (the shoemakers, weavers, merchants, bakers, stonemasons, and carpenters) abolished in the churches and convents of their district all masses, anniversaries, advowsons, and prebends. Three others (the tanners, smiths, and tailors) prepared to imitate them. The seven remaining companies were undecided, except the butchers, who were enthusiastic for the pope. Thus, the majority of the citizens had embraced the gospel. Many parishes throughout the canton had done the same, and the avoyer d'Erlach, that great adversary of the Reformation, could no longer keep the torrent within bounds.

Yet the attempt was made. The bailiffs were ordered to note the irregularities and dissolute lives of the monks and nuns. All women of loose morals were even turned out of the cloisters. But it was not against these abuses alone that the Reformation was levelled. It was against the institutions themselves and against the popery on which they were founded. The people ought therefore to decide. "The Bernese clergy," said they, "must be convoked, as at Zurich, and let the two doctrines be discussed in a solemn conference. We will proceed afterwards in conformity with the result."

On the Sunday following the festival of Saint Martin (November 11), the council and citizens unanimously resolved that a public disputation should take place at the beginning of the succeeding year. "The glory of God and His Word," said they, "will at length appear!" Bernese and strangers, priests and laymen, were invited by letter or by printed notice to come and discuss the controverted points, but the discussion was to be by Scripture alone, without the glosses of the ancients, at the same time renouncing all subtleties and abusive language. "Who knows," said they, "whether all the members of the ancient Swiss Confederation may not be thus brought to unity of faith?"

Thus, within the walls of Berne, the struggle was about to take place that would decide the fate of Switzerland, for the example of the Bernese must necessarily lead with it a great part of the Confederation.

The Five Cantons, alarmed at this intelligence, met at Lucerne, where they were joined by Friburg, Soleure, and Glaris. There was nothing either in the letter or in the spirit of the federal compact to obstruct religious liberty. "Every state," said Zurich, "is free to choose the doctrine that it desires to profess." The Waldstettes (inhabitants of the primitive democratic cantons Schwytz, Uri, Unterwalen, and Lucerne, to which Zug may be added), on the contrary, wished to deprive the cantons of this independence and to subject them to the federal majority and to the pope. They protested, therefore, in the name of the Confederation, against the proposed discussion. "Your ministers," wrote they to Berne, "dazzled and confounded at Baden by the brightness of truth, would desire by this new discussion to hide their shame, but we entreat you to desist from a plan so contrary to our ancient alliances."

"It is not we who have infringed them," replied Berne. "It is much rather your haughty missive that has destroyed them. We will not abandon the Word of our Lord Jesus Christ." Upon this the Roman cantons decided to refuse a safe-conduct to those who should proceed to Berne. This decision was giving token of sinister intentions.

The bishops of Lausanne, Constance, Basel, and Sion, being invited to the conference under pain of forfeiting all their privileges in the canton of Berne, replied that, since it was to be a disputation according to the Scriptures, they had nothing to do with it. Thus did these priests forget the words of one of the most illustrious Roman doctors of the fifteenth century: "In heavenly things man should be independent of his fellows, and trust in God alone."

The Catholic doctors followed the example of the bishops. Eck, Murner, Cochloeus, and many others said wherever they went, "We have received the letter of this leper, of this accursed heretic, Zwingli. They want to take the Bible for their judge, but has the Bible a voice against those who do it violence? We will not go to Berne. We will not crawl into that obscure corner of the world. We will not go and combat in that gloomy cavern, in that school of heretics. Let these villains come out into the open air and contend with us on level ground, if they have the Bible on their side, as they say." The emperor ordered the discussion to be adjourned, but on the very day of its opening, the council of Berne replied that, as every one was already assembled, delay would be impossible.

Then, despite the doctors and bishops, the Helvetic church assembled to decide upon its doctrines. The contest seemed unequal. On one side appeared the Roman hierarchy, a giant which had increased in strength during many centuries. On the other, there was at first but one weak and timid man, the modest Berthold Haller. "I cannot wield the sword of the Word," said he in alarm to his friends. "If you do not stretch out your hands to me, all is over." He then threw himself trembling at the feet of the Lord, and soon arose enlightened and exclaiming, "Faith in the Savior gives me courage and scatters all my fears."

A conference in Latin afterwards took place between William Farel and a Parisian doctor. The latter advanced a strange argument. "Christians," said he, "are enjoined to obey the Devil; for it is said, 'Submit unto thine adversary' (Matt. 5:25). Now, our adversary is the Devil. How much more, then, should we submit to the church!" Loud bursts of laughter greeted this remarkable syllogism. A discussion on baptism and other subjects terminated the conference.

The two councils decreed that the Mass should be abolished and that every one might remove from the churches the ornaments he had placed there. Immediately, twenty-five altars and a great number of images were destroyed in the cathedral, yet without disorder or bloodshed.

The hearts of the adherents of the papacy were filled with bitterness as they heard the objects of their adoration fall one after another. "Should any man," said John Schneider, "take away the altar of the Butchers' Company, I will take away his life." Peter Thorman compared the cathedral stripped of its ornaments to a stable. "When the good folks of the Oberland come to market," added he, "they will be happy to put up their cattle in it." And John Zehender, member of the Great Council, to show the little value he set on such a place of worship, entered it riding on a donkey, insulting and cursing the reform. A Bernese, who chanced to be there, said to him, "It is by God's will that these images have been pulled down."

"Say rather by the Devil's," replied Zehender. "When have you ever been with God so as to learn his will?" He was fined twenty livres and expelled from the council.

This reform was necessary. When Christianity in the fourth century had seen the favor of princes succeed to persecution, a crowd of heathens rushing into the church had brought with them the images, pomps, statues, and demigods of paganism, and a likeness of the mysteries of Greece and Asia, and above all of Egypt, and had banished the Word of Jesus Christ from the Christian oratories. This Word returning in the sixteenth century, a purification must necessarily take place, but it could not be done without grievous rents.

The departure of the strangers was drawing near. On January 28, the day after that on which the images and altars had been thrown down, while their piled fragments still encumbered here and there the porches and aisles of the cathedral, Zwingli crossed these eloquent ruins and once more ascended the pulpit in the midst of an immense crowd. In great emotion, directing his eyes by turns on these fragments and on the people, he said: "Victory has declared for the truth, but perseverance alone can complete the triumph. Christ persevered even until death. . . . Cornelius Scipio, after the disaster at Cannae, having learned that the generals surviving the slaughter meditated quitting Italy, entered the senate house, although not yet of senatorial age, and drawing his sword, constrained the affrighted chiefs to swear that they would not abandon Rome. Citizens of Berne, to you I address the same demand: Do not abandon Jesus Christ."

Then, turning toward the fragments that lay near him: "Behold," said he, "behold these idols! Behold them conquered, mute, and shattered before us! These corpses must be dragged to the shambles, and the gold you have spent upon such foolish images must henceforward be devoted to comforting in their misery the living images of God. Feeble souls, ye shed tears over these sad idols. Do ye not see that they break, do ye not hear that they crack like any other wood, or like any other stone? Look! Here is one deprived of its head." Zwingli pointed to the image, and all the people fixed their eyes upon it. "Here is another maimed of its arms. If this ill usage had done any harm to the saints that are in heaven and if they had the power ascribed to them, would you have been able, I pray, to cut off their arms and their heads?"

"Now, then," said the powerful orator in conclusion, "stand fast in the liberty wherewith Christ has made you free, and be not entangled again with the yoke of bondage (Gal. 5:1). Fear not! That God who has enlightened you will enlighten your confederates also, and Switzerland, regenerated by the Holy Ghost, shall flourish in righteousness and peace."

The words of Zwingli were not lost. The mercy of God called forth that of man. Some persons condemned to die for sedition were pardoned, and all the exiles were recalled. "Should we not have done so," said the council, "had a great prince visited us? Shall we not much more do so, now that the King of kings and the Redeemer of our souls has made his entry among us, bearing an everlasting amnesty?"

The Roman Catholic cantons, exasperated at the result of the discussion, sought to harass the return of the doctors. On arriving before Bremgarten, they found the gates closed. The bailiff Schütz, who had accompanied them with two hundred men-at-arms, placed two halberdiers before Zwingli's horse, two behind him, and one on each side. Then putting himself at the reformer's left hand, while the burgomaster Roust stationed himself on the right, he ordered the escort to proceed, lance in rest. The avoyers of the town, being intimidated, came to a parley. The gates were opened. The escort traversed Bremgarten amidst an immense crowd, and on February 1 reached Zurich without accident, which Zwingli reentered, says Luther, like a conqueror.

The Council of Berne, desirous of separating from the pope, relied upon the people. On January 30, messengers going from house to house convoked the citizens, and on February 2, the burgesses and inhabitants, masters and servants, uniting in the cathedral and forming but one family, with hands upraised to heaven, swore to defend the two councils in all they should undertake for the good of the state or of the church.

On February 7, 1528, the council published a general edict of reform and "threw for ever from the necks of the Bernese the yoke of the four bishops, who," said they, "know well how to shear their sheep, but not how to feed them."

At the same time the reformed doctrines were spreading among the people. In every quarter might be heard earnest and keen dialogues in which the pale and expiring Mass, stretched on her deathbed, was loudly calling for all her physicians and, finding their advice useless, at length dictating with a broken voice her last will and testament—which the people received with loud bursts of laughter.

The Reformation generally, and that of Berne in particular, has been reproached as being brought about by political motives. But, on the contrary, Berne, which of all the Helvetic states was the greatest favorite of the court of Rome—which had in its canton neither a bishop to dismiss nor a powerful clergy to humiliate—Berne, whose most influential families, the Weingartens, Manuels, Mays, were reluctant to sacrifice the pay and the service of the foreigner, and all whose traditions were conservative, ought to have opposed the movement. The Word of God was the power that overcame this political tendency.

At Berne, as elsewhere, it was neither a learned, nor a democratic, nor a sectarian spirit that gave birth to the Reformation. Undoubtedly the men of letters, the liberals, the sectarian enthusiasts rushed into the great struggle of the sixteenth century. But the duration of the reform would not have been long had it received its life from them. The primitive strength of Christianity, reviving after ages of long and complete prostration, was the creative principle of the Reformation, and it was erelong seen separating distinctly from the false allies that had presented themselves by consecrating the rights of the Word and of the Christian people.

But while we maintain that the Reformation was at Berne, as elsewhere, a truly Christian work, we are far from saying that it was not useful to the canton in a political sense. All the European states that embraced the Reformation were elevated, while those which combated it were lowered.

Chapter 21
Church and State

It was the will of God that at the very gates of His revived church there should be two great examples to serve as lessons for future generations. Luther and the German Reformation—declining the aid of the temporal power, rejecting the force of arms, and looking for victory only in the confession of truth—were destined to see their faith crowned with the most brilliant success; while Zwingli and the Swiss Reformation, stretching out their hands to the mighty ones of the earth and grasping the sword, were fated to witness a horrible, cruel, and bloody catastrophe fall upon the Word of God—a catastrophe which threatened to engulf the evangelical cause in the most furious whirlpool. God is a jealous God, and gives not His glory to another; He claims to perform His own work Himself and, to attain His ends, sets other springs in motion than those of a skillful diplomacy.

We are far from forgetting that we are called upon to relate facts and not to discuss theories, but there is a principle which the history we are narrating sets forth in capital letters. It is that professed in the gospel, where it says, *The weapons of our warfare are not carnal, but mighty through God!* In maintaining this truth we do not place ourselves on the ground of any particular school but on that of universal conscience and of the Word of God.

It was the very extension of the reform in Switzerland that exposed it to the dangers under which it sunk. So long as it was concentrated at Zurich, it continued a religious matter. But when it had gained Berne, Basel, Schaffhausen, St. Gall, Glaris, Appenzell, and numerous bailiwicks, it formed inter-cantonal relations, and—here was the error and misfortune—while the connection should have taken place between church and church, it was formed between state and state.

As soon as spiritual and political matters became mingled together, the latter took the upper hand. Zwingli erelong thought it his duty to examine not only doctrinal but also federal questions, and the illustrious reformer might be seen, unconscious of the snares beneath his feet, precipitating himself into a course strewn with rocks, at the end of which a cruel death awaited him.

The primitive Swiss cantons had resigned the right of forming new alliances without the consent of all, but Zurich and Berne had reserved the power. Zwingli thought himself therefore quite at liberty to promote an alliance with the evangelical states. Constance was the first city that gave her adhesion. But this Christian co-burghery, which might become the germ of a new confederation, immediately raised up numerous adversaries against Zwingli, even among the partisans of the Reformation.

There was yet time. Zwingli might withdraw from public affairs and occupy himself entirely with those of the gospel. But no one in Zurich had, like him, that application to labor, that correct, keen, and sure eye, so necessary for politicians. If he retired, the vessel of the state would be left without a pilot. Besides, he was convinced that political acts alone could save the reform. He resolved, therefore, to be at one and the same time the man of the state and of the church.

The registers prove that in his later years he took part in the most important deliberations. He was commissioned by the councils of his canton to write letters, compose proclamations, and draw up opinions. Already, before the dispute with Berne, looking upon war as possible, he had traced out a very detailed plan of defense, the manuscript of which is still in existence. In 1528 he did still more. He showed in a remarkable paper how the republic should act with regard to the empire, France, and other European states, and with respect to the several cantons and bailiwicks. Then, as if he had grown gray at the head of the Helvetic troops (and it is but just to remark that he had long lived among soldiers), he explained the advantages there would be in surprising the enemy and described even the nature of the arms and the manner of employing them. In truth, an important revolution was then taking place in the art of war. The pastor of Zurich is at once the head of the state and general of the army. This double—this triple—part of the reformer was the ruin of the Reformation and of himself.

Undoubtedly we must make allowances for the men of this age, who, being accustomed to seeing Rome wield two swords for so many centuries, did not understand that they must take up one and leave the other. We must acknowledge that the republican education of Zwingli had taught him to confound his country with his religion and that there was in this great man enough to fill up many lives. But we should also see in the great and terrible lesson that God gave him, a precept for all times and for every nation, and, finally, we should remember what is so often forgotten, "that the kingdom of Christ is not of this world."

The Roman Catholic cantons, on hearing of the new alliances of the reformed, felt a violent indignation. William of Diesbach, deputy from Berne at the diet, was forced to submit to the keenest reproaches. The sitting, for a while interrupted, was resumed immediately after his departure. "They may try to patch up the old faith," said the Bernese, as he withdrew. "It cannot, however, last any longer." In truth, they patched away with all their might, but with a sharp and envenomed needle that drew blood. Joseph Am-Berg of Schwytz and Jacques Stocker of Zug, bailiffs of Thurgovia, behaved with cruelty toward all who were attached to the gospel. They enforced against them fines, imprisonment, torture, the scourge, confiscation, and banishment. They cut out the ministers' tongues, beheaded them, or condemned them to be burnt. At the same time they took away the Bibles and all the evangelical books. And if any poor Lutherans, fleeing from Austria, crossed the Rhine and that low valley where its calm waters flow between the Alps of the Tyrol and of Appenzell—if these poor creatures, tracked by the lansquenets, came to seek a refuge in Switzerland, they were cruelly given up to their persecutors.

The heavier lay the hands of the bailiffs on Thurgovia and the Rheinthal, the greater conquests did the gospel make. The bishop of Constance wrote to the Five Cantons that if they did not act with firmness, all the country would embrace the reform. In consequence of this, the cantons convoked at Frauenfeld all the prelates, nobles, judges, and persons of note in the district; and a second meeting taking place six days after (December 6, 1528) at Weinfeld, deputies from Berne and Zurich entreated the assembly to consider the honor of God above all things and in no respect to care for the threats of the world. A great agitation followed upon this discourse. At last a majority called for the preaching of the Word of God. The people came to the same decision, and the Rheinthal, as well as Bremgarten, followed this example.

What was to be done? The flood had become hourly more encroaching. Must then the Forest Cantons open their valleys to it at last? Religious antipathies put an end to national antipathies, and these proud mountaineers, directing their looks beyond the Rhine, thought of invoking the succor of Austria, which they had vanquished at Morgarten and at Sempach. The fanatical German party that had crushed the revolted Swabian peasants was all-powerful on the frontiers. Letters were exchanged; messengers passed to and fro across the river. At last they took advantage of a wedding in high rank that was to take place at Feldkirch in Swabia, six leagues from Appenzell. On February 16, 1529, the marriage party, forming a brilliant cavalcade in the midst of which the deputies of the Five Cantons were concealed, made their entry into Feldkirch, and Am-Berg had an immediate interview with the Austrian governor. "The power of the enemies of our ancient faith had so increased," said the Swiss, "that the friends of the church can resist them no longer. We therefore turn our eyes to that illustrious prince who has saved in Germany the faith of our fathers."

This alliance was so very unnatural that the Austrians had some difficulty in believing it to be sincere. "Take hostages," said the Waldstettes. "Write the articles of the treaty with your own hands. Command and we will obey!"

"Very good!" replied the Austrians. "In two months you will find us again at Waldshut, and we will let you know our conditions."

A rumor of these negotiations which spread abroad excited great dissatisfaction, even in the partisans of Rome. In no place did it burst out with greater force than in the council of Zug. The opposing parties were violently agitated. They stamped their feet, started from their seats, and were nearly coming to blows, but hatred prevailed over patriotism. The deputies of the Forest Cantons appeared at Waldshut. They suspended the arms of their cantons by the side of those of the oppressors of Switzerland, decorated their hats with peacocks' feathers (the badge of Austria), and laughed, drank, and chattered with the Imperialists.

This strange alliance was at last concluded. "Whoever shall form new sects among the people," it ran, "shall be punished with death, and, if need be, with the help of Austria. This power, in case of emergency, shall send into Switzerland six thousand foot soldiers and four hundred horse, with all requisite artillery. If necessary, the reformed cantons shall be blockaded and all provisions intercepted." To the Catholic cantons, then, belongs the initiative of this measure so much decried. Finally, Austria guaranteed to the Waldstettes the possession not only of the common bailiwicks but also of all the conquests that might be made on the left bank of the Rhine.

Dejection and consternation immediately pervaded all Switzerland. This national complaint, which Bullinger has preserved, was sung in every direction:

> Wail, Helvetians, wail,
> For the peacock's plume of pride
> To the forest cantons' savage bull
> In friendship is allied.

All the cantons not included in this alliance, with the exception of Friburg, assembled in diet at Zurich and resolved to send a deputation to their mountain confederates, with a view to reconciliation. The deputation, admitted at Schwytz in the presence of the people, was able to execute its mission without tumult. At Zug there was a cry of "No sermon! No sermon!" At Altorf the answer was, "Would to God that your new faith was buried for ever!" At Lucerne they received this haughty reply: "We shall know how to defend ourselves, our children, and our children's children from the poison of your rebellious priests." It was at Unterwalden that the deputation met with the worst reception. "We declare our alliance at an end," said they. "It is we, it is the other Waldstettes who are the real Swiss. We graciously admitted you into our Confederation, and now you claim to become our masters! The emperor, Austria, France, Savoy, and Valais will assist us!" The deputies retired in astonishment, shuddering as they passed before the house of the secretary of state, where they saw the arms of Zurich, Berne, Basel, and Strasbourg hanging from a lofty gibbet.

The deputation had scarcely returned to Zurich and made their report, when men's minds were inflamed. Zwingli proposed to grant no peace to Unterwalden if it would not renounce foreign service, the alliance with Austria, and the government of the common bailiwicks. "No! No!" said Berne, that had just stifled a civil war in its own canton, "Let us not be so hasty. When the rays of the sun shine forth, each one wishes to set out, but as soon as it begins to rain, every man loses heart! The Word of God enjoins peace. It is not with pikes and lances that faith is made to enter the heart. For this reason, in the name of our Lord's sufferings, we entreat you to moderate your anger."

This Christian exhortation would have succeeded, if the fearful news that reached Zurich on the very day when the Bernese delivered their moderate speech had not rendered it unavailing.

On Saturday, May 22, Jacques Keyser, a pastor and father of a family in the neighborhood of the Greiffensee, after coasting the fertile shores of this little lake, crossed the rich pastures of the bailiwick of Gruningen, passed near the Teutonic house of Bubikon and the convent of Ruti, and reached that simple and wild district bathed by the upper part of Lake Zurich. Making his way to Oberkirk, a parish in the Gaster district between the two lakes of Zurich and Wallenstadt, of which he had been nominated pastor and where he was to preach on the morrow, he crossed on foot the lengthened and rounded flanks of the Buchberg, fronting the picturesque heights of the Ammon. He was confidently advancing into those woods which for many weeks he had often traversed without obstruction, when he was suddenly seized by six men posted there to surprise him, and carried off to Schwytz.

"The bailiffs," said they to the magistrates, "have ordered all innovating ministers to be brought before the tribunals. Here is one that we bring you." Although Zurich and Glaris interposed, and although the government of Gaster, where Keyser had been taken, did not then belong to Schwytz, the landsgemeinde desired a victim, and on May 29 they condemned the minister to be burnt alive. On being informed of his sentence, Keyser burst into tears. But when the hour of execution arrived, he walked cheerfully to death, freely confessed his faith, and gave thanks to the Lord even with his latest breath. "Go and tell them at Zurich how he thanks us!" said one of the Schwytz magistrates, with a sarcastic smile, to the Zurich deputies. Thus had a fresh martyr fallen under the hands of that formidable power that is "drunk with the blood of the saints."

The cup was full. The flames of Keyser's pile became the signal of war. Exasperated, Zurich uttered a cry that resounded through all the Confederation. Zwingli above all called for energetic measures. Everywhere—in the streets, in the councils, and even in the pulpits—he surpassed in daring even the most valiant captains. He spoke at Zurich; he wrote to Berne. "Let us be firm, and fear not to take up arms," said he. "This peace, which some desire so much, is not peace, but war, while the war that we call for is not war but peace. We thirst for no man's blood, but we will clip the wings of the oligarchy. If we shun it, the truth of the gospel and the ministers' lives will never be secure among us."

In every part of Europe, Zwingli beheld the mighty ones of the earth aiding one another to stifle the reviving animation of the church, and he thought that without some decisive and energetic movement, Christianity, overwhelmed by so many blows, would soon fall back into its ancient slavery. "Undoubtedly," said he, "we must trust in God alone, but when He gives us a just cause, we must also know how to defend it, and like Joshua and Gideon, shed blood in behalf of our country and our God."

Chapter 22
War of Religion

On Saturday, June 15, 1529, seven days after Keyser's martyrdom, all Zurich was in commotion. The moment was come when Unterwalden should send a governor to the common bailiwicks, and the images having been burnt in those districts, Unterwalden had sworn to take a signal revenge. Thus the consternation had become general. "Keyser's pile," thought they, "will be rekindled in all our villages." Many of the inhabitants flocked to Zurich, and on their alarmed and agitated features, one might, in imagination, have seen reflected the flames that had just consumed the martyr.

These unhappy people found a powerful advocate in Zwingli. The reformer imagined that he had at last attained the object he never ceased to pursue—the free preaching of the gospel in Switzerland. To inflict a final blow would, in his idea, suffice to bring this enterprise to a favorable issue.

"Greedy pensioners," said Zwingli to the Zurichers, "profit by the ignorance of the mountaineers to stir up these simple souls against the friends of the gospel. Let us therefore be severe upon these haughty chiefs. The mildness of the lamb would only serve to render the wolf more ferocious. Let us propose to the Five Cantons to allow the free preaching of the Word of the Lord, to renounce their wicked alliances, and to punish the abettors of foreign service. As for the Mass, idols, rites, and superstitions, let no one be forced to abandon them. It is for the Word of God alone to scatter with its powerful breath all this idle dust. Be firm, noble lords, and despite certain black horses, as black at Zurich as they are at Lucerne, but whose malice will never succeed in overturning the chariot of reform, we shall clear this difficult pass, and arrive at the unity of Switzerland and at unity of faith." Thus Zwingli, while calling for force against political abuses, asked only liberty for the gospel, but he desired a prompt intervention, in order that this liberty might be secured to it. Oecolampadius thought the same. "It is not a time for delay," said he. "It is not a time for parsimony and pusillanimity! So long as the venom shall not be utterly removed from this adder in our bosoms we shall be exposed to the greatest dangers."

The council of Zurich, led away by the reformer, promised the bailiwicks to support religious liberty among them, and no sooner had they learned that Anthony ab Acker of Unterwalden was proceeding to Baden with an army, than they ordered five hundred men to set out for Bremgarten with four pieces of artillery. This was June 5, and on the same evening, the standard of Zurich waved over the convent of Mouri.

The war of religion had begun. The horn of the Waldstettes reechoed afar in the mountains. Men were arming in every direction, and messengers were sent off in haste to invoke the assistance of the Valais and of Austria. Three days later (Tuesday, June 8), six hundred Zurichers under the command of Jacques Werdmuller set out for Rapperschwyl and the district of Gaster. On the morrow, four thousand men repaired to Kappel under the command of the valiant Captain George Berguer, to whom Conrad Schmidt, pastor of Kussnacht, had been appointed chaplain. "We do not wish you to go to the war," said Burgomaster Roust to Zwingli, "for the pope, the Archduke Ferdinand, the Roman cantons, the bishops, the abbots, and the prelates hate you mortally. Stay with the council; we have need of you."

"No," replied Zwingli, who was unwilling to confide so important an enterprise to any one. "When my brethren expose their lives I will not remain quietly at home by my fireside. Besides, the army also requires a watchful eye that looks continually around it." Then, taking down his glittering halberd which he had carried (as they say) at Marignan and placing it on his shoulder, the reformer mounted his horse and set out with the army. The walls, towers, and battlements were covered with a crowd of old men, children, and women, among whom was Anna, Zwingli's wife.

Zurich had called for the aid of Berne. But that city, whose inhabitants showed little disposition for a religious war, and which besides was not pleased at seeing the increasing influence of Zurich, replied, "Since Zurich has begun the war without us, let her finish it in like manner." The evangelical states were disunited at the very moment of struggle.

The Roman Catholic cantons did not act thus. It was Zug that issued the first summons, and the men of Uri, of Schwytz, and of Unterwalden had immediately begun to march. On June 8, the great banner floated before the townhouse of Lucerne, and on the next day the army set out to the sound of the antique horns that Lucerne pretended to have received from the Emperor Charlemagne.

On June 10, the Zurichers, who were posted at Kappel, sent a herald at daybreak to Zug, who was commissioned, according to custom, to denounce to the Five Cantons the rupture of the alliance. Immediately Zug was filled with cries and alarm. This canton, the smallest in Switzerland, not having yet received all the confederate contingents, was not in a condition to defend itself. The people ran to and fro, sent off messengers, and hastily prepared for battle. The warriors fitted on their armor, the women shed tears, and the children shrieked.

Already the first division of the Zurich army, amounting to two thousand men, under the command of William Thoming and stationed near the frontier below Kappel, was preparing to march when they observed in the direction of Baar a horseman pressing the flanks of his steed and galloping up as fast as the mountain which he had to ascend would permit. It was Aebli, landamman of Glaris. "The Five Cantons are prepared," said he, as he arrived, "but I have prevailed upon them to halt, if you will do the same. For this reason I entreat my lords and the people of Zurich, for the love of God and the safety of the Confederation, to suspend their march at the present moment." As he uttered these words, the brave Helvetian shed tears. "In a few hours," continued he, "I shall be back again. I hope, with God's grace, to obtain an honorable peace and to prevent our cottages from being filled with widows and orphans."

Aebli was known to be an honorable man, friendly to the gospel, and opposed to foreign service. His words, therefore, moved the Zurich captains, who resolved to halt. Zwingli alone, motionless and uneasy, beheld in his friend's intervention the machinations of the adversary. Austria, occupied in repelling the Turks and unable to succor the Five Cantons, had exhorted them to peace. This, in Zwingli's opinion, was the cause of the propositions brought to them by the Landamman of Glaris. So at the moment Aebli turned round to return to Zug, Zwingli, approaching him, said with earnestness, "Landamman, you will render to God an account of all this. Our adversaries are caught in a sack, and hence they give you sweet words. By and by they will fall upon us unawares, and there will be none to deliver us."

Replied the landamman, "I have confidence in God that all will go well. Let each one do his best." And he departed.

The army, instead of advancing upon Zug, now began to erect tents along the edge of the forest and the brink of the torrent, a few paces from the sentinels of the Five Cantons; while Zwingli, seated in his tent, silent, sad, and in deep thought, anticipated some distressing news from hour to hour.

He had not long to wait. The deputies of the Zurich council came to give reality to his fears. Berne, maintaining the character that it had so often filled as representative of the federal policy, declared that if Zurich or the cantons would not make peace, they would find means to compel them. This state at the same time convoked a diet at Arau and sent five thousand men into the field under the command of Sebastian Diesbach. Zwingli was struck with consternation.

Aebli's message, supported by that of Berne, was sent back by the council to the army, for, according to the principles of the time, "wherever the banner waves, there is Zurich."

"Let us not be staggered," cried the reformer, ever decided and firm. "Our destiny depends upon our courage. Today they beg and entreat, and in a month, when we have laid down our arms, they will crush us. Let us stand firm in God. Before all things, let us be just. Peace will come after that." But Zwingli, transformed to a statesman, began to lose the influence which he had gained as a servant of God. Many could not understand him and asked if what they had heard was really the language of a minister of the Lord.

While Zurich was sending deputies to Arau, the two armies received reinforcements. The men of Thurgovia and St. Gall joined their banners to that of Zurich. The Valaisans and the men of St. Gothard united with the Roman Catholic cantons. The advanced posts were in sight of each other at Thun, Leematt, and Goldesbrunnen, on the delightful slopes of the Albis.

Never, perhaps, did Swiss cordiality shine forth brighter with its ancient luster. The soldiers called to one another in a friendly manner, and shook hands, styling themselves confederates and brothers. "We shall not fight," said they. "A storm is passing over our heads, but we will pray to God, and he will preserve us from every harm." Scarcity afflicted the army of the Five Cantons, while abundance reigned in the camp of Zurich. Some young famishing Waldstettes one day passed the outposts. The Zurichers made them prisoners, conducted them to the camp, and then sent them back laden with provisions.

At another time, some warriors of the Five Cantons, having placed a bucket filled with milk on the frontier line, cried out to the Zurichers that they had no bread. The latter came down immediately and cut their bread into the enemies' milk, upon which the soldiers of the two parties began with jokes to eat out of the same dish—some on this side, some on that. The Zurichers were delighted that, notwithstanding the prohibition of their priests, the Waldstettes ate with heretics. When one of the troop took a morsel that was on the side of his adversaries, the latter sportively struck him with their spoons and said, "Do not cross the frontier!" Thus did these good Helvetians make war upon one another, and hence it was that the Burgomaster Sturm of Strasbourg, one of the mediators, exclaimed, "You confederates are a singular people! When you are disunited, you live still in harmony with one another, and your ancient friendship never slumbers."

The most perfect order reigned in the camp of Zurich. Every day Zwingli, the commander Schmidt, Zink the abbot of Kappel, or some other minister preached among the soldiers. No oath or dispute was heard. All disorderly women were turned out of the camp; prayers were offered up before and after every meal; and each man obeyed his chiefs. There were no dice, no cards, no games calculated to excite quarrels; but psalms, hymns, national songs, bodily exercise, wrestling, or pitching the stone were the military recreations of the Zurichers. The spirit that animated the reformer had passed into the army.

The assembly at Arau, transported to Steinhausen in the neighborhood of the two camps, decreed that each army should hear the complaints of the opposite party. The reception of the deputies of the Five Cantons by the Zurichers was tolerably calm. It was not so in the other camp.

On June 15, fifty Zurichers, surrounded by a crowd of peasants, proceeded on horseback to the Waldstettes. The sound of the trumpet, the roll of the drum, and repeated salvos of artillery announced their arrival. Nearly twelve thousand men of the smaller cantons, in good order, with uplifted heads and arrogant looks, were under arms. Escher of Zurich spoke first, and many persons from the rural districts enumerated their grievances after him, which the Waldstettes thought exaggerated. "When have we ever refused you the federal right?" asked they.

"Yes, yes!" replied Funk, Zwingli's friend, "we know how you exercise it. That pastor [Keyser] appealed to it, and you referred him—to the executioner!"

"Funk, you would have done better to have held your tongue," said one of his friends. But the words had slipped out. A dreadful tumult suddenly arose. All the army of the Waldstettes was in agitation. The most prudent begged the Zurichers to retire promptly and protected their departure.

At length the treaty was concluded on June 26, 1529. Zwingli did not obtain all he desired. Instead of the free preaching of the Word of God, the treaty stipulated only liberty of conscience. It declared that the common bailiwicks should pronounce for or against the reform by a majority of votes. Without decreeing the abolition of foreign pensions, it was recommended to the Roman Catholic cantons to renounce the alliance formed with Austria. The Five Cantons were to pay the expenses of the war, Murner was to retract his insulting words, and an indemnity was secured to Keyser's family.

An incontrovertible success had just crowned the warlike demonstration of Zurich. The Five Cantons felt it. Gloomy, irritated, silently champing the bit that had been placed in their mouths, their chiefs could not decide upon giving up the deed of their alliance with Austria. Zurich immediately recalled her troops, the mediators redoubled their solicitations, and the Bernese exclaimed, "If you do not deliver up this document, we will ourselves go in procession and tear it from your archives." At last it was brought to Kappel on June 26, two hours after midnight. All the army was drawn out at eleven in the forenoon, and they began to read the treaty. The Zurichers looked with astonishment at its breadth and excessive length, and the nine seals which had been affixed, one of which was in gold. But scarcely had a few words been read, when Aebli, snatching the parchment, cried out, "Enough, enough!"

"Read it, read it!" said the Zurichers, "we desire to learn their treason!" But the bailiff of Glaris replied boldly, "I would rather be cut in a thousand pieces than permit it." Then dashing his knife into the parchment, he cut the treaty in pieces in the presence of Zwingli and the soldiers and threw the fragments to the secretary, who committed them to the flames.

The banners were immediately struck. The men of Unterwalden retired in anger. Those of Schywtz swore they would for ever preserve their ancient faith; while the troops of Zurich returned in triumph to their homes. But the most opposite thoughts agitated Zwingli's mind. "I hope," said he, doing violence to his feelings, "that we bring back an honorable peace to our dwellings. It was not to shed blood that we set out. God has once again shown the great ones of the earth that they can do nothing against us." Whenever he gave way to his natural disposition, a very different order of thoughts took possession of his mind. He was seen walking apart in deep dejection and anticipating the most gloomy future. In vain did the people surround him with joyful shouts. "This peace," said he, "which you consider a triumph, you will soon repent of, striking your breasts." It was at this time that, venting his sorrow, he composed, as he was descending the Albis, a celebrated hymn often repeated to the sound of music in the fields of Switzerland, among the burghers of the confederate cities, and even in the palaces of kings.

> Do Thou direct Thy chariot, Lord,
> And guide it at Thy will;
> Without Thy aid our strength is vain,
> And useless all our skill.
> Look down upon Thy saints brought low,
> And prostrate laid beneath the foe.

> Beloved Pastor, who hast saved
> Our souls from death and sin,
> Uplift Thy voice, awake Thy sheep
> That slumbering lie within
> Thy fold, and curb with Thy right hand,
> The rage of Satan's furious band.

> Send down Thy peace, and banish strife,
> Let bitterness depart;
> Revive the spirit of the past
> In every Switzer's heart:
> Then shall Thy church forever sing
> The praises of her heavenly King.

An edict, published in the name of the confederates, ordered the revival everywhere of the old friendship and brotherly concord, but decrees are powerless to work such miracles.

This treaty of peace was nevertheless favorable to the reform. Undoubtedly, it met with violent opposition in some places. The nuns of the vale of St. Catherine in Thurgovia, deserted by their priests and excited by some noblemen beyond the Rhine, who styled them in their letters, "Chivalrous women of the house of God," sang mass themselves and appointed one of their number preacher to the convent. Certain deputies from the Protestant cantons having had an interview with them, the abbess and three of the nuns secretly crossed the river by night, carrying with them the papers of the monastery and the ornaments of the church. But such isolated resistance as this was unavailing. Already in 1529 Zwingli was able to hold a synod in Thurgovia, which organized the church there, and he decreed that the property of the convents should be consecrated to the instruction of pious young men in sacred learning. Thus concord and peace seemed at last to be reestablished in the Confederation.

Chapter 23
"The Beginning of Sorrows"

Whenever a conqueror abandons himself to his triumph, in that very confidence he often finds destruction. Zurich and Zwingli were to exemplify this mournful lesson of history. Taking advantage of the national peace, they redoubled their exertions for the triumph of the gospel. This was a legitimate zeal, but it was not always wisely directed. To attain the unity of Switzerland by unity of faith was the object of the Zurichers. But they had forgotten that forcing a unity causes it to break into pieces and that freedom is the only medium in which contrary elements can be dissolved and a salutary union established. While Rome aims at unity by anathemas, imprisonment, and the stake, Christian truth demands unity through liberty.

Some persons, however, had at that time a glimpse of what might have saved Switzerland and the Reformation—the *autonomy,* self-government, of the church and its independence of political interests. Had they been wise enough to decline the secular power to secure the triumph of the gospel, it is probable that harmony might have been gradually established in the Helvetic cantons and that the gospel would have conquered by its divine strength. The power of the Word of God presented chances of success that were not afforded by pikes and muskets. The energy of faith, the influence of charity, would have proved a securer protection to Christians against the burning piles of the Waldstettes than diplomatists and men-at-arms.

But it was too late to tread in this path which would have prevented so many disasters. The Reformation had already entered upon the stormy ocean of politics with all her sails set, and terrible misfortunes were gathering over her. Zwingli's proud and piercing eyes, his harsh features, his bold step all proclaimed in him a resolute mind and the man of action. His prompt and penetrating looks were turned to the right and to the left, to the cabinets of kings and the councils of the people, while they should have been directed solely to God. As early as 1527, Zwingli, observing how all the powers were rising against the Reformation, had conceived the plan of a co-burghery or Christian state, which should unite all the friends of the Word of God in one holy and powerful league. This was so much the easier as Zwingli's reformation had won over Strasbourg, Augsburg, Ulm, Reutlingen, Lindau, Memmingen, and other towns of Upper Germany. Constance in December 1527, Berne in June 1528, St. Gall in November of the same year, Bienne in January 1529, Mulhausen in February, Basel in March, Schaffhausen in September, and Strasbourg in December entered into this alliance.

This political phase of Zwingli's character is in the eyes of some persons his highest claim to glory; we do not hesitate to acknowledge it as his greatest fault. The reformer, deserting the paths of the apostles, allowed himself to be led astray by the perverse example of Catholicism. The primitive church never opposed their persecutors except with the sentiments derived from the gospel of peace. Faith was the only sword by which it vanquished the mighty ones of the earth. Zwingli felt clearly that by entering into the ways of worldly politicians, he was leaving those of a minister of Christ. He therefore sought to justify himself. "No doubt, it is not by human strength," said he; "it is by the strength of God alone that the Word of the Lord should be upheld. But God often makes use of men as instruments to succor men. Let us therefore unite, and from the sources of the Rhine to Strasbourg let us form but one people and one alliance."

Zwingli played two parts at once—he was a reformer and a magistrate. But these are two characters that ought not to be united, no more than those of a minster and of a soldier. We will not altogether blame the soldiers and the magistrates; in forming leagues and drawing the sword, even for the sake of religion, they act according to their point of view, although it is not the same as ours. But we must decidedly blame the Christian minister who becomes a diplomatist or a general.

And in truth, from that hour Zwingli advanced more and more along the fatal path into which he was led by his character, his patriotism, and his early habits. Stunned by so many violent shocks, attacked by his enemies and by his brethren, he staggered and his head grew dizzy. From this period, the reformer almost entirely disappears, and we see in his place the politician, the great citizen, who, beholding a formidable coalition preparing its chains for every nation, stands up energetically against it.

The emperor had just formed a close alliance with the pope. In Zwingli's opinion, if his deadly schemes were not opposed, it would be all over with the Reformation, with religious and political liberty, and even with the Confederation itself. "The emperor," said he, "is stirring up friend against friend, enemy against enemy: and then he endeavors to raise out of this confusion the glory of the papacy, and, above all, his own power. . . . Then, when the confusion shall have become general, he will fall upon Germany, will offer himself as a mediator, and ensnare princes and cities by fine speeches, until he has them all under his feet."

Away, then, without delay! Should they wait until Charles V claimed the ancient castle of Hapsburg? The papacy and the empire, it was said at Zurich, are so confounded together that one cannot exist or perish without the other. Whoever rejects Catholicism should reject the empire, and whoever rejects the emperor should reject the pope.

It appears that Zwingli's thoughts went even beyond a simple resistance. When once the gospel had ceased to be his principal study, there was nothing that could arrest him. "A single individual," said he, "must not take it into his head to dethrone a tyrant. This would be a revolt, and the kingdom of God commands peace, righteousness, and joy. But if a whole people with common accord, or if the majority at least, rejects him, without committing any excess, it is God Himself who acts." Charles V was at that time a tyrant in Zwingli's eyes, and the reformer hoped that Europe, awakening at length from its long slumber, would be the hand of God to hurl the emperor from his throne.

The Five Cantons accelerated with their might those fatal days of anger and of vengeance. They were irritated at the progress of the gospel throughout the Confederation, while the

PROGENIES·DIVVM·QVINTVS·SIC·CAROLVS·ILLE
IMPERII·CAESAR·LVMINA·ET·ORA·TVLIT.
AET   SVAE   X̄X̄XI
ANN · M̄ D̄ · X̄X̄XI

Charles V, emperor of the Holy Roman Empire (modern Germany), was a powerful leader of the Catholic forces in Europe against the Protestant Reformation.

peace they had signed became every day more irksome to them. "We shall have no repose," said they, "until we have broken these bonds and regained our former liberty."

A general diet was convoked at Baden for January 8, 1531. The Five Cantons then declared that if justice was not done to their grievances, particularly with respect to the abbey of St. Gall, they would no more appear in diet. "Confederates of Glaris, Schaffhausen, Friburg, Soleure, and Appenzell," cried they, "aid us in making our ancient alliances respected, or we will ourselves contrive the means of checking this guilty violence, and may the Holy Trinity assist us in this work!"

They did not confine themselves to threats. The treaty of peace had expressly forbidden all insulting language, "for fear," it said, "that by insults and calumnies, discord should again be excited, and greater troubles than the former should arise." Thus was concealed in the treaty itself the spark whence the conflagration was to proceed. In fact, to restrain the rude tongues of the Waldstettes was impossible.

Two Zurichers, the aged prior Ravensbühler and the pensioner Gaspard Godli, who had been compelled to renounce, the one his convent, and the other his pension, especially aroused the anger of the people against their native city. They used to say everywhere in these valleys, and with impunity, that the Zurichers were heretics; that there was not one of them who did not indulge in unnatural sins, and who was not a robber at the very least; that Zwingli was a thief, a murderer, and an arch-heretic; and that, on one occasion at Paris (where Zwingli had never been), he had committed a horrible offence. "I shall have no rest," said a pensioner, "until I have thrust my sword up to the hilt in the heart of this impious wretch."

They went still further. Passing from words to deeds, the Five Cantons persecuted the poor people among them who loved the Word of God, flung them into prison, imposed fines upon them, brutally tormented them, and mercilessly expelled them from their country. The people of Schwytz did even worse. Not fearing to announce their sinister designs, they appeared at a landsgemeinde wearing pine-branches in their hats, in sign of war, and no one opposed them. "The Abbot of St. Gall," said they, "is a prince of the empire and holds his investiture from the emperor. Do they imagine that Charles V will not avenge him?" Secret councils were continually held in one place or another. New alliances were sought with the Valais, the pope, and the emperor.

At the sight of these alarming manifestations, the evangelical cities were in commotion. They first assembled at Basel in February 1531, then at Zurich in March. "What is to be done?" said the deputies from Zurich, after setting forth their grievances. "How can we punish these infamous calumnies, and force these threatening arms to fall?"

"We understand," replied Berne, "that you would have recourse to violence, but think of these secret and formidable alliances that are forming with the pope, the emperor, the King of France, with so many princes, in a word with all the priests' party, to accelerate our ruin. Think on the innocence of so many pious souls in the Five Cantons, who deplore these acts. Think how easy it is to begin a war, but that no one can tell when it will end."

"Let us therefore send a deputation to the Five Cantons," continued Berne. "Let us call upon them to punish these infamous calumnies in accordance with the treaty, and if they refuse, let us break off all intercourse with them."

"What will be the use of this mission?" asked Basel. "Do we not know the brutality of this people? And is it not to be feared that the rough treatment to which our deputies will be exposed may make the matter worse? Let us rather convoke a general diet." Schaffhausen and St. Gall having concurred in this opinion, Berne summoned a diet at Baden for April 10, at which deputies from all the cantons were assembled.

Many of the principal men among the Waldstettes disapproved of the violence of the retired soldiers and of the monks. They saw that these continually repeated insults would injure their cause. "The insults of which you complain," said they to the diet, "afflict us no less than you. We shall know how to punish them, and we have already done so. But there are violent men on both sides. The other day a man of Basel met on the high road a person who was coming from Berne and learned that he was going to Lucerne. "To go from Berne to Lucerne," exclaimed he, "is passing from a father to an arrant knave!" The mediating cantons invited the two parties to banish every cause of discord.

But the war of the Chatelain of Musso having then broken out, Zwingli and Zurich, who saw in it the first act of a vast conspiracy destined to stifle the reform in every place, called their allies together. "We must waver no longer," said Zwingli. "The rupture of the alliance on the part of the Five Cantons and the unheard-of insults with which they load us impose upon us the obligation of marching against our enemies before the emperor, who is still detained by the Turks, shall have expelled the landgrave, seized upon Strasbourg, and subjugated even ourselves."

The warlike tone of Zurich alarmed its confederates. Basel proposed a summons, and then, in case of refusal, the rupture of the alliance. Schaffhausen and St. Gall were frightened even at this step. "The mountaineers, so proud, indomitable, and exasperated," said they, "will accept with joy the dissolution of the Confederation, and then shall we be more advanced?" Such was the posture of affairs, when, to the great astonishment of all, deputies from Uri and Schwytz made their appearance. They were coldly received. The cup of honor was not offered to them, and they had to walk, according to their own account, in the midst of the insulting cries of the people. They unsuccessfully endeavored to excuse their conduct. "We have long been waiting," was the cold reply of the diet, "to see your actions and your words agree." The men of Schwytz and of Uri returned in sadness to their homes, and the assembly broke up, full of sorrow and distress.

Zwingli beheld with pain the deputies of the evangelical towns separating without having come to any decision. He no longer desired only a reformation of the church. He wished for a transformation in the confederacy, and it was this latter reform that he now was preaching from the pulpit. He was not the only person who desired it. For a long time the inhabitants of the most populous and powerful towns of Switzerland had complained that the Waldstettes, whose contingent of men and money was much below theirs, had an equal share in the deliberations of the diet and in the fruits of their victories. The Five Cantons, by means of their adherents, had the majority. Now Zwingli thought that the reins of Switzerland should be placed in the hands of the great cities, and, above all, in those of the powerful cantons of Berne and Zurich.

And indeed the animated words of the patriot reformer passed from the church where they had been delivered into the councils and the halls of the guilds, into the streets and the fields. The burning words that fell from this man's lips kindled the hearts of his fellow citizens. The electric spark, escaping with noise and commotion, was felt even in the most distant cottage. The ancient traditions of wisdom and prudence seemed forgotten. Public opinion declared itself energetically.

On April 29 and 30, a number of horsemen rode hastily out of Zurich. They were envoys from the council, commissioned to remind all the allied cities of the encroachment of the Five Cantons and to call for a prompt and definitive decision. Reaching their several destinations, the messengers recapitulated the grievances. "Take care," said they in conclusion, "great dangers are impending over all of us. The emperor and King Ferdinand are making vast preparations. They are about to enter Switzerland with large sums of money, and with a numerous army."

Zurich joined actions to words. This state, being resolved to make every exertion to establish the free preaching of the gospel in those bailiwicks where it shared the sovereignty with the Roman Catholic cantons, desired to interfere by force wherever negotiations could not prevail. The federal rights, it must be confessed, were trampled under foot at St. Gall, in Thurgovia, and in the Rheinthal, and Zurich substituted arbitrary decisions in their place that excited the indignation of the Waldstettes to the highest degree. Thus the number of enemies to the reform kept increasing. The tone of the Five Cantons became daily more threatening, and the inhabitants of the canton of Zurich, whom their business called into the mountains, were loaded with insults, and sometimes badly treated. These violent proceedings excited in turn the anger of the reformed cantons.

Zwingli traversed Thurgovia, St. Gall, and the Tockenburg, everywhere organizing synods, taking part in their proceedings, and preaching before excited and enthusiastic crowds. In all parts he met with confidence and respect. At St. Gall, an immense crowd assembled under his windows, and a concert of voices and instruments expressed the public gratitude in harmonious songs. "Let us not abandon ourselves," he repeated continually, "and all will go well." It was resolved that a meeting should be held at Arau on May 12 to deliberate on a posture of affairs that daily became more critical. This meeting was to be the beginning of sorrows.

Chapter 24
Between War and Peace

Zwingli's scheme with regard to the establishment of a new Helvetian constitution did not prevail in the diet of Arau. Perhaps it was thought better to see the result of the crisis. Perhaps a more Christian, a more federal view—the hope of procuring the unity of Switzerland by unity of faith—occupied men's minds more than the preeminence of the cities. In truth, if a certain number of cantons remained with the pope, the unity of the Confederation would be destroyed, and it might be forever. But if all the Confederation was brought over to the same faith, the ancient Helvetic unity would be established on the strongest and surest foundation. Now was the time for acting—or never; and there must be no fear of employing a violent remedy to restore the whole body to health.

Nevertheless, the allies shrank back at the thought of restoring religious liberty or political unity by means of arms. To escape from the difficulties in which the Confederation was placed, they sought a middle course between war and peace. "There is no doubt," said the deputies from Berne, "that the behavior of the cantons with regard to the Word of God fully authorizes an armed intervention. But the perils that threaten us on the side of Italy and the empire, the danger of arousing the lion from his slumber, the general want and misery that afflict our people, the rich harvests that will soon cover our fields and which the war would infallibly destroy, the great number of pious men among the Waldstettes, and whose innocent blood would flow along with that of the guilty—all these motives enjoin us to leave the sword in the scabbard. Let us rather close our markets against the Five Cantons. Let us refuse them corn, salt, wine, steel, and iron. We shall thus impart authority to the friends of peace among them, and innocent blood will be spared." The meeting separated forthwith to carry this intermediate proposition to the different evangelical cantons, and on May 15 again assembled at Zurich.

Convinced that the means apparently the most violent were nevertheless both the surest and the most humane, Zurich resisted the Bernese proposition with all its might. "By accepting this proposition," said they, "we sacrifice the advantages that we now possess, and we give the Five Cantons time to arm themselves and to fall upon us first. Let us take care that the emperor does not then assail us on one side, while our ancient confederates attack us on the other. A just war is not in opposition to the Word of God, but this is contrary to it—taking the bread from the mouths of the innocent as well as the guilty, straitening by hunger the sick, the aged, pregnant women, children, and all who are deeply afflicted by the injustice of the Waldstettes. We should beware of exciting by this means the anger of the poor and transforming into enemies many who at the present time are our friends and our brothers!"

We must acknowledge that this language, which was Zwingli's, contained much truth. But the other cantons, and Berne in particular, were immovable. "When we have once shed the blood of our brothers," said they, "we shall never be able to restore life to those who have lost it, while, from the moment the Waldstettes have given us satisfaction, we shall be able to put an end to all these severe measures. We are resolved not to begin the war." There were no means of running counter to such a declaration. The Zurichers consented to refuse supplies to the Waldstettes, but it was with hearts full of anguish, as if they had foreseen all that this deplorable measure would cost them.

It was agreed that the severe step that was now about to be taken should not be suspended except by common consent, and that, as it would create great exasperation, each one should hold himself prepared to repel the attacks of the enemy. Zurich and Berne were commissioned to notify this determination to the Five Cantons. Zurich, discharging its task with promptitude, immediately forwarded an order to every bailiwick to suspend all communication with the Waldstettes, commanding them at the same time to abstain from ill-usage and hostile language. Thus the Reformation, becoming imprudently mixed up with political combinations, marched from fault to fault. It pretended to preach the gospel to the poor and was now about to refuse them bread.

On the Sunday following, the resolution was published from the pulpits. Zwingli walked toward his, where an immense crowd was waiting for him. If at this moment the true character of a minister of the gospel had awakened within him—if Zwingli with his powerful voice had called on the people to humiliation before God, to forgiveness of trespasses, and to prayer, safety might yet have dawned on brokenhearted Switzerland. But it was not so. More and more, the Christian disappeared in the reformer, and the citizen alone remained. He saw clearly that every delay could ruin Zurich, and after having made his way through the congregation and closed the book of the Prince of Peace, he hesitated not to attack the resolution which he had just communicated to the people and to preach war on the very festival of the Holy Ghost.

"He who fears not to call his adversary a criminal," said he in his usual forcible language, "must be ready to follow the word with a blow. If he does not strike, he will be stricken. Men of Zurich! You deny food to the Five Cantons, as to evildoers. Well! let the blow follow the threat, rather than reduce poor innocent creatures to starvation. If, by not taking the offensive, you appear to believe that there is not sufficient reason for punishing the Waldstettes and yet you refuse them food and drink, you will force them by this line of conduct to take up arms, to raise their hands, and to inflict punishment upon you. This is the fate that awaits you."

These words of the eloquent reformer moved the whole assembly. Zwingli so influenced and misled all the people that there were few souls Christian enough to feel how strange it was, that on the very day when they were celebrating the outpouring of the Spirit of peace and love upon the Christian church (Whitsunday), the mouth of a minister of God should utter a provocation to war. They looked at this sermon only in a political point of view. "It is a seditious discourse; it is an excitement to civil war!" said some. "No," replied others, "it is the language that the safety of the state requires!" All Zurich was agitated. "Zurich has too much fire," said Berne. "Berne has too much cunning," replied Zurich. Zwingli's gloomy prophecy was too soon to be fulfilled.

No sooner had the reformed cantons communicated this pitiless decree to the Waldstettes than they hastened its execution, and Zurich showed the greatest strictness respecting it. Not only the markets of Zurich and of Berne but also those of the free bailiwicks of St. Gall, of the Tockenburg, of the district of Sargans and of the valley of the Rhine, a country partly under the sovereignty of the Waldstettes, were shut against the Five Cantons. A formidable power had suddenly encompassed with barrenness, famine, and death the noble founders of Helvetian liberty.

Their last hope was in Wesen and the Gastal. Neither Berne nor Zurich had anything to do there. Schwytz and Glaris alone ruled over them, but the power of their enemies had penetrated everywhere. A majority of thirteen votes had declared in favor of Zurich at the landsgemeinde of Glaris, and Glaris closed the gates of Wesen and of the Gastal against Schwytz. In vain did Berne itself cry out, "How can you compel subjects to refuse supplies to their lords?" In vain did Schwytz raise its voice in indignation. Zurich immediately sent gunpowder and bullets to Wesen. It was upon Zurich, therefore, that fell all the odium of a measure which that city had at first so earnestly combated.

At Arau, at Bremgarten, at Mellingen, in the free bailiwicks were several carriages laden with provisions for the Waldstettes. They were stopped, unloaded, and upset. With them, barricades were erected on the roads leading to Lucerne, Schwytz, and Zug. Already a year of dearth had made provisions scarce in the Five Cantons. Already had a frightful epidemic, the Sweating Sickness, scattered everywhere despondency and death. But now the evil increased, and the poor inhabitants of these mountains beheld unheard-of calamities approach with hasty steps. No more bread for their children—no more wine to revive their exhausted strength—no more salt for their flocks and herds! Everything failed them that man requires for subsistence. One could not see such things and be a man, without feeling his heart wrung.

In the confederate cities, and out of Switzerland, numerous voices were raised against this implacable measure. What good can result from it? Did not St. Paul write to the Romans: "If thine enemy hunger, feed him; if he thirst, give him drink: for in so doing thou shalt heap coals of fire on his head"? And when the magistrates wished to convince certain refractory communes of the utility of the measure, they cried, "We desire no religious war. If the Waldstettes will not believe in God, let them stick to the Devil!"

But it was especially in the Five Cantons that earnest complaints were heard. The most pacific individuals, and even the secret partisans of the reform, seeing famine invade their habitations, felt the deepest indignation. The enemies of Zurich skillfully took advantage of this disposition. They fostered these murmurs, and soon the cry of anger and distress reechoed from all the mountains. In vain did Berne represent to the Waldstettes that it is more cruel to refuse men the nourishment of the soul than to cut off that of the body. "God," replied these mountaineers in their despair, "causes the fruits of the earth to grow freely for all men!" They were not content with groaning in their cottages and venting their indignation in the councils. They filled all Switzerland with complaints and menaces. "They wish to employ famine to tear us from our ancient faith. They wish to deprive our wives and our children bread, that they may take from us the liberty we derive from our forefathers. When did such things ever take place in the bosom of the Confederation? Did we not see, in the last war, the confederates with arms in their hands and who were ready to draw the sword, eating together from the same dish? They tear in pieces old friendships—they trample our ancient manners under foot—they violate treaties—they break alliances. . . . We invoke the charters of our ancestors. Help! . . . Wise men of our people, give us your advice, and all you who know how to handle the sling and the sword, come and maintain with us the sacred possessions, for which our fathers, delivered from the yoke of the stranger, united their arms and their hearts."

At the same time the Five Cantons sent into Alsace, Brisgau, and Swabia to obtain salt, wine, and bread, but the administration of the cities was implacable. The orders were everywhere given and everywhere strictly executed. Zurich and the other allied cantons intercepted all communication and sent back to Germany the supplies that had been forwarded to their brethren. The Five Cantons were like a vast fortress, all the issues from which are closely guarded by watchful sentinels. The afflicted Waldstettes, on beholding themselves alone with famine between their lakes and their mountains, had recourse to the observances of their worship. All sports, dances, and every kind of amusement were interdicted. Prayers were directed to be offered up, and long processions covered the roads of Einsidlen and other resorts of pilgrims. They assumed the belt, and staff, and arms of the brotherhood to which they each belonged. Each man carried a chaplet in his hands and repeated paternosters. The mountains and the valleys reechoed with their plaintive hymns.

But the Waldstettes did still more. They grasped their swords. They sharpened the points of their halberds. They brandished their weapons in the direction of Zurich and of Berne and exclaimed with rage, "They block up their roads, but we will open them with our right arms!" No one replied to this cry of despair. But there is a just Judge in heaven to whom vengeance belongs, and who would soon reply in a terrible manner, by punishing those misguided persons, who, forgetful of Christian mercy and making an impious mixture of political and religious matters, pretended to secure the triumph of the gospel by famine and by armed men.

Some attempts were made to arrange matters, but these very efforts proved a great humiliation for Switzerland and for the reform. It was not the ministers of the gospel, it was France—more than once an occasion of discord to Switzerland—that offered to restore peace. Every proceeding calculated to increase its influence among the cantons was of service to its policy. On May 14, Maigret and Dangertin (the latter of whom had received the gospel truth, and consequently did not dare return to France), after some allusions to the spirit which Zurich had shown in this affair—a spirit little in accordance with the gospel—said to the council, "The king our master has sent you two gentlemen to consult on the means of preserving concord among you. If war and tumult invade Switzerland, all the society of the Helvetians will be destroyed, and whichever party is the conqueror, he will be as much ruined as the other." Zurich having replied that if the Five Cantons would allow the free preaching of the Word of God, the reconciliation would be easy, the French secretly sounded the Waldstettes, whose answer was, "We will never permit the preaching of the Word of God as the people of Zurich understand it."

These more or less interested exertions of the foreigners having failed, a general diet became the only chance of safety that remained for Switzerland. One was accordingly convoked at Bremgarten. It was opened in presence of deputies from France, from the Duke of Milan, from the Countess of Neufchatel, from the Grisons, Valais, Thurgovia, and the district of Sargans; it met on five different occasions, on June 14 and 20, on July 9, and on August 10 and 23. The chronicler Bullinger, who was pastor of Bremgarten, delivered an oration at the opening, in which he earnestly exhorted the confederates to union and peace.

A gleam of hope for a moment cheered Switzerland. The blockade had become less strict. Friendship and good neighborhood had prevailed in many places over the decrees of the state. Unusual roads had been opened across the wildest mountains to convey supplies to the Waldstettes. Provisions were concealed in bales of merchandise, and while Lucerne imprisoned and tortured its own citizens who were found with the pamphlets of the Zurichers, Berne punished but slightly the peasants who had been discovered bearing food for Unterwalden and Lucerne. Glaris shut its eyes on the frequent violation of its orders. The voice of charity, that had been momentarily stifled, pleaded with fresh energy the cause of their confederates before the reformed cantons.

But the Five Cantons were inflexible. "We will not listen to any proposition before the raising of the blockade," said they. "We will not raise it," replied Berne and Zurich, "before the gospel is allowed to be freely preached, not only in the common bailiwicks, but also in the Five Cantons." This was undoubtedly going too far, even according to the natural law and the principles of the Confederation. The councils of Zurich might consider it their duty to have recourse to war for maintaining liberty of conscience in the common bailiwicks. But it was unjust; it was a usurpation to constrain the Five Cantons in a matter that concerned their own territory. Nevertheless the mediators succeeded, not without much trouble, in drawing up a plan of conciliation that seemed to harmonize with the wishes of both parties. The conference was broken up, and this project was hastily transmitted to the different states for their ratification.

The diet met a few days after, but the Five Cantons persisted in their demand, without yielding in any one point. In vain did Zurich and Berne represent to them that, by persecuting the reformed, the cantons violated the treaty of peace. In vain did the mediators exhaust their strength in warnings and entreaties. The Waldstettes at last broke up the third conference by declaring that, far from opposing the evangelical truth, they would maintain it, as it had been taught by the Redeemer, by His holy apostles, by the four doctors, and by their holy mother, the church—a declaration that seemed a bitter irony to the deputies from Zurich and Berne. Nevertheless Berne, turning toward Zurich as they were separating, observed, "Beware of too much violence, even should they attack you!"

This exhortation was unnecessary. The strength of Zurich had passed away. The first appearance of the Reformation and of the reformers had been greeted with joy. The people, who groaned under a twofold slavery, believed they saw the dawn of liberty. But their minds, abandoned for ages to superstition and ignorance, being unable immediately to realize the hopes they had conceived, a spirit of discontent soon spread among the masses. The change by which Zwingli, ceasing to be a man of the gospel, became the man of the state, took away from the people the enthusiasm necessary to resist the terrible attacks they would have to sustain.

The enemies of the reform had a fair chance against it, as soon as its friends abandoned the position that gave them strength. Besides, Christians could not have recourse to famine and to war to secure the triumph of the gospel without their consciences becoming troubled. The Zurichers "walked not in the Spirit, but in the flesh; now, the works of the flesh are hatred, variance, emulations, wrath, strife, seditions." The danger without was increasing, while within, hope, union, and courage were far from being augmented. Men saw on the contrary the gradual disappearance of that harmony and lively faith which had been the strength of the reform. The Reformation had grasped the sword, and that very sword pierced its heart.

Occasions of discord were multiplied in Zurich. By the advice of Zwingli, the number of nobles was diminished in the two councils because of their opposition to the gospel, and this measure spread discontent among the most honorable families of the canton. The millers and bakers were placed under certain regulations which the dearth rendered necessary, and a great part of the townspeople attributed this proceeding to the sermons of the reformer and became irritated against him. Rodolph Lavater, bailiff of Kibourg, was appointed captain-general, and the officers who were of longer standing than he were offended. Many who had been formerly the most distinguished by their zeal for the reform now openly opposed the cause they had supported. The ardor with which the ministers of peace demanded war spread in every quarter a smothered dissatisfaction, and many persons gave vent to their indignation. This unnatural confusion of church and state, which had corrupted Christianity after the age of Constantine, was hurrying on the ruin of the Reformation. The majority of the Great Council, ever ready to adopt important and salutary resolutions, was destroyed. The old magistrates, who were still at the head of affairs, allowed themselves to be carried away by feelings of jealousy against men whose nonofficial influence prevailed over theirs. All those who hated the doctrine of the gospel, whether from love of the world or from love to the pope, boldly raised their heads in Zurich. The partisans of the monks, the friends of foreign service, the malcontents of every class, coalesced in pointing out Zwingli as the author of all the sufferings of the people.

Zwingli was heartbroken. He saw that Zurich and the Reformation were hastening to their ruin, and he could not check them. How could he do so, since, without suspecting it, he had been the principal accomplice in these disasters? There was but one means of safety for Zurich and for Zwingli. He should have retired from the political stage and fallen back on that kingdom which is not of this world. He should, like Moses, have kept his hands and his heart night and day raised toward heaven and energetically preached repentance, faith, and peace. But religious and political matters were united in the mind of this great man by such old and dear ties that it was impossible for him to distinguish their line of separation. This confusion had become his dominant idea. The Christian and the citizen were for him one and the same character, and hence it resulted that all resources of the state—even cannons—were to be placed at the service of the Truth. When one peculiar idea thus seizes upon a man, we see a false conscience formed within him, which approves of many things condemned by the Word of the Lord.

This was now Zwingli's condition. War appeared to him legitimate and desirable, and if that was refused, he had only to withdraw from public life. He was for everything or nothing. He therefore on July 26 appeared before the Great Council. "For eleven years," said he, "I have been preaching the gospel among you and have warned you faithfully and paternally of the woes that are hanging over you, but no attention has been paid to my words. The friends of foreign alliances, the enemies of the gospel, are elected to the council, and while you refuse to follow my advice, I am made responsible for every misfortune. I cannot accept such a position, and I ask for my dismission."

The council shuddered as they heard these words. All the old feelings of respect which they had so long entertained for Zwingli were revived. To lose him now was to ruin Zurich. The burgomaster and the other magistrates received orders to persuade him to recall his fatal resolution. The conference took place on the same day. Zwingli asked time for consideration. For three days and three nights he sought the road that he should follow. He groaned and cried to the Lord. He would have put away the cup of bitterness that was presented to his soul, but could not gather up the resolution. At length the sacrifice was accomplished, and the victim was placed shuddering upon the altar. Three days after the first conference, Zwingli reappeared in the council. "I will stay with you," said he, "and I will labor for the public safety—until death!"

From this moment he displayed new zeal. On the one hand, he endeavored to revive harmony and courage in Zurich. On the other, he set about arousing and exciting the allied cities to increase and concentrate all the forces of the Reformation. He had thought that by consenting to remain at the head of affairs, he would recover all his ancient influence. But he was deceived. The people desired to see him there, and yet they would not follow him. The Zurichers daily became more and more indisposed toward the war which they had at first demanded and identified themselves with the passive system of Berne. Zwingli remained for some time stupefied and motionless before this inert mass, which his most vigorous exertions could not move. But soon discovering in every quarter of the horizon the prophetic signs, precursors of the storm about to burst upon the ship of which he was the pilot, he uttered cries of anguish and showed the signal of distress.

"I see," exclaimed he one day to the people from the pulpit, whither he had gone to give utterance to his gloomy forebodings, "that the most faithful warnings cannot save you. You will not punish the pensioners of the foreigner. . . . They have too firm a support among us! A chain is prepared—behold it entire—it unrolls link after link. Soon will they bind me to it, and more than one pious Zuricher with me. . . . It is against me they are enraged! I am ready; I submit to the Lord's will. But these people shall never be my masters. . . . As for thee, O Zurich, they will give thee thy reward. They will strike thee on the head. Thou willest it. Thou refusest to punish them. Well! it is they who will punish thee. But God will not the less preserve his Word, and their haughtiness shall come to an end." Such was Zwingli's cry of agony, but the hearts of the Zurichers were so hardened that the sharpest arrows of the reformer could not pierce them, and they fell at his feet blunted and useless.

But events were pressing on, and they justified all his fears. The Five Cantons had rejected every proposition that had been made to them. "Why do you talk of punishing a few wrongs?" they had replied to the mediators. "It is a question of quite another kind. Do you not require that we should receive back among us the heretics whom we have banished and tolerate no other priests than those who preach conformable to the Word of God? We know what that means. No, we will not abandon the religion of our fathers, and if we must see our wives and our children deprived of food, our hands will know how to conquer what is refused to us. To that we pledge our bodies—our goods—our lives." It was with this threatening language that the deputies quitted the diet of Bremgarten. They had proudly shaken the folds of their mantles, and war had fallen from them.

The terror was general, and the alarmed citizens beheld everywhere frightful portents, terrific signs, apparently foreboding the most horrible events. In the western quarter of the heavens there appeared a frightful comet (Halley's comet), whose immense train of a pale yellow color turned toward the south. At the time of its setting, this apparition shone in the sky like the fire of a furnace. One night—on August 15 as it would appear—Zwingli and George Müller, former abbot of Wettingen, being together in the cemetery of the cathedral, both fixed their eyes upon this terrific meteor. "This ominous globe," said Zwingli, "is come to light the path that leads to my grave. It will be at the cost of my life and of many good men with me. Although I am rather shortsighted, I foresee great calamities in the future. The truth and the church will mourn, but Christ will never forsake us."

Chapter 25
An Avalanche Impending

The Five Cantons, assembled in diet at Lucerne, appeared full of determination, and war was decided upon. "We will call upon the cities to respect our alliances," said they, "and if they refuse, we will enter the common bailiwicks by force to procure provisions, and unite our banners in Zug to attack the enemy." The Waldstettes were not alone. The nuncio, being solicited by his Lucerne friends, had required that auxiliary troops, paid by the pope, should be put in motion toward Switzerland, and he announced their near arrival.

These resolutions carried terror into Switzerland. The mediating cantons met again at Arau and drew up a plan that should leave the religious question just as it had been settled by the treaty of 1529. Deputies immediately bore these propositions to the different councils. Lucerne haughtily rejected them. "Tell those who sent you," was the reply, "that we do not acknowledge them as our schoolmasters. We would rather die than yield the least thing to the prejudice of our faith."

The mediators returned to Arau, trembling and discouraged. This useless attempt increased the disagreement among the reformed and gave the Waldstettes still greater confidence. Zurich, so decided for the reception of the gospel, now became daily more irresolute. The members of the council distrusted each other. The people felt no interest in this war, and Zwingli, notwithstanding his unshaken faith in the justice of his cause, had no hope for the struggle that was about to take place. Berne, on its side, did not cease to entreat Zurich to avoid precipitation. "Do not let us expose ourselves to the reproach of too much haste, as in 1529," was the general remark in Zurich. "We have sure friends in the midst of the Waldstettes. Let us wait until they announce to us, as they have promised, some real danger."

It was soon believed that these temporizers were right. In fact the alarming news ceased. That constant rumor of war, which incessantly came from the Waldstettes, discontinued. There were no more alarms! No more fears! Deceitful omen! Over the mountains and valleys of Switzerland hung a gloomy and mysterious silence, the forerunner of the tempest.

While those at Zurich were sleeping, the Waldstettes were preparing to conquer their rights by force of arms. The chiefs, closely united to each other by common interests and dangers, found a powerful support in the indignation of the people. In a diet of the Five Cantons, held at Brunnen on the banks of the Lake of Lucerne, opposite Grutli, the alliances of the Confederation were read; and the deputies, having been summoned to declare by their votes whether they thought the war just and lawful, all raised their hands with a shudder. Immediately the Waldstettes had prepared their attack with the profoundest mystery. All the passes had been guarded. All communication between Zurich and the Five Cantons had been rendered impossible. The friends upon whom the Zurichers had reckoned on the banks of the Lakes Lucerne and Zug, and who had promised them intelligence, were like prisoners in their mountains. The terrible avalanche was about to slip from the icy summits of the mountain and to roll into the valleys, even to the gates of Zurich, overthrowing everything in its passage, without the least forewarning of its fall.

The mediators had returned, discouraged, to their cantons. A spirit of imprudence and of error—sad forerunner of the fall of republics as well as of kings—had spread over the whole city of Zurich. The council had at first given orders to call out the militia. Then, deceived by the silence of the Waldstettes, it had imprudently revoked the decree, and Lavater, the commander of the army, had retired in discontent to Rybourg and indignantly thrown far from him that sword which they had commanded him to leave in the scabbard.

Whatever were the exertions of the Waldstettes, they could not entirely stifle the rumor of war which from chalet to chalet called all their citizens to arms. God permitted a cry of alarm—a single one, it is true—to resound in the ears of the people of Zurich. On October 4, a little boy, who knew not what he was doing, succeeded in crossing the frontier of Zug and presented himself with two loaves at the gate of the reformed monastery of Kappel, situated in the farthest limits of the cantons of Zurich. He was led to the abbot, to whom the child gave the loaves without saying a word.

The superior, with whom there chanced to be at that time a councilor from Zurich (Henry Peyer, sent by his government) turned pale at the sight. "If the Five Cantons intend entering by force of arms into the free bailiwicks," had said these two Zurichers to one of their friends of Zug, "you will send your son to us with one loaf. But you will give him two if they are marching at once upon the bailiwicks and upon Zurich." The abbot and the councilor wrote with all speed to Zurich. "Be upon your guard! Take up arms," said they, but no credit was attached to this information. The council was at that time occupied in taking measures to prevent the supplies that had arrived from Alsace from entering the cantons. Zwingli himself, who had never ceased to announce war, did not believe it. "These pensioners are really clever fellows," said the reformer. "Their preparations may be after all nothing but a French maneuver."

He was deceived. Four days were to accomplish the ruin of Zurich.

On Sunday, October 8, a messenger appeared at Zurich and demanded, in the name of the Five Cantons, letters of perpetual alliance. The majority saw in this step nothing but a trick, but Zwingli began to discern the thunderbolt in the black cloud that was drawing near. He was in the pulpit. It was the last time he was destined to appear in it.

At the same moment a messenger arrived in haste from Mulinen, commander of the Knights-Hospitallers of St. John at Hitzkylch. "On Friday, October 6," said he to the councils of Zurich, "the people of Lucerne planted their banner in the Great Square. Two men that I sent to Lucerne have been thrown into prison. Tomorrow morning, Monday, October 9, the Five Cantons will enter the bailiwicks. Already the country people, frightened and fugitive, are running to us in crowds."

"It is an idle story," said the councils. Nevertheless, they recalled commander in chief Lavater, who sent off a trusty man (nephew of James Winckler) with orders to repair to Kappel, and if possible, as far as Zug to reconnoiter the arrangements of the cantons.

The Waldstettes were in reality assembling round the banner of Lucerne. The people of this canton; the men of Schwytz, Uri, Zug, and Unterwalden; refugees from Zurich and Berne; and a few Italians, formed the main body of the army, which had been raised to invade the free bailiwicks. Two manifestos were published—one addressed to the cantons, the other to foreign princes and nations.

The Five Cantons energetically set forth the attacks made upon the treaties, the discord sown throughout the Confederation, and finally the refusal to sell them provisions—a refusal whose only aim was (according to them) to excite the people against the magistrates and to establish the reform by force. "It is not true," added they, "that—as they are continually crying out—we oppose the preaching of the truth and the reading of the Bible. As obedient members of the church, we desire to receive all that our holy mother receives. But we reject the books and the innovations of Zwingli and his companions."

Hardly had the messengers charged with these manifestos departed before the first division of the army began to march, and they arrived in the evening in the free bailiwicks. The soldiers, having entered the deserted churches and seen the images of the saints removed and the altars broken, had their anger kindled. They spread like a torrent over the whole country, pillaged everything they met with, and were particularly enraged against the houses of the pastors, where they destroyed the furniture with oaths and maledictions. At the same time the division that was to form the main army marched upon Zug, thence to move upon Zurich.

Kappel, at three leagues from Zurich and about a league from Zug, was the first place they would reach in the Zurich territory after crossing the frontier of the Five Cantons. Near the Albis, between two hills of similar height, the Granges on the north, and the Ifelsberg on the south, in the midst of delightful pastures, stood the ancient and wealthy convent of the Cistercians, in whose church were the tombs of many ancient and noble families of these districts. The Abbot Wolfgang Joner, a just and pious man, a great friend of the arts and letters, and a distinguished preacher, had reformed his convent in 1527. Full of compassion, rich in good works, particularly toward the poor of the canton of Zug and the free bailiwicks, he was held in great honor throughout the whole country. He predicted what would be the termination of the war. Yet as soon as danger approached, he spared no labor to serve his country.

It was on Sunday night that the abbot received positive intelligence of the preparations at Zug. He paced up and down his cell with hasty steps. Sleep fled from his eyes. He drew near his lamp, and, addressing his intimate friend, Peter Simmler, who succeeded him and who was then residing at Kylchberg, a village on the borders of the lake, about a league from the town, he hastily wrote these words: "The great anxiety and trouble which agitate me prevent me from busying myself with the management of the house, and induce me to write to you all that is preparing. The time is come. . . . the scourge of God appears. . . . After many journeys and inquiries, we have learned that the Five Cantons will march today [Monday] to seize upon Hitzkylch, while the main army assembles its banners at Baar, between Zug and Kappel. Those from the valley of the Adige and the Italians will arrive today or tomorrow." This letter, through some unforeseen circumstance, did not reach Zurich till the evening.

Meanwhile, the messenger whom Lavater had sent—the nephew of J. Winckler—creeping on his belly, gliding unperceived past the sentinels, and clinging to the shrubs that overhung the precipices, had succeeded in making his way where no road had been cleared. On arriving near Zug, he had discovered with alarm the banner and the militia hastening from all sides at beat of drum. Then traversing again these unknown passes, he had returned to Zurich with this information.

It was high time that the bandage should fall from the eyes of the Zurichers, but the delusion was to endure until the end. The council which was called together met in small number. "The

Five Cantons," said they, "are making a little noise to frighten us and to make us raise the blockade." The council, however, decided on sending Colonel Rodolph Dumysen and Ulrich Funk to Kappel to see what was going on; and each one, tranquillized by this unmeaning step, retired to rest.

They did not slumber long. Every hour brought fresh messages of alarm to Zurich.

"The banners of four cantons are assembled at Zug," said they. "They are only waiting for Uri. The people of the free bailiwicks are flocking to Kappel and demanding arms. . . . Help!"

Before the break of the day, the council was again assembled, and it ordered the convocation of the Two Hundred. An old man, whose hair had grown gray on the battlefield and in the council of the state—the banneret John Schweitzer—raising his head enfeebled by age and darting the last beam, as it were, from his eyes, exclaimed, "Now—at this very moment, in God's name, send an advanced guard to Kappel, and let the army, promptly collecting round the banner, follow it immediately."

He said no more, but the charm was not yet broken. "The peasants of the free bailiwicks," said some, "we know to be hasty and easily carried away. They make the matter greater than it really is. The wisest plan is to wait for the report of the councilors." In Zurich there was no longer either arm to defend or head to advise.

It was seven o'clock in the morning, and the assembly was still sitting, when Rodolph Gwerb, pastor of Rifferschwyl, near Kappel, arrived in haste. "The people of the lordship of Knonau," said he, "are crowding round the convent and loudly calling for chiefs and for aid. The enemy is approaching. Will our lords of Zurich (say they) abandon themselves, and us with them? Do they wish to give us up to slaughter?" The pastor, who had witnessed these mournful scenes, spoke with animation. The councilors, whose infatuation was to be prolonged to the last, were offended at his message. "They want to make us act imprudently," replied they, turning in their armchairs.

They had scarcely ceased speaking before a new messenger appeared, wearing on his features the marks of the greatest terror.

It was Schwytzer, landlord of the Beech Tree on Mount Albis. "My lords Dumysen and Funk," said he, "have sent me to you with all speed to announce to the council that the Five Cantons have seized upon Hitzkylch, and that they are now collecting all their troops at Baar. My lords remain in the bailiwicks to aid the frightened inhabitants."

This time the most confident turned pale. Terror, so long restrained, passed like a flash of lightning through every heart. Hitzkylch was in the power of the enemy, and the war had begun.

It was resolved to expedite to Kappel a flying camp of six hundred men with six guns, but the command was intrusted to George Godli, whose brother was in the army of the Five Cantons, and he was enjoined to keep on the defensive. Godli and his troops had just left the city when the captain-general Lavater, summoning into the hall of the Smaller Council the old banneret Schweitzer; William Toning, captain of the arquebusiers; J. Dennikon, captain of the artillery; Zwingli; and some others, said to them, "Let us deliberate promptly on the means of saving the canton and the city. Let the tocsin immediately call out all the citizens."

The captain-general feared that the councils would shrink at this proceeding, and he wished to raise the landsturm (veteran reserve) by the simple advice of the chiefs of the army and of Zwingli. "We cannot take it upon ourselves," said they. "The two councils are still sitting; let us lay this proposition before them." They hastened toward the place of meeting, but there were only a few members of the Smaller Council on the benches. "The consent of the Two Hundred is necessary," said they. Again a new delay, and the enemies were on their march. Two hours after noon, the Great Council met again, but only to make long and useless speeches. At length the resolution was taken, and at seven in the evening the tocsin began to sound in all the country districts. Treason united with this dilatoriness, and persons who pretended to be envoys from Zurich stopped the landsturm in many places, as being contrary to the opinion of the council. A great number of citizens went to sleep again.

It was a fearful night. The thick darkness, a violent storm, the alarm bell ringing from every steeple, the people running to arms, the noise of swords and guns, the sound of trumpets and of drums, combined with the roaring of the tempest, the distrust, discontent, and even treason, which spread affliction in every quarter, the sobs of women and of children, the cries which accompanied many a heart-rending adieu, an earthquake that occurred about nine o'clock at night, as if nature herself had shuddered at the blood that was about to be spilt, and that violently shook the mountains and the valleys: all increased the terrors of this fatal night, a night to be followed by a still more fatal day.

While these events were passing, the Zurichers encamped on the heights of Kappel about one thousand men fixed their eyes on Zug and upon the lake, attentively watching every movement. On a sudden, a little before night, they perceived a few barks filled with soldiers coming from the side of Arth; they were rowing across the lake toward Zug. Their number increased—one boat followed another—and soon they distinctly heard the bellowing of the Bull (the horn) of Uri and discerned the banner. The barks drew near Zug. They were moored to the shore, which was lined with an immense crowd. The warriors of Uri and the arquebusiers of the Adige sprang up and leaped on shore, where they were received with acclamations, and took up their quarters for the night. Behold the enemies assembled! The council was informed with all speed.

The agitation was still greater at Zurich than at Kappel. The confusion was increased by uncertainty. The enemy attacking them on different sides at once, they knew not where to carry assistance. Two hours after midnight, five hundred men with four guns quitted the city for Bremgarten, and three or four hundred men with five guns for Wadenschwyl. They turned to the right and to the left, while the enemy was in front.

Alarmed at its own weakness, the council resolved to apply without delay to the cities of the Christian co-burghery. "As this revolt," wrote they, "has no other origin than the Word of God, we entreat you once—twice—thrice, as loudly, as seriously, as firmly, and as earnestly, as our ancient alliances and our Christian co-burghery permit and command us to do—to set forth without delay with all your forces. Haste! Act as promptly as possible—the danger is yours as well as ours." Thus spake Zurich, but it was already too late.

At break of day the banner was raised before the townhouse. Instead of flaunting proudly in the wind, it hung drooping down the staff, a sad omen that filled many minds with fear. Lavater took up his station under this standard, but a long period elapsed before a few hundred soldiers could be got together. In the square and in all the city, disorder and confusion prevailed. The troops, fatigued by a hasty march or by long waiting, were faint and discouraged.

At ten o'clock only seven hundred men were under arms. The selfish, the lukewarm, the friends of Rome and of the foreign pensioners had remained at home. A few old men who had more courage than strength—several members of the two councils who were devoted to the holy cause of God's Word, many ministers of the church who desired to live and die with the reform, the boldest of the townspeople and a certain number of peasants, especially those from the neighborhood of the city—such were the defenders who, wanting that moral force so necessary for victory, incompletely armed, and without uniform, crowded in disorder around the banner of Zurich.

The army should have numbered at least four thousand men. They waited still. The usual oath had not been administered, and yet courier after courier arrived, breathless and in disorder, announcing the terrible danger that threatened Zurich. All this disorderly crowd was violently agitated; they no longer waited for the commands of their chiefs, and many without taking the oath had rushed through the gates. About two hundred men thus set out in confusion. All those who remained prepared to depart.

Zwingli was now seen issuing from a house before which a horse was stamping impatiently. It was his own. His look was firm, but dimmed by sorrow. He parted from his wife, his children, and his numerous friends, without deceiving himself, and with a bruised heart. Fifteen days before the attack of the Waldstettes, he had said from the pulpit, "I know the meaning of all this. I am the person specially pointed at. All this comes to pass—in order that I may die." The council, according to an ancient custom, had called upon him to accompany the army as its chaplain. Zwingli did not hesitate. He prepared himself without surprise and without anger, with the calmness of a Christian who places himself confidently in the hands of his God. If the cause of reform was doomed to perish, he was ready to perish with it.

Surrounded by his weeping wife and friends, by his children who clung to his garments to detain him, he quitted that house where he had tasted so much happiness. At the moment that his hand was upon his horse, just as he was about to mount, the animal violently started back several paces, and when he was at last in the saddle, it refused for a time to move, rearing and prancing backwards. Many in Zurich at that time thought, "It is a bad omen! A Roman would go back!" Zwingli, having at last mastered his horse, gave the reins, applied the spur, started forward, and disappeared.

At eleven o'clock the flag was struck, and all who remained in the square, about five hundred men, began their march along with it. The greater part were torn with difficulty from the arms of their families and walked sad and silent, as if they were going to the scaffold instead of battle. There was no order—no plan. The men were isolated and scattered, some running before, some after the colors, their extreme confusion presenting a fearful appearance, so much so that those who remained behind—the women, the children, and the old men—filled with gloomy forebodings, beat their breasts as they saw them pass. Zwingli, armed according to the usage of the chaplains of the Confederation, rode mournfully behind this distracted multitude. Myconius, when he saw him, was nigh fainting. Zwingli disappeared, and Myconius remained behind to weep.

He did not shed tears alone. In all quarters were heard lamentations, and every house was changed into a house of prayer. In the midst of this universal sorrow, one woman remained silent. Her only cry was a bitter heart, her only language the mild and suppliant eye of faith. This was Anna, Zwingli's wife. She had seen her husband depart—her son, her brother, a great number of intimate friends and near relations, whose approaching death she foreboded. But her soul, strong as that of her husband, offered to God the sacrifice of her holiest affections. Gradually the defenders of Zurich precipitated their march, and the tumult died away in the distance.

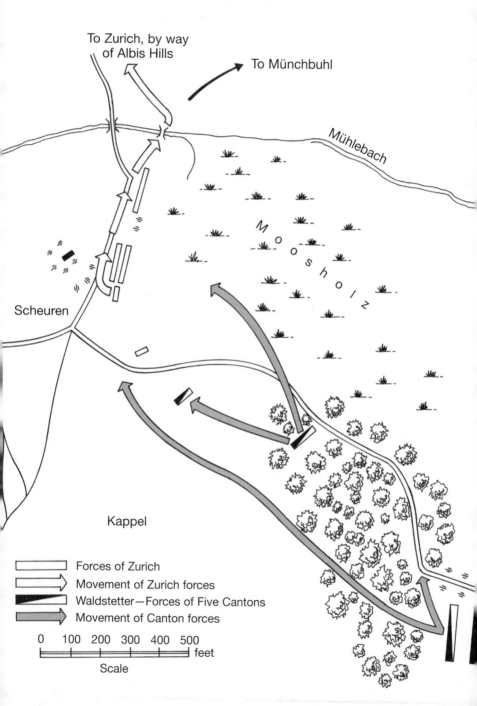

The Battle of Kappel
October 11, 1531

To Zurich, by way
of Albis Hills

To Münchbuhl

Mühlebach

Moosholz

Scheuren

Kappel

☐ Forces of Zurich
▷ Movement of Zurich forces
◣ Waldstetter—Forces of Five Cantons
➤ Movement of Canton forces

0 100 200 300 400 500
├───┼───┼───┼───┼───┤ feet
Scale

Chapter 26
Clash at Kappel

This night, which was so stormy in Zurich, had not been calmer among the inhabitants of Kappel. They had received the most alarming reports one after another. It was necessary to take up a position that would allow the troops assembled round the convent to resist the enemy's attack until the arrival of the reinforcements that were expected from the city. They cast their eyes on a small hill, which, lying to the north toward Zurich and traversed by the high road, presented an uneven but sufficiently extensive surface. A deep ditch that surrounded it on three sides defended the approaches, but a small bridge, the only issue on the side of Zurich, rendered a precipitate retreat very dangerous. On the southwest was a wood of beech trees. On the south, in the direction of Zug, was the highroad and a marshy valley. "Lead us to the Granges," cried all the soldiers. They were conducted thither. The artillery was stationed near some ruins. The line of battle was drawn up on the side of the monastery and of Zug, and sentinels were placed at the foot of the slope.

Meantime, the signal was given at Zug and Baar. The drums beat. The soldiers of the Five Cantons took up their arms. A universal feeling of joy animated them. The churches were opened, the bells rang, and the serried ranks of the cantons entered the cathedral of St. Oswald, where mass was celebrated and the host offered up for the sins of the people. All the men of the army began their march at nine o'clock, with banners flying. Eight thousand men marched in order of battle. All the picked men of the Five Cantons were there. Fresh and active after a quiet night, and having only one short league to cross before reaching the enemy, these haughty Waldstettes advanced with a firm and regular step under the command of their chiefs.

On reaching the common meadow of Zug, they halted to take the oath. Every hand was upraised to heaven, and all swore to avenge themselves. They were about to resume their march when some aged men made signs to them to stop. "Comrades," said they, "we have long offended God. Our blasphemies, our oaths, our wars, our revenge, our pride, our drunkenness, our adulteries, the gold of the stranger to whom our hands have been extended, and all the disorders in which we have indulged, have so provoked His anger, that if He should punish us today, we should only receive the dessert [sic] of our crimes." The emotion of the chiefs had passed into the ranks. All the army bent the knee in the midst of the plain. Deep silence prevailed, and every soldier, with bent head, crossed himself devoutly and repeated in a low voice five paters, as many aves, and the credo. One might have said that they were for a time in the midst of a vast and still desert. Suddenly the noise of an immense crowd was again heard. The army rose up. "Soldiers," said the captains, "you know the cause of this war. Bear your wives and your children continually before your eyes."

Then the chief usher (grand sautier) of Lucerne, wearing the colors of the canton, approached the chiefs of the army. They placed in his hands the declaration of war, dated on that very day and sealed with the arms of Zug. He then set off on horseback, preceded by a trumpeter, to carry this paper to the commander of the Zurichers.

It was eleven in the morning. The Zurichers soon discovered the enemy's army and cast a sorrowful glance on the small force they were able to oppose to it. Every minute the danger increased. All bent their knees and raised their eyes to heaven, and every Zuricher uttered a cry from the bottom of his heart, praying for deliverance from God. As soon as the prayer was ended, they got ready for battle. There were at that time about twelve hundred men under arms.

At noon, the trumpet of the Five Cantons sounded not far from the advanced posts. Godli, having collected the members of the two councils who happened to be with the army as well as the commissioned and noncommissioned officers, and having ranged them in a circle, ordered the secretary Rheinhard to read the declaration of which the sautier of Lucerne was the bearer. After the reading, Godli opened a council of war. "We are few in number, and the forces of our adversaries are great," said Landolt, bailiff of Marpac, "but I will here await the enemy in the name of God."

"Wait!" cried the captain of the halberdiers, Rodolph Zigler. "Impossible! Let us rather take advantage of the ditch that cuts the road to effect our retreat, and let us everywhere raise a levee en masse." This was in truth the only means of safety. But Rudi Gallmann, considering every step backwards as an act of cowardice, cried out, stamping his feet forcibly on the earth and casting a fiery glance around him, "Here—here shall be my grave!"

"It is now too late to retire with honor," said other officers. "This day is in the hands of God. Let us suffer whatever He lays upon us." It was put to the vote.

The members of the council had scarcely raised their hands in token of assent when a great noise was heard around them. "The captain! The captain!" cried the soldier from the outposts who arrived in haste.

"Silence, silence!" replied the ushers driving him back, "they are holding a council!"

"It is no longer time to hold a council," replied the soldier. "Conduct me immediately to the captain."

"Our sentinels are falling back," cried he with an agitated voice, as he arrived before Godli. "The enemy is there—they are advancing through the forest with all their forces and with great tumult." He had not ceased speaking before the sentinels, who were in truth retiring on all sides, returned and ran up the hill, and the army of the Five Cantons was soon seen climbing the slope of Ifelsberg in face of the Granges and pointing their guns. The leaders of the Waldstettes were examining the position and seeking to discover by what means their army could reach that of Zurich. The Zurichers were asking themselves the same question. The nature of the ground prevented the Waldstettes from passing below the convent, but they could arrive by another quarter. Ulrich Bruder, under-bailiff of Husen in the canton of Zurich, fixed his anxious look on the beech wood. "It is thence that the enemy will fall upon us!"

"Axes—axes!" immediately cried several voices. "Let us cut down the trees!" Godli, the abbot, and several others were opposed to this. "If we stop up the wood by throwing down the trees, we shall ourselves be unable to work our guns in that direction," said they.

"Well! At least let us place some arquebusiers in that quarter."

"We are already so small a number," replied the captain, "that it will be imprudent to divide the forces." Neither wisdom nor courage was to save Zurich. They once more invoked the help of God and waited in expectation.

At one o'clock the Five Cantons fired the first gun. The ball, passing over the convent, fell below the Granges. A second passed over the line of battle. A third struck a hedge close to the ruins. The Zurichers, seeing the battle was begun, replied with courage, but the slowness and awkwardness with which the artillery was served in those days prevented any great loss being inflicted on either side.

When their enemies perceived this, they ordered their advanced guard to descend from Ifelsberg and to reach the Granges through the meadow. Soon the whole army of the cantons advanced in this direction, but with difficulty and over bad roads. Some arquebusiers of Zurich came and announced the disorder of the cantons. "Brave Zurichers," cried Rudi Gallmann, "if we attack them now, it is all over with them."

At these words some of the soldiers prepared to enter the wood on the left, to fall upon the disheartened Waldstettes. But Godli, perceiving this movement, cried out, "Where are you going? Do you not know that we have agreed not to separate?" He then ordered the skirmishers to be recalled, so that the wood remained entirely open to the enemy. They were satisfied with discharging a few random shots from time to time to prevent the cantons from establishing themselves there. The firing of the artillery continued until three o'clock and announced far and wide, even to Bremgarten and Zurich, that the battle had begun.

In the meanwhile the great banner of Zurich and all those who surrounded it, among whom was Zwingli, came advancing in disorder toward the Albis. For a year past the gaiety of the reformer had entirely disappeared. He was grave, melancholy, easily moved, having a weight on his heart that seemed to crush it. No one had ever observed in him any irritation. On the contrary, he had received with mildness the counsels that had been offered and had remained tenderly attached to men whose convictions were not the same as his own. He was now advancing mournfully along the road to Kappel, and John Maaler of Winterthour, who was riding a few paces behind him, heard his groans and sighs, intermingled with fervent prayers. If anyone spoke to him, he was found firm and strong in the peace that proceeds from faith, but he did not conceal his conviction that he should never see his family or church again. Thus advanced the forces of Zurich. A woeful march—resembling rather a funeral procession than an army going to battle.

As they approached they saw express after express galloping along the road from Kappel, begging the Zurichers to hasten to the defense of their brothers.

At Adliswyl, having passed the bridge under which flow the impetuous waters of the Sihl and traversed the village through the midst of women, children, and old men, who, standing before their cottages, looked with sadness on this disorderly troop, they began to ascend the Albis. They were about halfway from Kappel when the first cannon shot was heard. They stopped. They listened. A second, a third succeeded. There was no longer any doubt. The glory, the very existence of the republic, was endangered, and they were not present to defend it! The blood curdled in their veins. On a sudden they aroused, and each one began to run to the support of his brothers.

But the road over the Albis was much steeper than it is in our days. The badly harnessed artillery could not ascend it. The old men and citizens, little habituated to marching and covered with weighty armor, advanced with difficulty, and yet they formed the greater portion of the troops. They were seen stopping one after another, panting and exhausted, along the sides of the road near the thickets and ravines of the Albis, leaning against a beech or an ash tree and looking with dispirited eyes to the summit of the mountain covered with thick pines.

They resumed their march, however. The horsemen and the most intrepid of the foot soldiers hastened onwards and, having reached the "Beech Tree" on the top of the mountain, they halted to take counsel.

What a prospect then extended before their eyes. Zurich, the lake and its smiling shores—those orchards, those fertile fields, those vine-clad hills, almost the whole of the canton, alas, soon, perhaps, was to be devastated by the forest bands.

Scarcely had these noble-minded men begun to deliberate, when fresh messengers from Kappel appeared before them exclaiming, "Hasten forward!" At these words many of the Zurichers prepared to gallop toward the enemy. Toning, the captain of the arquebusiers, stopped them. "My good friends," cried he to them, "against such great forces what can we do alone? Let us wait here until our people are assembled, and then let us fall upon the enemy with the whole army."

"Yes, if we had an army," bitterly replied the captain-general, who, in despair of saving the republic, thought only of dying with glory. "But we have only a banner and no soldiers."

"How can we stay calmly upon these heights," said Zwingli, "while we hear the shots that are fired at our fellow citizens? In the name of God I will march toward my brother warriors, prepared to die in order to save them."

"And I too," added the aged banneret Schweitzer. "As for you," continued he, turning with a contemptuous look toward Toning, "wait till you are a little recovered."

"I am quite as much refreshed as you," replied Toning, the color mantling on his face, "and you shall soon see whether I cannot fight." All hastened their steps toward the field of battle.

The descent was rapid. They plunged into the woods, passed through the village of Husen, and at length arrived near the Granges. It was three o'clock when the banner crossed the narrow bridge that led thither, and there were so few soldiers round it that everyone trembled as he beheld this venerated standard thus exposed to the attacks of so formidable an enemy. The army of the Cantons was at that moment deploying before the eyes of the newcomers. Zwingli gazed upon this terrible spectacle. Behold, then, these phalanxes of soldiers. A few minutes more, and the labors of eleven years would be destroyed perhaps forever.

A citizen of Zurich, one Leonard Bourkhard, who was ill-disposed toward the reformer, said to him in a harsh tone, "Well, Master Ulrich, what do you say about this business? Are the radishes salt enough? . . . Who will eat them now?"

"I," replied Zwingli, "and many a brave man who is here in the hands of God, for we are His in life and in death."

"And I too—I will help to eat them," resumed Bourkhard immediately, ashamed of his brutality. "I will risk my life for them." And he did so, and many others with him.

It was four o'clock. The sun was sinking rapidly. The Waldstettes did not advance, and the Zurichers began to think that the attack would be put off till the morrow. In fact, the chiefs of the Five Cantons, seeing the great banner of Zurich arrive, the night near at hand, and the impossibility of crossing under the fire of the Zurichers the marsh and the ditch that separated the combatants, were looking for a place in which their troops might pass the night. "If at this moment any mediators had appeared," says Bullinger, "their proposals would have been accepted."

The Waldstette soldiers, observing the hesitation of their chiefs, began to murmur loudly. "The big ones abandon us," said one. "The captains fear to bite the fox's tail," said another. "Not to attack them," they all cried, "is to ruin our cause." During this time, a daring man was preparing the skillful maneuver that was to decide the fate of the day. A warrior of Uri, John Jauch, formerly bailiff of Sargans, a good marksman and experienced soldier, having taken a few men with him, moved toward the right of the army of the Five Cantons, crept into the midst of the clump of beech trees that, by forming a semicircle to the east, united the hill of Ifelsberg to that of the Granges, found the wood empty, arrived to within a few paces of the Zurichers, and there, hidden behind the trees, remarked unperceived the smallness of their numbers and their want of caution. Then, stealthily retiring, he went to the chiefs at the very moment the discontent was on the point of bursting out. "Now is the time to attack the enemy," he cried.

Replied Troguer, captain-in-chief of Uri, "You do not mean to say that we should set to work at so late an hour. Besides, the men are preparing their quarters, and everybody knows what it cost our fathers at Naples and Marignan for having commenced the attack a little before night. And then it is Innocent's day, and our ancestors have never given battle on a feast day."

"Don't think about the Innocents of the calendar," replied Jauch, "but let us rather remember the innocents that we have left in our cottages." Gaspard Godli of Zurich, brother of the commander of the Granges, added his entreaties to those of the warrior of Uri. "We must either beat the Zurichers tonight," said he, "or be beaten by them tomorrow. Take your choice."

All was unavailing. The chiefs were inflexible, and the army prepared to take up its quarters. Upon this the warrior of Uri drew his sword and cried, "Let all true confederates follow me." Then hastily leaping to his saddle, he spurred his horse into the forest. Immediately arquebusiers, soldiers from the Adige, and many other warriors of the Five Cantons, especially from Unterwalden—in all about three hundred men, rushed into the wood after him.

At this sight, Jauch no longer doubted the victory of the Waldstettes. He dismounted and fell upon his knees, "for," says Tschudi, "he was a man who feared God." All his followers did the same and together invoked the aid of God, of His holy mother, and of all the heavenly host. They then advanced, but soon the warrior of Uri, wishing to expose no one but himself, halted his troops and glided from tree to tree to the verge of the wood. Observing that the enemy was as incautious as ever, he rejoined his arquebusiers, led them stealthily forward, and posted them silently behind the trees of the forest, enjoining them to take their aim so as not to miss their men. During this time the chiefs of the Five Cantons, foreseeing that this rash man was about to bring on the action, decided against their will, and collected their soldiers around the banners.

Chapter 27
Death of a Reformer

The Zurichers, fearing that the enemy would seize upon the road that led to their capital, were then directing part of their troops and their guns to a low hill by which the capital was commanded. At the very moment that the invisible arquebusiers stationed among the beech trees were taking their aim, this detachment passed near the little wood. The deepest silence prevailed in this solitude. Each one posted there picked out the man he desired to bring down, and Jauch exclaimed, "In the name of the Holy Trinity—of God the Father, the Son, and the Holy Ghost—of the Holy Mother of God, and of all the heavenly host—fire!" At the word, the deadly balls issued from the wood, and a murderous carnage in the ranks of Zurich followed this terrible discharge.

The battle, which had begun four hours ago and which had never appeared to be a serious attack, now underwent an unforeseen change. The sword was not again to be returned to the scabbard until it had been bathed in torrents of blood. Those of the Zurichers who had not fallen at this first discharge lay flat on the ground so that the balls passed over their heads, but they soon sprang up, saying, "Shall we allow ourselves to be butchered? No! let us rather attack the enemy!" Lavater seized a lance and, rushing into the foremost rank exclaimed, "Soldiers, uphold the honor of God and of our lords, and behave like brave men!"

Zwingli was there also with halberd in hand. "Master Ulrich," said Bernard Sprungli, "speak to the people and encourage them."

"Warriors!" said Zwingli, "fear nothing. If we are this day to be defeated, still our cause is good. Commend yourselves to God!"

The Zurichers quickly turned the artillery they were dragging to another quarter and pointed it against the wood, but their bullets, instead of striking the enemy, reached only the top of the trees and tore off a few branches that fell upon the skirmishers.

Rychmuth, the landamman of Schwytz, came up at a gallop to recall the volunteers, but seeing the battle begun, he ordered the whole army to advance. Immediately the five banners moved forward.

But already Jauch's skirmishers, rushing from among the trees, had fallen impetuously upon the Zurichers, charging with their long and pointed halberds. "Heretics! Sacrilegists!" cried they, "We have you at last!"

"Man-sellers, idolaters, impious papists!" replied the Zurichers, "Is it really you?" At first, a shower of stones fell from both parties and wounded several. Immediately they came to close quarters. The resistance of the Zurichers was terrible. Each struck with the sword or with the halberd. At last the soldiers of the Five Cantons were driven back in disorder. The Zurichers advanced, but in so doing lost the advantages of their position and got entangled in the marsh.

In the meantime, the army of the Five Cantons hastened through the wood. Burning with courage and with anger, they eagerly quickened their steps. From the midst of the beech trees there resounded a confused and savage noise—a frightful murmur. In vain did the bravest of the Zurichers offer an intrepid resistance. The Waldstettes had the advantage in every quarter. "They are surrounding us," cried some. "Our men are fleeing," said others. A man from the canton of Zug, mingling with the Zurichers and pretending to be of their party, exclaimed, "Fly, fly, brave Zurichers, you are betrayed!" Even the hand of Him who is the disposer of battles turned against this people. Thus was it also in times of old that God frequently chastised His own people of Israel by the Assyrian sword. A panic-terror seized upon the bravest, and the disorder spread everywhere with frightful rapidity.

In the meanwhile, the aged Schweitzer had raised the great banner with a firm hand, and all the picked men of Zurich were drawn up around it. But soon their ranks were thinned. John Kammli, charged with the defense of the standard, having observed the small number of combatants that remained upon the field of battle, said to the banneret, "Let us lower the banner, my lord, and save it, for our people are flying shamefully."

"Warriors, remain firm," replied the aged banneret, whom no danger had ever shaken. The disorder augmented—the number of fugitives increased every minute. The old man stood fast, amazed and immovable as an aged oak beaten by a frightful hurricane. He received unflinchingly the blows that fell upon him and alone resisted the terrible storm.

Kammli seized him by the arm. "My lord," said he again, "lower the banner, or else we shall lose it. There is no more glory to be reaped here!"

The banneret, who was already mortally wounded, exclaimed, "Alas! must the city of Zurich be so punished!" Then, dragged off by Kammli, who held him by the arm, he retreated as far as the ditch. The weight of years, and the wounds with which he was covered, did not permit him to cross it. He fell in the mire at the bottom, still holding the glorious standard, whose folds dropped on the other bank.

The enemy ran up with loud shouts, being attracted by the colors of Zurich, as the bull by the gladiator's flag. Kammli, seeing this, unhesitatingly leaped to the bottom of the ditch and laid hold of the stiff and dying hands of his chief, in order to preserve the precious ensign that they tightly grasped. But it was in vain. The hands of the aged Schweitzer would not loose the standard.

"My lord banneret," cried this faithful servant, "it is no longer in your power to defend it." The hands of the banneret, already stiffened in death, still refused, upon which Kammli violently tore away the sacred standard, leaped upon the other bank, and rushed with his treasure far from the steps of the enemy. The last Zurichers at this moment reached the ditch. They fell one after another upon the expiring banneret, and thus hastened his death.

Kammli, however, had received a wound from a gunshot and his march was retarded; soon the Waldstettes surrounded him with their swords. The Zuricher, holding the banner in one hand, and his sword in the other, defended himself bravely. One of the Waldstettes caught hold of the staff; another seized the flag itself and tore it. Kammli with one blow of his sword cut down the former, and striking around him, called out, "To the rescue, brave Zurichers! Save the honor and the banner of our lords."

The assailants increased in number, and the warrior was about to fall, when Adam Naeff of Wollenwyd rushed up sword in hand, and the head of the Waldstette who had torn the colors rolled upon the plain, and his blood gushed out upon the flag of Zurich. Dumysen, member of the Smaller Council, supported Naeff with his halberd, and both dealt such lusty blows that they succeeded in disengaging the standard-bearer. He, although dangerously wounded, sprang forward, holding the blood-stained folds of the banner in one hand, which he carried off hastily, dragging the staff behind him. With fierce look and fiery eye, he thus passed, sword in hand, through the midst of friends and enemies. He crossed plains, woods, and marshes, everywhere leaving traces of his blood, which flowed from numerous wounds.

Two of his enemies, one from Schwytz—the other from Zug—were particularly eager in his pursuit. "Heretic! Villain!" cried they, "Surrender and give us the banner."

"You shall have my life first," replied the Zuricher. Then the two hostile soldiers, who were embarrassed by their cuirasses, stopped a moment to take them off. Kammli took advantage of this to get in advance. He ran. Huber, Dumysen, and Dantzler of Naenikon were at his side. They all four thus arrived near Husen, halfway up the Albis. They had still to climb the steepest part of the mountain. Huber fell covered with wounds. Dumysen, the colonel-general, who had fought as a private soldier, almost reached the church of Husen, and there he dropped lifeless. Two of his sons, in the flower of youth, soon lay stretched on the battlefield that had drunk their father's blood.

Kammli took a few steps farther, but halted erelong, exhausted and panting, near a hedge that he would have to clear, and discovered his two enemies and other Waldstettes running from all sides, like birds of prey, toward the wavering standard of

Zurich. The strength of Kammli was sinking rapidly and his eyes grew dim as thick darkness surrounded him. A hand of lead fastened him to the ground. Then, mustering all his expiring strength, he flung the standard on the other side of the hedge, exclaiming, "Is there any brave Zuricher near me? Let him preserve the banner and the honor of our lords! As for me, I can do no more!" He cast a last look to heaven and added: "May God be my helper!" He fell exhausted by this last effort. Dantzler, who came up, flung away his sword, sprung over the hedge, seized the banner, and cried, "With the aid of God, I will carry it off." He then rapidly climbed the Albis and at last placed the ancient standard of Zurich in safety.

The enemy were victorious at all points. The soldiers of the Five Cantons, and particularly those of Unterwalden long hardened in the wars of the Milanese, showed themselves more merciless toward their confederates than they had ever been toward foreigners. At the beginning of the battle, Godli had taken flight, and soon after he quitted Zurich forever. Lavater, the captain-general, after having fought valiantly, had fallen into the ditch. He was dragged out by a soldier and escaped.

The most distinguished men of Zurich fell one after another under the blows of the Waldstettes. Rudi Gallman found the glorious tomb he had wished for, and his two brothers stretched beside him left their father's house desolate. Toning, captain of the arquebusiers, died for his country as he had foretold. All the pride of the population of Zurich, seven members of the Smaller Council, 19 members of the Two Hundred, 65 citizens of the town, 417 from the rural districts: the father in the midst of his children, the son surrounded by his brothers, lay on the field.

Gerold Meyer of Knonau, son of Anna Zwingli, at that time twenty-two years of age and already a member of the council of Two Hundred, a husband and a father, had rushed into the foremost ranks with all the impetuosity of youth. "Surrender, and your life shall be spared," cried some of the warriors of the Five Cantons, who desired to save him. "It is better for me to die with honor than to yield with disgrace," replied the son of Anna, and immediately struck by a mortal blow, he fell and expired not far from the castle of his ancestors.

The ministers were those who paid proportionally the greatest tribute on this bloody day. The sword that was at work on the heights of Kappel thirsted for their blood. Twenty-five of them fell beneath its stroke. The Waldstettes trembled with rage whenever they discovered one of these heretical preachers and sacrificed him with enthusiasm, as a chosen victim to the Virgin and the saints. There has, perhaps, never been any battle in which so many men of the Word of God have fallen. Almost everywhere, the pastors had marched at the head of their flocks. One might have said that Kappel was an assembly of Christian churches rather than an army of Swiss companies. The Abbot Joner, receiving a mortal wound near the ditch, expired in sight of his own monastery. The people of Zug, in pursuit of the enemy, uttered a cry of anguish as they passed his body, remembering all the good he had done them. Schmidt of Kussnacht, stationed on the field of battle in the midst of his parishioners, fell surrounded by forty of their bodies. Geroldsek, John Haller, and many other pastors, at the head of their flocks, suddenly met in a terrible and unforeseen manner the Lord whom they had preached.

But the death of one individual far surpassed all others. Zwingli was at the post of danger, the helmet on his head, the sword hanging at his side, the battle-axe in his hand. (The chaplains of the Swiss troops still wear a sword. Zwingli did not make use of his arms.) Scarcely had the action begun, when, as he stooped to console a dying man, a stone hurled by the vigorous arm of a Waldstette struck him on the head and closed his lips. Yet Zwingli arose, when two other blows which hit him successively on the leg threw him down again. Twice more he stood up, but a fourth time he received a thrust from a lance. He staggered, and sinking beneath so many wounds, fell on his knees. Zwingli once more uplifted that head which had been so bold and gazing with calm eye upon the trickling blood exclaimed, "What matters this misfortune? They may indeed kill the body, but they cannot kill the soul!" These were his last words.

He had scarcely uttered them ere he fell backwards. There, under a tree, in a meadow, he remained lying on his back, with clasped hands and eyes upturned to heaven.

The death of Zwingli, a romanticized artist's conception

While the bravest were pursuing the scattered soldiers of Zurich, the stragglers of the Five Cantons had pounced like hungry ravens on the field of battle. Torches in hand, these wretches prowled among the dead, casting looks of irritation around them, and lighting up the features of their expiring victims by the dull glimmering of these funeral torches. They turned over the bodies of the wounded and the dead. They tortured and stripped them. If they found any who were still sensible, they cried out, "Call upon the saints and confess to our priests!" If the Zurichers, faithful to their creed, rejected these cruel invitations, these men, who were as cowardly as they were fanatical, pierced them with their lances or dashed out their brains with the butt-ends of their arquebuses. The Roman Catholic historian, Salat of Lucerne, makes a boast of this. "They were left to die like infidel dogs, or were slain with the sword or the spear, that they might go so much the quicker to the Devil, with whose help they had fought so desperately."

If any of the soldiers of the Five Cantons recognized a Zuricher against whom they had any grudge, with dry eyes, disdainful mouth, and features changed by anger, they drew near the unhappy creature, writhing in the agonies of death, and said, "Well! Has your heretical faith preserved you? Ah ha! it was pretty clearly seen today who had the true faith. . . . Today we have dragged your gospel in the mud, and you too, even you are covered with your own blood. God, the Virgin, and the saints have punished you." Scarcely had they uttered these words before they plunged their swords into their enemy's bosom. "Mass or death!" was their watchword.

Thus triumphed the Waldstettes. It is in the furnace of trial that the God of the gospel conceals the pure gold of His most precious blessings. This punishment was necessary to turn aside the church of Zurich from the "broad ways" of the world and lead it back to the "narrow ways" of the Spirit and the life. In a political history, a defeat like that of Kappel would be styled a great misfortune. But in a history of the church of Jesus Christ, such a blow, inflicted by the hand of the Father Himself, ought rather to be called a great blessing.

Meanwhile, Zwingli lay extended under the tree, near the road by which the mass of the people was passing. The shouts of the victors, the groans of the dying, those flickering torches borne from corpse to corpse, Zurich humbled, the cause of reform lost—all cried aloud to him that God punishes His servants when they have recourse to the arm of man.

Two of the soldiers who were prowling over the field of battle came near the reformer without recognizing him. "Do you wish for a priest to confess yourself?" asked they. Zwingli, without speaking (for he had not strength), made signs in the negative. "If you cannot speak," replied the soldiers, "at least think in thy heart of the Mother of God and call upon the saints!" Zwingli again shook his head and kept his eyes still fixed on heaven. Upon this the irritated soldiers began to curse him. "No doubt," said they, "you are one of the heretics of the city!" One of them, being curious to know who it was, stooped down and turned Zwingli's head in the direction of a fire that had been lighted near the spot. The soldier immediately let him fall to the ground. "I think," said he, surprised and amazed, "I think it is Zwingli!"

At this moment Captain Fockinger of Unterwalden, a veteran and a pensioner, drew near. He had heard the first words of the soldier. "Zwingli!" exclaimed he, "That vile heretic Zwingli! That rascal, that traitor!" Then raising his sword, so long sold to the stranger, he struck the dying Christian on the throat, exclaiming in a violent passion, "Die, obstinate heretic!" Yielding under this last blow, the reformer gave up the ghost; he was doomed to perish by the sword of a mercenary. "Precious in the sight of the Lord is the death of his saints."

The soldiers ran to other victims. All did not show the same barbarity. The night was cold. A thick hoarfrost covered the fields and the bodies of the dying. The Protestant historian, Bullinger, informs us that some Waldstettes gently raised the wounded in their arms, bound up their wounds, and carried them to the fires lighted on the field of battle. "Ah!" cried they, "why have the Swiss thus slaughtered one another!"

The main body of the army had remained on the field of battle near the standards. The soldiers conversed around the fires, interrupted from time to time by the cries of the dying. During this time the chiefs, assembled in the convent, sent messengers to carry the news of their signal victory to the confederate cantons and to the Roman Catholic powers of Germany.

At length the day appeared. The Waldstettes spread over the field of battle, running here and there, stopping, contemplating, struck with surprise at the sight of their most formidable enemies stretched lifeless on the plain, but sometimes also shedding tears as they gazed on corpses which reminded them of old and sacred ties of friendship. At length they reached the pear tree under which Zwingli lay dead, and an immense crowd collected around it. His countenance still beamed with expression and with life. "He has the look," said Bartholomew Stocker of Zug, who had loved him, "of a living rather than of a dead man. Such was he when he kindled the people by the fire of his eloquence."

All eyes were fixed upon the corpse. John Schonbrunner, formerly canon of Zurich, who had retired to Zug at the epoch of the Reformation, could not restrain his tears. "Whatever may have been thy creed," said he, "I know, Zwingli, that thou hast been a loyal confederate! May thy soul rest with God!"

But the pensioners of the foreigner, on whom Zwingli had never ceased to make war, required that the body of the heretic should be dismembered and a portion sent to each of the Five Cantons. "Peace be to the dead! and God alone be their judge!" exclaimed the avoyer Golder and the landamman Thoss of Zug. Cries of fury answered their appeal and compelled them to retire. Immediately the drums beat to muster. The dead body was tried, and it was decreed that it should be quartered for treason against the Confederation and then burnt for heresy. The executioner of Lucerne carried out the sentence. Flames consumed Zwingli's disjointed members; the ashes of swine were mingled with his; and a lawless multitude rushing upon his remains, flung them to the four winds of heaven.

Zwingli was dead. A great light had been extinguished in the church of God. Mighty by the Word as were the other reformers, he had been more so than they in action, but this very power had been his weakness, and he had fallen under the weight of his own strength. Zwingli was not forty-eight years old when he died. If the might of God always accompanied the might of man, what would he not have done for the Reformation in Switzerland, and even in the empire. But Zwingli had wielded an arm that God had forbidden. His body was no more than a handful of dust in the palm of a soldier.

Chapter 28
Dishonor, Peace, and the Faith Preserved

Fear-filled darkness hung over Zurich during the night that followed the afflicting day of Kappel. It was seven in the evening when the first news of the disaster arrived. Vague but alarming reports spread at first with the rapidity of lightning. It was known that a terrible blow had been inflicted, but not of what kind. Soon a few wounded men, who arrived from the field of battle, cleared up the frightful mystery.

"Then," said Bullinger, "there arose suddenly a loud and horrible cry of lamentation and tears, bewailing and groaning." The consternation was so much the greater because no one had expected such a disaster.

The Christian portion, convinced that Zurich was fighting in a good cause, had not doubted that victory would be on the side of truth. Thus their first stupefaction was succeeded by a violent outburst of rage. With blind fury, the mob accused all their chiefs and loaded with insults even those who had defended their country at the price of their blood. An immense crowd—agitated, pale, and bewildered—filled all the streets of the city. They met; they questioned and replied. They questioned again, and the answer could not be heard, for the shouts of the people interrupted or drowned the voice of the speakers.

The councilors who had remained in Zurich repaired in haste to the town hall. The people, who had already assembled there in crowds, looked on with threatening eyes. Accusations of treason burst from every mouth, and the patricians were pointed out to the general indignation. They must have victims. "Before going to fight against the enemy on the frontiers," said the mob, "we should defend ourselves against those who are within our walls."

Sorrow and fear excited the minds of all. That savage instinct of the populace, which in great calamities leads them, like a wild beast, to thirst for blood, was violently aroused.

A hand from the midst of the crowd pointed out the council hall, and a harsh and piercing voice exclaimed, "Let us chop off the heads of some of the men who sit in these halls, and let their blood ascend to heaven, to beg for mercy in behalf of those whom they have slain."

But this fury was nothing in comparison with that which broke out against the ministers, against Zwingli, and all those Christians who were the cause (said they) of the ruin of the country. Fortunately, the sword of the Waldstettes had withdrawn them from the rage of their fellow citizens. Nevertheless, there still remained some who could pay for the others. Leo Juda, whom Zwingli's death was about to raise to the head of religious affairs, had scarcely recovered from a serious illness. It was on him they rushed. They threatened; they pursued him. A few worthy citizens carried him off and hid in their houses. The rage of these madmen was not appeased. They continued shouting that atonement must be made for the slaughter at Kappel by a still more frightful slaughter within the very walls of the city.

On a sudden, grief succeeded rage, and sobs choked the utterance of the most furious. All those whose relatives had marched to Kappel imagined that they were among the number of the victims. Old men, women, and children went forth in the darkness by the glimmering light of torches, with haggard eyes and hurried steps. As soon as each wounded man arrived, they questioned him with trembling voice about those whom they were seeking. Some replied, "I saw him fall close by my side." "He was surrounded by so many enemies," said others, "that there was no chance of safety for him." At these words, the distracted family members dropped their torches and filled the air with shrieks and groans.

Anna Zwingli had heard from her house the repeated discharges of artillery. As wife and mother, she had passed in expectation many long hours of anguish, offering fervent prayers to heaven. At length the most terrible accounts, one after another, burst upon her.

In the midst of those whose cries of despair re-echoed along the road to Kappel was Oswald Myconius, who inquired with anxiety what had become of his friend. Soon he heard one of the unfortunate wretches who had escaped from the massacre, relating to those around him that Zwingli had fallen.

Zwingli is dead! The cry was repeated. It ran through Zurich with the rapidity of lightning and at length reached the unhappy widow. Anna fell on her knees. But the loss of her husband was not enough. God had inflicted other blows. Messengers following each other at short intervals announced to her the death of her son Gerold of Knonau, of her brother the bailiff of Reinhard, of her son-in-law Antony Wirz, of John Lutschi, the husband of her dear sister, and the death of all her most intimate friends. This woman remained alone—alone with her God, alone with her young children, who, as they saw her tears, wept also and threw themselves into their mother's arms.

On a sudden, the alarm bell rang. The council, distracted by the most contrary opinions, had at last resolved to summon all the citizens toward the Albis. But the sound of the tocsin re-echoing through the darkness, the lamentable stories of the wounded, and the distressful groans of bereaved families still further increased the tumult. A numerous and disorderly troop of citizens rushed along the road to Kappel. Among them was the Valaisan, Thomas Plater. Here he met with a man who had but one hand and others who supported their wounded and bleeding heads with both hands. Farther still was a soldier whose bowels protruded from his body. In front of these unhappy creatures, peasants were walking with lighted torches, for the night was very dark. Plater wished to return, but he could not, for sentinels placed on the bridge over the Sihl allowed persons to quit Zurich but permitted no one to reenter.

On the morrow, the news of the disgraceful treatment of Zwingli's corpse aroused the anger of all Zurich. His friends exclaimed, "These men may fall upon his body, they may kindle their piles and brand his innocent life . . . but he lives—

this invincible hero lives in eternity and leaves behind him an immortal monument of glory that no flames can destroy. God, for whose honor he has labored, even at the price of his blood, will make his memory eternal." Thus Zurich consecrated to Zwingli a funeral oration of tears and sighs, of gratitude and cries of anguish.

Zurich rallied her forces. John Steiner had collected on the Albis some scattered fragments of the army for the defense of the pass. They bivouacked around their fires on the summit of the mountain, and all were in disorder. Plater, benumbed with cold, had drawn off his boots to warm his feet at the watch fire. On a sudden an alarm was given, the troop was hastily drawn up, and while Plater was getting ready, a trumpeter, who had escaped from the battle, seized his halberd. Plater took it back and stationed himself in the ranks. Before him stood the trumpeter, without hat or shoes, and armed with a long pole. Such was the army of Zurich.

The chief captain, Lavater, rejoined the army at daybreak. Gradually the allies came up: 1,500 Grisons, under the orders of the captain-general Frey of Zurich; 1,500 Thurgovians; 600 Tockenburgers; and other auxiliaries besides soon formed an army of 12,000 men. All, even children, ran to arms. The council gave orders that these young folks should be sent back to share in the domestic duties with the women.

Another reverse erelong augmented the desolation of the reformed party. While the troops of Berne, Zurich, Basel, and Bienne, amounting to 24,000 men, were assembling at Bremgarten, the Five Cantons entrenched themselves at Baar, near Zug. But Zwingli was missing from the reformed army, and he would have been the only man capable of inspiring them with courage. A gust of wind threw down a few fir trees in the forests where the Zurichers were encamped and caused the death of some soldiers, and they saw in this the signal of fresh reverses.

Frey called loudly for battle, but the Bernese commandant Diesbach refused. Upon this, the Zurich captain set off in the night of October 23 at the head of 4,000 men of Zurich, Schaffhausen, Basel, and St. Gall; and while the Bernese were sleeping quietly, he turned the Waldstettes, drove their outposts beyond the Sihl and took his station on the heights that overlook the Goubel. His imprudent soldiers, believing victory to be certain, proudly waved their banners and then sank into a heavy sleep.

The Waldstettes had observed all. On October 24, at two in the morning, by a bright moonlight, they quitted their camp in profound silence, leaving their fires burning, and wearing white shirts that they might recognize one another in the obscurity. Their watchword was "Mary, the mother of God." They glided stealthily into a pine forest, near which the reformed troops were encamped. The men stationed at the advanced guard of the Zurichers, having perceived the enemy, ran up to the fires to arouse their friends, but they had scarcely reached the third fire before the Waldstettes appeared, uttering a frightful shout. The army of the cities at first made a vigorous resistance, and many of the white shirts fell, covered with blood, but this did not continue for long. The bravest of the Zurichers fell, with the valiant Frey at their head, and the rout became general. Eight hundred men were left lying on the field of battle.

In the midst of these afflictions, the Bernese remained stubborn and motionless. Francis Kolb, who, notwithstanding his advanced age, had accompanied the Bernese contingent as chaplain, reproached in a sermon the negligence and cowardice of his party. "Your ancestors," said he, "would have swum across the Rhine, and you—this little stream stops you! They went to battle for a word, and you, even the gospel cannot move. For us it remains only to commit our cause to God." Many voices were raised against the imprudent old man, but others took up his defense. The captain, James May, being as indignant as the aged chaplain at the delays of his fellow citizens, drew his sword, and thrusting it into the folds of the Bernese banner, pricked the bear that was represented on it and cried out in the presence of the whole army, "You knave, will you not show your claws?" But the bear remained motionless.

Already about two thousand Italian soldiers, sent by the pope and commanded by the Genoese De l'Isola, had unfolded their seven standards and united near Zug with the army of the Five

Cantons. Auxiliary troops, diplomatic negotiations, and even missionaries to convert the heretics were not spared. The bishop of Veroli arrived in Switzerland in order to bring back the Lutherans to the Roman faith by means of his friends and of his money. The Roman politicians hailed the victory at Kappel as the signal of the restoration of the papal authority, not only in Switzerland but also throughout the whole of Christendom. At last this presumptuous Reformation was about to be repressed. Everything seemed advancing toward a grand catastrophe. The Tockenburgers made peace and retired. The Thurgovians followed them, and next the people of Gaster. The evangelical army was thus gradually disbanded. The severity of the season was joined to these dissensions. Continual storms of wind and rain drove the soldiers to their homes.

Upon this, the Five Cantons with the undisciplined bands of the Italian general Isola threw themselves on the left bank of the Lake of Zurich. The alarm bell was rung on every side. The peasants retired in crowds into the city with their weeping wives, their frightened children, and their cattle that filled the air with sullen lowings. A report too was circulated that the enemy intended laying siege to Zurich. The country people in alarm declared that if the city refused to make terms, they would make a treaty on their own account.

The peace party prevailed in the council. Deputies were elected to negotiate. "Above all things, preserve the gospel, and then our honor, as far as may be possible." Such were their instructions. On November 16, the deputies from Zurich arrived in a meadow situated near the frontier, on the banks of the Sihl, in which the representatives of the Five Cantons awaited them. They proceeded to the deliberations.

"In the name of the most honorable, holy, and divine Trinity," began the treaty. "Firstly, we the people of Zurich bind ourselves and agree to leave our trusty and well-beloved confederates of the Five Cantons, their well-beloved co-burghers of the Valais, and all their adherents lay and ecclesiastic in their true and indubitable Christian faith, renouncing all evil intention, wiles, and stratagems. And, on our side, we of the Five Cantons, agree to leave our confederates of Zurich and their allies in possession of their faith." At the same time, Rapperschwyl, Gaster, Wesen, Bremgarten, Mellingen, and the common bailiwicks were abandoned to the Five Cantons.

Zurich had preserved its faith, and that was all. The treaty having been read and approved of, the plenipotentiaries got off their horses, fell upon their knees, and called upon the name of God. Then the new captain-general of the Zurichers, Escher, a hasty and eloquent old man, rising up, said as he turned toward the Waldstettes, "God be praised that I can again call you my well-beloved confederates!" and approaching them, he shook hands successively with the terrible victors at Kappel. All eyes were filled with tears. Each took with trembling hand the bottle suspended at his side and offered a draught to one of the chiefs of the opposite party. Shortly after, a similar treaty was concluded with Berne.

Chapter 29
Aftermath and a New Dawn

The restoration of Catholicism immediately commenced in Switzerland, and Rome showed herself everywhere proud, exacting, and ambitious.

After the Battle of Kappel, the Catholic minority at Glaris had resumed the upper hand. It marched with Schwytz against Wesen and the district of the Gaster. On the eve of the invasion, at midnight, twelve deputies came and threw themselves at the feet of the Schwytzer chiefs, who were satisfied with confiscating the national banners of these two districts, with suppressing their tribunals, annulling their ancient liberties, and condemning some to banishment and others to pay a heavy fine. Next, the Mass, the altars, and the images were everywhere reestablished.

It was especially on Bremgarten, Mellingen, and the free bailiwicks that the cantons proposed to inflict a terrible vengeance. Since Berne had recalled its army, Mutschli, the avoyer of Bremgarten, followed Diesbach as far as Arau. In vain did the former remind the Bernese that it was only according to the orders of Berne and Zurich that Bremgarten had blockaded the Five Cantons. "Bend to circumstances," replied the general.

On this, the wretched Mutschli, turning away from the pitiless Bernese, exclaimed, "The prophet Jeremiah has well said, 'Cursed be he that trusteth in man!'" The Swiss and Italian bands entered furiously into these flourishing districts, brandishing their weapons, inflicting heavy fines on all the inhabitants, compelling the gospel ministers to flee, and at the point of the sword restoring everywhere the Mass, idols, and altars.

On the other side of the lake, the misfortune was still greater. On November 18, while the reformed of Rapperschwyl were sleeping peacefully in reliance on the treaties, an army from

Schwytz silently passed the wooden bridge nearly two thousand feet long which crosses the lake and was admitted into the city by the Roman party. On a sudden, the reformed awoke at the loud pealing of the bells and the tumultuous voices of the Catholics. The greater part quitted the city. One of them, however, by name Michael Wohlgemuth, barricaded his house, placed arquebuses at every window, and repelled the attack. The exasperated enemy brought up some heavy pieces of artillery, besieged this extemporaneous citadel in regular form, and Wohlgemuth was soon taken and put to death in the midst of horrible tortures.

Nowhere had the struggle been more violent than at Soleure. The two parties were drawn up in battle array on each side of the Aar, and the Roman Catholics had already discharged one ball against the opposite bank with another about to follow, when the avoyer Wenge, throwing himself on the mouth of the cannon, cried out earnestly, "Fellow citizens, let there be no bloodshed, or else let me be your first victim!" The astonished multitude dropped their arms, but seventy evangelical families were obliged to emigrate, and Soleure returned under the papal yoke.

The deserted cells of St. Gall, Muri, Einsidlen, Wettingen, Rheinau, St. Catherine, Hermetschwyll and Guadenthall witnessed the triumphant return of Benedictines, Franciscans, Dominicans, and all the Roman militia. Priests and monks, intoxicated with their victory, overran country and town, and prepared for new conquests.

The wind of adversity was blowing with fury. The evangelical churches fell one after another, like the pines in the forest whose fall before the battle of the Goubel had raised such gloomy presentiments. The Five Cantons, full of gratitude to the virgin, made a solemn pilgrimage to her temple at Einsidlen. The chaplains celebrated anew their mysteries in this desolated sanctuary. The abbot, who had no monks, sent a number of youths into Swabia to be trained up in the rules of the order, and this famous chapel, which Zwingli's voice had converted into a sanctuary for the Word, became for Switzerland the center of the power and of the intrigues of the papacy.

But this was not enough. At the very time that these flourishing churches were falling to the ground, the reform witnessed the extinction of its brightest lights. A blow from a stone had slain the energetic Zwingli on the field of battle, and the rebound reached the pacific Oecolampadius at Basel, in the midst of a life that was wholly evangelical. The death of his friend, the severe judgments with which they pursued his memory, the terror that had suddenly taken the place of the hopes he had entertained of the future—all these sorrows rent the heart of Oecolampadius.

He recovered, however, sufficient energy to defend the memory of his brother. "It was not," said he, "on the heads of the most guilty that the wrath of Pilate and the tower of Siloam fell. The judgment began in the house of God. Our presumption has been punished. Let our trust be placed now on the Lord alone, and this will be an inestimable gain." Oecolampadius declined the call of Zurich to take the place of Zwingli. "My post is here," said he, as he looked upon Basel.

He was not destined to hold it long. Illness fell upon him in addition to so many afflictions. The plague was in the city. A violent inflammation attacked him, and erelong a tranquil scene succeeded the tumult of Kappel. A peaceful death calmed the agitated hearts of the faithful, and replaced by sweet and heavenly emotions the terror and distress with which a horrible disaster had filled them.

On hearing of the danger of Oecolampadius, all the city was plunged into mourning. A crowd of men of every age and of every rank rushed to his house. "Rejoice," said the reformer with a meek look, "I am going to a place of everlasting joy." He then commemorated the death of our Lord with his wife, his relations, and domestics, who shed floods of tears. "This supper," said the dying man, "is a sign of my real faith in Jesus Christ my Redeemer."

On the morrow he sent for his colleagues. "My brethren," said he, "the Lord is there; He calls me away. Oh! my brethren, what a black cloud is appearing on the horizon—what a tempest is approaching! Be steadfast. The Lord will preserve his own."

He then held out his hand, and all these faithful ministers clasped it with veneration.

On November 23, he called his children around him, the eldest of whom was barely three years old. "Eusebius, Irene, Alethea," said he to them, as he took their little hands, "love God who is your Father." Their mother having promised for them, the children retired with his blessing.

The night that followed this scene was his last. All the pastors were around his bed: "What is the news?" asked Oecolampadius of a friend who came in.

"Nothing," was the reply.

"Well," said the faithful disciple of Jesus, "I will tell you something new." His friends awaited in astonishment. "In a short time I shall be with the Lord Jesus." One of his friends now asking him if he was incommoded by the light, he replied, putting his hand on his heart, "There is light enough here." The day began to break; he repeated in a feeble voice Psalm 51, "Have mercy upon me, O God, according to thy loving-kindness." Then remaining silent, as if he wished to recover strength, he said, "Lord Jesus, help me!" The ten pastors fell on their knees around his bed with uplifted hands. The death of this servant of the Lord was like his life, full of light and peace.

Zwingli and Oecolampadius had fallen. There was a great void and great sorrow in the church of Christ. Dissensions vanished before these two graves, and nothing could be seen but tears. Luther himself was moved. On receiving the news of these two deaths, he called to mind the days he had passed with Zwingli and Oecolampadius at Marburg. The blow inflicted on him by their sudden decease was such, that many years after he said to Bullinger, "Their death filled me with such intense sorrow that I was near dying myself."

The youthful Henry Bullinger, threatened with the scaffold, had been compelled to flee from Bremgarten, his native town, with his aged father, his colleagues, and sixty of the principal inhabitants, who abandoned their houses to be pillaged by the Waldstettes. Three days after this, he was preaching in the cathedral of Zurich. "No, Zwingli is not dead," exclaimed Myconius, "or, like the phoenix, he has risen again from his ashes." Bullinger was unanimously chosen to succeed the great reformer. He adopted Zwingli's orphaned children, Wilhelm, Regula, and Ulrich, and endeavoured to supply the place of their father. This young man, scarcely twenty-eight years of age, and who presided forty years with wisdom and blessing over this church, was everywhere greeted as the apostle of Switzerland.

Yet as the sea roars long after the violent tempest has subsided, so the people of Zurich were still in commotion. Many were agitated from on high. They came to themselves. They acknowledged their error. The weapons of their warfare had been carnal. They were now of a contrite and humble spirit. They arose and went to their Father and confessed their sin. In those days there was great mourning in Zurich. Some, however, stood up with pride, protested by the mouth of their ministers against the work of the diplomatists, and boldly stigmatized the shameful compact. "If the shepherds sleep, the dogs must bark," exclaimed Leo Juda in the cathedral of Zurich. "My duty is to give warning of the evil they are about to do to my Master's house."

Nothing could equal the sorrow of this city, except the exultation of the Waldstettes. The noise of drums and fifes, the firing of guns, the ringing of bells had long resounded on the banks of their lakes and even to their highest valleys. Now the noise was less, but the effect greater. The Five Cantons, in close alliance with Friburg and Soleure, formed a perpetual league for the defense of the ancient Christian faith with the bishop of Sion and the tithings of the Valais, and henceforward carried their measures in the federal affairs with boldness. But a deep conviction was formed at that period in the hearts of the Swiss Reformed. "Faith comes from God," said they. "Its success does not depend on the life or death of a man. Let our adversaries boast of our ruin; we will boast only in the Cross."

"God reigns," wrote Berne to Zurich, "and He will not permit the bark to founder." This conviction was of more avail than the victory of Kappel.

Thus the Reformation, having deviated from the right path, was driven back by the very violence of the assault into its first course, having no other power than the Word of God. We have taken a few stones and piled them as a monument on the battle-field of Kappel, in order to remind the church of the great lesson which this terrible catastrophe teaches. As we bid farewell to this sad scene, we inscribe on these monumental stones, on the one side, these words from God's Book: "Some trust in chariots, and some in horses: but we will remember the name of the Lord our God. They are brought down and fallen: but we are risen and stand upright." And on the other, this declaration of the Head of the church: "My kingdom is not of this world."

If, from the ashes of the martyrs at Kappel, a voice could be heard, it would be in these very words of the Bible that these noble confessors would address the Christians of our days. That the church has no other king than Jesus Christ; that she ought not to meddle with the policy of the world, derive from it her inspiration, and call for its swords, its prisons, its treasures; that she will conquer by the spiritual powers which God has deposited in her bosom, and, above all, by the reign of her adorable Head; that she must not expect upon earth thrones and mortal triumphs; but that her march resembles that of her King, from the manger to the cross, and from the cross to the crown—such is the lesson to be read on the bloodstained page that has crept into our simple and evangelical narrative.

But if God teaches his people great lessons, He also gives them great deliverances. The bolt had fallen from heaven. The Reformation seemed to be little better than a lifeless body, cumbering the ground, whose dissevered limbs were about to be reduced to ashes. But God raises up the dead. New and more glorious destinies were awaiting the gospel of Jesus Christ at the foot of the Alps.

At the southwestern extremity of Switzerland, in a great valley which the white giant of the mountains points out from afar; on the banks of the Leman lake, at the spot where the Rhône, clear and blue as the sky above it, rolls its majestic waters; on a small hill that the foot of Caesar had once trod, and on which the steps of another conqueror, of a Gaul—John Calvin of Noyon—were destined erelong to leave their ineffaceable and glorious traces, stood an ancient city, Geneva, as yet covered with the dense shadows of Catholicism; but which God was about to raise to be a beacon to the church and a bulwark to Christendom.

After the death of Zwingli, John Calvin of Geneva became the major leader of
the Swiss Reformation, carrying on where the fallen Zwingli had left off.

Editor's Afterword

Jean Rilliet called Ulrich Zwingli the "third man" of the Reformation, highlighting the fact that Zwingli has generally ranked behind Martin Luther and John Calvin in historical importance. Indeed, one might even call him the "forgotten man" of the Reformation. There are Lutheran churches and Calvinistic churches today, but no church that calls itself "Zwinglian."

But as the preceding pages have shown, Zwingli played a leading role in the Protestant Reformation. He pioneered the reform of Switzerland, anticipating the work of Calvin that would follow in Geneva. Zwingli went further than Luther in eliminating the vestiges of medieval Catholicism from the church. All those who today affirm the doctrines of justification by faith alone, the priesthood of all believers, and the sole authority of Scripture will readily acknowledge their debt to Zwingli.

Zwingli was born in a shepherd's cottage and was reared among shepherds. Appropriately, the image of the shepherd well symbolizes the Swiss reformer. The apostle Peter exhorted the elders in the church to "feed the flock of God" and to be "ensamples to the flock," waiting for that "chief Shepherd" to reward them with a "crown of glory" (I Pet. 5:1-4). Pastor Zwingli saw himself clearly as shepherd to the flock of Zurich. When he opposed the Swiss practice of selling themselves as mercenary soldiers, for example, Zwingli was not just offering a political reform. He sought to spare his sheep from slaughter.

One can understand Zwingli better when one realizes that for him there was no difference between being the shepherd of the church in Zurich and being shepherd of all the citizens of that city. Zwingli, like most of the reformers, still believed in the union of church and state. There was no difference between church and city—Zwingli was pastor of all.

This fact helps explain one of the blots on Zwingli's reputation, his treatment of the Anabaptists. By rejecting the state church, the Anabaptists appeared to be not only religious dissenters but also political revolutionaries. To protect his sheep, Zwingli mistakenly thought, the city must treat the Anabaptists as wolves among the flock of God.

Modern readers may be surprised at how negatively Merle d'Aubigné portrays the Anabaptists. Like most writers before the twentieth century, Merle viewed the Anabaptists as radicals and revolutionaries. Only in more recent time have historians presented a more balanced picture of the Anabaptist movement. Still, Merle's account reminds readers that there were extremist elements among the Anabaptists. But even Merle cannot countenance the harsh treatment Zurich and other cities inflicted on the Anabaptists, and he used their situation to argue for religious liberty.

Zwingli, unfortunately, never understood such arguments. Merle d'Aubigné, on the other hand, not only understood them but also advanced them. In his native Switzerland in the nineteenth century, Merle was one of another group of reformers who successfully advanced the cause of religious liberty and the separation of church and state. The historian was quick to cite the warnings that the Reformation offered of the dangers of close ties between church and state. The melancholy fate of Ulrich Zwingli on the fields of Kappel was, to Merle, one such dreadful warning.

For God and His People: Ulrich Zwingli and the Swiss Reformation is the second biography I have compiled from the writings of Swiss church historian Jean Henri Merle d'Aubigné. Like the first volume, *The Triumph of Truth: A Life of Martin Luther,* this work allows readers to understand the life and contribution of an important leader of the Reformation. In addition, they can perhaps understand why Merle's eloquent writings were bestsellers in their day. It is my hope that through the marvelously readable prose of J. H. Merle d'Aubigné, modern Christians will learn why they should remember the "forgotten man of the Reformation," the Swiss reformer Ulrich Zwingli.

Glossary

abbot—the superior of a monastery

acolyte—a devoted follower

advowson—the right of presentation to a vacant benefice

almshouse—a poorhouse

Ambrosian—of, pertaining to, or instituted by St. Ambrose

amman—a bailiff

anathema—an ecclesiastical ban, curse, or excommunication

arquebus—a heavy portable matchlock gun

arquebusier—a soldier armed with an arquebus

Augean stables—legendary stables so dirty that Hercules diverted a river to clean them

ave—a Roman Catholic prayer, which in Latin begins *"Ave Maria"* (Hail, Mary)

avoyer—the first magistrate of some Swiss cantons

bailiff—a minor court official entrusted with maintenance of order in the court and in his jurisdiction; a magistrate

bailiwick—the office or district of a bailiff

banneret—a small banner; a title borne by certain officers in some Swiss cantons

batz—a unit of money worth about three cents, usually silver

benefice—a church office endowed with assets that provide a living

bull—an official document of the Roman Catholic church issued by the pope

burgomaster—the principal magistrate of a city or town

canon—a member of a chapter of priests serving in a cathedral or collegiate church

canton—a small territorial division of a country

celibacy—sexual abstinence, especially for religious vows

chancery—a court of public record

chaplet—a rosary

coadjutor—an assistant to a bishop

colloquy—a formal conversation

the Confederation—the united Swiss cantons

confessional—a small enclosed stall in which a priest hears confessions

consistory—a council, a tribunal

credo—the Apostle's or Nicene Creed, which begins with the word *credo* (I believe)

crown—a unit of money, gold or silver, worth about five shillings

crozier—a staff with a crook or a cross at the end, carried by or before an abbot, a bishop, or an archbishop as a symbol of office

curate—a cleric who assists a rector or vicar

dean—a Roman Catholic priest who oversees a group of parishes within a diocese

decretal—a decree, especially a papal letter that gives a decision on a point of canon law

Diet of Worms—a council of political authorities held in Worms in 1521 for the purpose of questioning Martin Luther about his beliefs

diocese—the district underneath the jurisdiction of a bishop

ducal cap—a highly ornamented headpiece showing rank, such as a duke might wear

ducat—a unit of money, often gold, worth four to ten shillings

episcopal—of or relating to church government by a bishop

Eucharist—a sacramental act of worship in which bread and wine are consecrated and consumed in remembrance of Jesus' death; communion

excommunication—to deprive of the right of church membership by ecclesiastical authority

expiatory—making amends or reparation (specifically for sins)

feast of Whitsuntide—the feast of Pentecost and the following days

florin—a unit of money, often gold, worth two to six shillings

grapnel—an iron shaft with claws at one end thrown by a rope and used for grasping and holding

halberd—a weapon having an axelike blade and a steel spike mounted on the end of a long shaft

halberdier—a soldier armed with a halberd

Hellenize—to make Greek in character, culture, or civilization

Helvetian—Swiss; relating to an area between the Alps and the Jura Mountains

indulgence—papers validated by the pope alleged to remit the punishment for sins

landamman—the chief magistrate of certain cantons or smaller administrative districts

landgrave—a man in medieval Germany who had jurisdiction over a particular territory

landsgemeinde—a local authority or governing body

landsturm—a general levy in time of war to build a militia of men not serving in the army

lansquenet—a soldier armed with a lance, often a mercenary

Lent—the forty weekdays from Ash Wednesday until Easter observed as a season of penance

Lutheran—a follower of the teachings of Martin Luther

mailed—armored

manifesto—a public declaration of principles, policies, or intentions, especially of a political nature

mitre—liturgical headdress of a bishop

mysticism—the experience of mystical communion

nuncio—a papal representative in a foreign court

oligarch—a member of a small governing faction

oligarchy—government by a few, especially a small faction of persons or families

ozier—a species of willow with tough, pliant branches

parochial—supported by or located in a parish

pater—the Lord's Prayer, which in Latin begins *Pater nostre* (Our Father)

phalanx—a formation of infantry using overlapping shields as a means of protection

plenipotentiary—a diplomat invested with full authority

pontiff—the pope or a bishop

prebend—a stipend or benefice

presbyterian—of or relating to ecclesiastical government by presbyters

procurator-fiscal—one authorized to manage the affairs of another (finances)

purgatory—a term that Roman Catholics use to describe a place of penance for sins that the redeemed must pass through after death before entering heaven

Rome—the Roman Catholic Church; the center of government of the Roman Catholic Church

sacerdotal—of or relating to the priesthood; priestly

sacrilegist—one who profanes something sacred

sacraments—any of the traditional seven rites of the Roman Catholic Church said to confer sanctifying grace

Saxony—a region of Northern Germany

schultheiss—a mayor

see—the official jurisdiction of a bishop; a diocese

shilling—a unit of money worth about twelve pennies

Shrove Tuesday—the day before Ash Wednesday

ultramontane—supporting papal policy in ecclesiastical or political matters

vicar—a priest who acts for or represents another cleric

vicar-general—a priest acting as a deputy to a bishop

Whitmonday—the day after Pentecost

Index

A

ab Acker, Anthony
 leader of an army proceeding to Baden at the beginning of the First War of Kappel, 190

Adrian VI
 pope (1522-1523) who bribed Zwingli, hoping to win him over, 102

Aebli
 landamman of Glaris who strove for peace in the First War of Kappel, 191, 192, 195

Albert
 archbishop; cardinal of Mentz who persuaded Capito to join his court, 56, 69

Am Ort
 a bailiff present at Hottinger's trial, 116

Am-Berg, Joseph
 bailiff of Thurgovia who cruelly persecuted followers of the Reformers, 119, 183, 184

Am-Grutt, Joachim
 undersecretary of state who opposed abolishing the mass in Zurich, 127

Ambrose
 ancient church father whose writings Zwingli studied, 13

Amerbach, Bruno
 printer who died of the plague in Basel, 53

Anselm, 42

Augustine
 ancient church father whose writings Zwingli studied, 13, 35

B

Battli, Melchior
 one of the ecclesiastical deputies sent to Zurich from the bishop of Constance (April 7, 1522), 75

Berguer, George
 Zurich deputy who led 2700 Zurichers to fight for the pope in Italy, 71, 95

Blaurock, George Jacob
 Anabaptist who was expelled from Zurich and eventually burned by Roman Catholics of Tyrol, 133, 137

Boschenstein, John
 scholar who directed Zwingli in the study of Hebrew, 67

Bourkhard, Leonard
 citizen of Zurich, 239

Brendi, Doctor
 one of the ecclesiastical deputies sent to Zurich from the bishop of Constance (April 7, 1522), 75, 77

Brentz
 eyewitness of the Marburg debate, 161

Brodtlein
 pastor of Zollikon, 133

Bruder, Ulrich
 under-bailiff of Husen, 235

Brunner, Conrad
 friend of Zwingli who died of the plague in Basel, 50, 53

Bucer
 friend of Zwingli and participant in the Marburg debate, 154, 163-64

Bullinger
 dean of Bremgarten who

M

Maaler, John
man of Zurich who rode behind Zwingli to Kappel, 237

Macrinus
master of the school of
Solere; friend of the
Reformation, 91

Maigret
French proponent of peace in
Switzerland, 214

Manz, Felix
Anabaptist; executed at the
order of Zurich's government,
132, 133, 137

May, James
captain of Bernese forces,
255

Megander, 127

Meili, John
Zwingli's uncle; abbot of the
convent of Fischingen, 2

Meili, Margaret
Zwingli's mother, 2

Melancthon, Philipp
theologian of Wittenburg;
companion of Luther, 54, 153

Meyer von Knonau, Gerold
son of John Meyer von
Knonau who died when
Gerold was about three; later
became Zwingli's adopted son
and died with him on the
field of Kappel, 68, 69, 245,
253

Meyer von Knonau, John
father of Gerold; Anna
Zwingli's first husband, 68

Meyer, Sebastian
reformer of Berne, 89, 94

Mulinen
commander of the Knights-
Hospitallers of St. John at
Hitzkylch, 223

Müller, George
abbott of Wettingon, 220

Murner, Thomas
Carmelite monk of Lucerne;
slandered Zwingli at the
Baden disputation and lam-
pooned the reformers in his
Almanac of Heretics, 146,
171, 175

Myconius, Felix
son of Oswald Myconius, 16,
112

Myconius, Oswald
devoted friend of Zwingli
with whom he studied at
Basel under Erasmus; introduced Zwingli to Zurich; became the headmaster of the
collegiate school of Lucerne
and a diligent proponent of
reform; rejected at Lucerne;
later taught and preached at
Zurich, 15, 16, 29, 31, 32, 54,
56, 57, 62, 65-67, 89, 92-96,
99, 103, 112, 113, 127, 129,
145, 230, 253, 262

N

Naeff, Adam
man of Zurich who defended
Zurich's standard at Kappel,
244

Napoleon, 49

Nicholas II, 133

O

Oecolampadius
John Hausschein, student of
Erasmus, preacher at Basel;
debated Dr. Eck at Baden and
joined Zwingli and Bucer at
the Marburg debate; sup-
ported Zurich's use of arms;
died of the plague shortly